MW00795857

Author: Ray Holder

ISBN 9780692728789

TABLE OF CONTENTS

Final Exam

Answer Keys

Glossary

INTRODUCTION

"Calculation" is a commonly used but undefined term in the NEC®. Typically, the term is used to relate to a logical order of steps or procedures to follow to arrive at a mathematical conclusion.

"Practical Calculations for Electricians" is designed to give a clear, concise easy to-use review of the basics of solving mathematical problems the electrician may encounter in his/her day-to-day work experiences or on electrical examinations. Introducing each topic, defining key terms, and "walking" through each sample problem in a step-by-step manner gives the electrician insight and understanding to solving these mathematical problems.

This book is not intended to be used as a design specification manual for untrained persons for electrical projects but, it does reflect the MINIMUM standards set forth by the NEC®. In this text you will not encounter mathematical tasks usually performed by an electrical engineer, nor will you encounter "trick questions" whose sole purpose is to confuse you.

Whether you purchased this book for exam preparation, continuing education, or simply to advance your knowledge, remember: LEARN MORE, EARN MORE.

HOW TO STUDY

Before beginning to study, get into the right frame of mind, be relaxed. Study in a quiet place that is conducive to learning. If such a place is not available, go to your local library. It is important that you have a quiet, relaxed atmosphere in which to study.

It is much better to study many short lengths of time than attempt to study fewer, longer lengths of time. Try to study a little while, say about an hour, every evening. You will need the support and understanding of your family to set aside this much needed time.

As you study this "Practical Calculations for Electricians" textbook and other references, highlight important points with a highlighter. It makes it easier to locate NEC® references when studying or taking an examination.

Use a straight edge, such as a six inch ruler when using the NEC® tables and charts. A very common mistake is to get on the wrong line when using these tables; if this happens, the result is an incorrect answer.

Use tabs on the major sections of your NEC®, this makes it easier and takes less time to locate these major sections while studying, on the job, or during an examination.

TYPICAL QUESTIONS

The following examples are intended to illustrate typical questions that the student may encounter.

<u>Example 1</u>

You are to install a single-phase, 240-volt, 7,500 VA commercial rated electric fryer in a restaurant. What load, in amperes, will the electric fryer draw?

A. 20.80 amperes
B. 31.25 amperes
C. 62.50 amperes
D. 27.50 amperes

Here you are asked to determine the current flow in the conductors serving the fryer using the information given. Power is expressed as 7,500 VA and voltage is 240. The formula to be used is I = P/E. Substitute the values given; I = 7,500 VA ÷ 240 volts = 31.25 amperes; the answer is **B**.

<u>Example 2</u>

A single-phase, 240-volt, 5 hp, Design B, 40°C rise motor has a FLA of 25 amperes indicated on the nameplate. The MINIMUM rating of the overload device used to protect this motor as required by the NEC® is _____.

A. 32.50 amperes
B. 28.25 amperes
C. 31.25 amperes
D. 35.00 amperes

Here the "question" is in the form of an incomplete statement. Your task is to select the choice that best completes the statement. In this case, you should have selected **C** since Section 430.6(A)(2) of the NEC® specifies motor overload protection shall be based on the motor nameplate rating and Section 430.32(A)(1) specifies the overload device shall be selected to trip at a value of not more than 125% of the motor nameplate full-load current rating, if the motor has a marked temperature rise of not over 40°C.
FLA = 25 amperes x 125% = 31.25 amperes

<u>Example 3</u>

Taking all exceptions into consideration, the largest standard size inverse time circuit breaker allowed to provide short-circuit, branch-circuit and ground-fault protection for a 5 hp, 230 volt, single-phase, continuous-duty motor has a standard rating of _____.

A. 110 amperes
B. 100 amperes
C. 70 amperes
D. 60 amperes

Again, the "question" is in the form of an incomplete statement and your task is to select the choice that best completes the statement. In this case, you are to find an exception. You have to select the MAXIMUM size circuit breaker the NEC® permits for overcurrent protection of the motor, you should have selected **A** because Section 430.6(A)(1) states, to determine the ampere rating of overcurrent protection for single-phase motors the FLC should be determined from Table 430.248, and Section 430.52(C)(1) Ex. 2(c) specifies the rating of an inverse time circuit breaker shall in no case exceed 400% of the full-load current motor. FLC = 28 amperes x 400% = 112 amperes. Section 240.6(A) of the NEC® indicates a circuit breaker with a 110 ampere rating to be the next standard size with a lower value. If a circuit breaker of a higher value was selected, you would exceed 400% of the full-load current motor.

HOW TO USE THIS BOOK

You can use this book in any way that fits your personal style for study and/or review. You must decide what works best with your needs. You can either study the text from cover to cover or just look for the information you need and keep it for further reference. However, it is suggested you first completely read the book to get a better understanding of all the concepts and steps involved.

Each "unit" contained in this book consist of related information to specific topics, followed by examples. First, read the related information, look at the example while covering up the answer and try to solve the problem. Then, look at the answer to see if you are correct.

At the end of each unit you will find a **"Self-Assessment Quiz"**, used to determine your understanding of the concepts contained in the unit of study. Review your answers with the **"ANSWER KEY"** located at the back of the book. When you get a question incorrect, do further study in that area. This will help you identify your strengths and weaknesses. When you discover you are weaker in some areas than others, you will find that further study is necessary in those areas.

The "final exam" consist of ninety (90) questions; journeyman electricians should get at least sixty-four (64), 70%, of the questions correct; Master electricians should get at least sixty-nine (69), 75%, of the questions correct for a passing score.

Complete only one unit contained in this book during an allotted study period; this way you do no get "burned out" and fatigued. This also helps you to develop good study habits. **Good Luck!**

ABOUT THE AUTHOR

H. Ray Holder has worked in the electrical industry for over fifty years as an apprentice, journeyman, master, field engineer, estimator, business manager, contractor, inspector, consultant, and instructor.

Mr. Holder is a graduate of Texas State University and holds a Bachelor of Science Degree in Occupational Education. He also holds a lifetime teaching certificate from the Texas Education Agency, in the field of Vocational Education.

He is a certified instructor of electrical trades. His classes are presented in a simplified, easy-to-understand format for electricians.

Since 1965, Mr. Holder has taught over 30,000 students at Austin Community College and the University of Texas, at Austin, Texas, Odessa College, at Odessa, Texas, Technical-Vocational Institute of Albuquerque, New Mexico, Howard College, at San Angelo, Texas and in the public school systems in Ft. Worth and San Antonio, Texas, as well as conducted electrical seminars throughout the United States. He is currently the Director of Education for Electrical Seminars, Inc.

Mr. Holder is a former member of the National Fire Protection Association, International Association of Electrical Inspectors and retired member of the International Brotherhood of Electrical Workers.

OTHER TITLES AVAILABLE BASED ON THE 2014 NEC®

Electricians Practice Calculations Exams 978-1-935834-09-0	ISBN
Electricians Exam Book	ISBN
Texas Electricians Practice Exams & Study Guide	ISBN

OTHER TITLES AVAILABLE BASED ON THE 2011 NEC®

Electricians Practice Calculations Exams	ISBN
Electricians Exam Book	ISBN
Electricians Handbook of NEC® Questions	ISBN

USEFUL FORMULAS

To Find	Single Phase	Three Phase	Direct Current
Amperes when kVA is known	$\frac{kVA \times 1{,}000}{E}$	$\frac{kVA \times 1{,}000}{E \times 1.732}$	not applicable
Amperes when horsepower is known	$\frac{hp \times 746}{E \times \%Eff. \times PF.}$	$\frac{hp \times 746}{E \times 1.732 \times \%Eff. \times PF.}$	$\frac{hp \times 746}{E \times \%Eff.}$
Amperes when Kilowatts are known	$\frac{kW \times 1{,}000}{E \times PF.}$	$\frac{kW \times 1{,}000}{E \times 1.732 \times PF.}$	$\frac{kW \times 1{,}000}{E}$
Kilowatts	$\frac{I \times E \times PF.}{1{,}000}$	$\frac{I \times E \times 1.732 \times PF.}{1{,}000}$	$\frac{I \times E}{1{,}000}$
Kilovolt Amperes	$\frac{I \times E}{1{,}000}$	$\frac{I \times E \times 1.732}{1{,}000}$	not applicable
Horsepower	$\frac{I \times E \times \%Eff. \times PF.}{746}$	$\frac{I \times E \times 1.732 \times \%Eff. \times PF.}{746}$	$\frac{I \times E \times \%Eff.}{746}$
Watts	$E \times I \times PF.$	$E \times I \times 1.732 \times PF.$	$E \times I$

I = Amperes
E = Volts
kW = Kilowatts
kVA = Kilovolt-Amperes

hp = Horsepower
%Eff.= Percent Efficiency
PF. = Power Factor

Power – "Pie" Circle Formulas

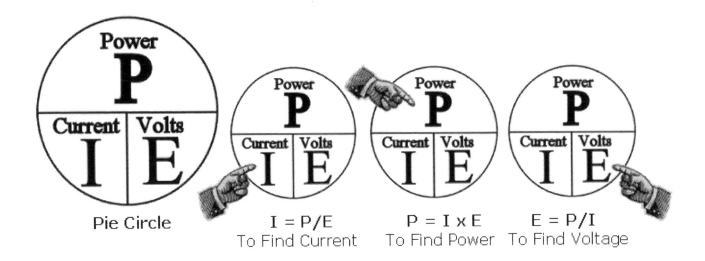

Pie Circle

I = P/E
To Find Current

P = I x E
To Find Power

E = P/I
To Find Voltage

Ohms Law Circle Formulas

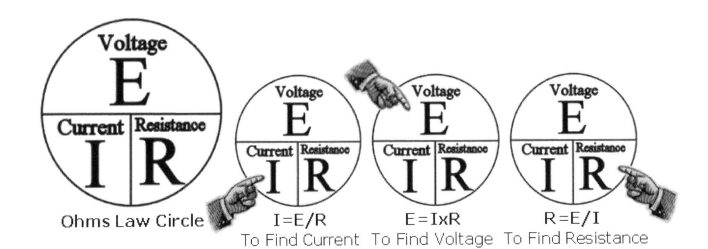

Ohms Law Circle

I = E/R
To Find Current

E = I x R
To Find Voltage

R = E/I
To Find Resistance

Power Factor Triangle Formulas

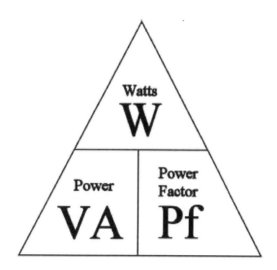

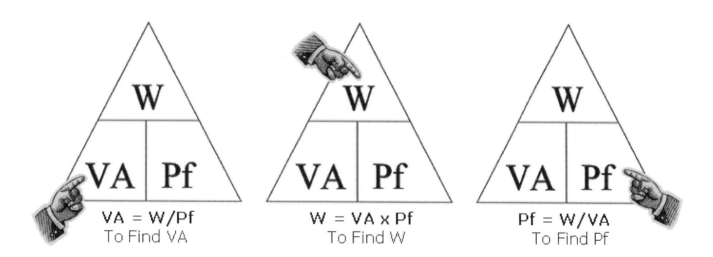

VA = W/Pf
To Find VA

W = VA x Pf
To Find W

Pf = W/VA
To Find Pf

VOLTAGE DROP FORMULAS

Formula Definitions:

VD = Volts dropped from a circuit.

2 = Multiplying factor for single-phase circuits. The 2 represents the conductor length in a single-phase circuit.

1.732 = Multiplying factor for three-phase circuits. The square root of 3 represents the conductor length in a three-phase circuit. The only difference between the single-phase and three-phase formulas is that "1.732" has replaced "2".

K = Approximate resistance of the conductor per mil foot. A mil foot is a wire 1 foot long and one mil in diameter. The approximate K value for copper wire is **12.9** ohms and for aluminum wire is **21.2** per mil foot.

I = Current or amperage draw of the load.

D = The distance from the source voltage to the load.

CM = Circular mil area of the conductor. (Chapter 9, Table 8)

*NOTE – When determining wire size, distance or current, VD is the actual volts that can be dropped from the circuit. The recommended percentage for a branch-circuit is 3%. Example: 3% of 120 volts is 3.6 volts. DO NOT enter 3% in the VD position.

To find voltage drop in a single-phase circuit.

$$VD = \frac{2 \times K \times I \times D}{CM}$$

To find wire size in a single-phase circuit.

$$CM = \frac{2 \times K \times I \times D}{VD}$$

To find distance in a single-phase circuit.

$$D = \frac{CM \times VD}{2 \times K \times I}$$

To find MAXIMUM current in amperes in a single-phase circuit.

$$I = \frac{CM \times VD}{2 \times K \times D}$$

UNIT 1

BASIC ELECTRICAL FORMULAS

Upon successfully completing this unit of study, the student will be familiar with the concepts and application of Ohm's Law, power formulas and power factor.

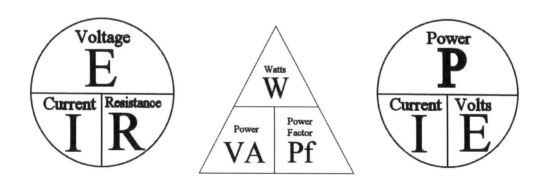

UNIT 1

BASIC ELECTRICAL FORMULAS

PIE CIRCLE FORMULAS

RELATED INFORMATION:

- The **PIE** formula circle illustrates the relationship between **power, current and voltage**.

- Power may be expressed as true power such as, **watts, kilowatts, kW** or **horsepower**; power may also be expressed in terms as apparent power such as, **volt-amps, VA, kilo volt-amps** or **kVA**.

- The letter "**P**" represents power.

- The letter "**I**" represents current.

- The letter "**E**" represents voltage.

- The letter "**k**" is the abbreviation of kilo or one thousand (1,000).

- One **kW** equals 1,000 watts.

- One **kVA** equals 1,000 volt-amps.

- One **horsepower** equals 746 watts.

➢ Formulas used to determine the available power for a single-phase circuit, load or an electrical system are:

P = I x E

P = current x volts

P – volts x amps

P = VA

P = kVA

kW = $\dfrac{\text{current x volts}}{1,000}$

kVA = $\dfrac{\text{current x volts}}{1,000}$

EXAMPLE – Determine the available power, in VA, for a 100 ampere, 240 volt, single-phase circuit.

        A. 2,400 VA
        B. 24,000 VA
        C. 240,000 VA
        D. 2.40 VA

ANSWER – (B)   24,000 VA

        VA = I x E
        VA = 100 amperes x 240 volts = 24,000 VA

EXAMPLE – Determine the apparent power, in kVA, for a 150 ampere, 120/240 Volt, single-phase electrical system.

        A. 36 kVA
        B. 3.60 kVA
        C. 360 kVA
        D. 3,600 kVA

ANSWER – (A)   36 kVA

        kVA = $\dfrac{\text{I x E}}{1,000}$

        kVA = $\dfrac{\text{150 amps x 240 volts}}{1,000}$ = $\dfrac{36,000}{1,000}$ = 36 kVA

➤ Formulas used to determine the available power for three-phase circuits, loads or electrical systems are:

P = I x E x 1.732

P = current x volts x 1.732

P = volts x 1.732 x amps

P = VA x 1.732

kW = $\dfrac{\text{current x volts x 1.732}}{1,000}$

kVA = $\dfrac{\text{current x volts x 1.732}}{1,000}$

EXAMPLE – Determine the available power, in VA, for a 100 ampere 208Y/120 volt, three-phase circuit.

    A. 3,603 VA
    B. 36,026 VA
    C. 360,260 VA
    D. 20,800 VA

ANSWER – (B)   36,026 VA

    VA = I x E x 1.732
    VA = 100 amps x 208 volts x 1.732 = 36,026 VA

    *Note – In this situation we are to use 208 volts and multiply by 1.732 (the square root of 3), because we are to balance the load   in the three current-carrying conductors.

EXAMPLE – A load that draws 50 amperes when connected to a 208Y/120 volt, three-phase source has a kW rating of _____.

    A. 18 kW
    B. 1.8 kW
    C. 180 kW
    D. 1,800 kW

ANSWER – (A)   18 kW

    kW = $\dfrac{\text{current x volts x 1.732}}{1,000}$
    kW = $\dfrac{50 \times 208 \times 1.732}{1,000}$ = $\dfrac{18,013}{1,000}$ = 18 kW

➢ Current may be expressed in terms such as **amps**, **amperes**, **full-load current**, **FLC**, **full-load amps**, **FLA**, **load in amps** or **amperes**, **amperage**, **amperage draw** or **line load**.

➢ The letter "I" represents the intensity of the current.

➢ Formulas used to determine the current in a single-phase circuit, load or an electrical system are:

$$I = \frac{P}{E}$$

$$I = \frac{power}{voltage}$$

$$I = \frac{watts}{volts}$$

$$I = \frac{kW \times 1,000}{volts}$$

$$I = \frac{VA}{volts}$$

$$I = \frac{kVA \times 1,000}{volts}$$

EXAMPLE – Determine the current, in amperes, for a 120 volt, single-phase branch circuit that has only six (6) 100 watt incandescent luminaries (lighting fixtures) connected.

    A. 5 amperes
    B. 15 amperes
    C. 20 amperes
    D. 2 amperes

ANSWER – (A)   5 amperes

$$I = \frac{watts}{volts} \quad I = \frac{600}{120} = 5 \text{ amperes}$$

EXAMPLE – Determine the current, in amperes, of a 2.4 kW load connected to a 240 volt, single-phase source.

    A. .01 ampere

B. 1 ampere
C. 100 amperes
D. 10 amperes

ANSWER – (D)   10 amperes

$$I = \frac{2.4\ kW \times 1,000}{240} = \frac{2,400}{240} = 10\ amperes$$

➢ Formulas used to determine the current in a three (3)-phase circuit, load, or an electrical system are:

$$I = \frac{P}{E \times 1.732}$$

$$I = \frac{power}{volts \times 1.732}$$

$$I = \frac{watts}{volts \times 1.732}$$

$$I = \frac{kW \times 1,000}{volts \times 1.732}$$

$$I = \frac{VA}{volts \times 1.732}$$

$$I = \frac{kVA \times 1,000}{volts \times 1.732}$$

EXAMPLE – A 36,026 VA load connected to a 208Y/120-volt, three-phase circuit will draw _____ of current per phase.

A. 10 amperes
B. 173 amperes
C. 250 amperes
D. 100 amperes

ANSWER – (D)   100 amperes

$$I = \frac{VA}{E \times 1.732}$$
$$I = \frac{36,026\ VA}{208\ volts \times 1.732} = \frac{36,026}{360.25} = 100\ amperes$$

EXAMPLE – A balanced 60 kVA load connected to a 480Y/277-volt three-phase electrical system will have a full-load current draw of _____ per phase.

A. 72 amperes
B. 125 amperes
C. 720 amperes
D. 80 amperes

ANSWER – (A)   72 amperes

$$I = \frac{kVA \times 1,000}{volts \times 1.732}$$

$$I = \frac{60\ kVA \times 1,000}{480\ volts \times 1.732} = \frac{60,000}{831.36} = 72\ amperes$$

POWER FACTOR

RELATED INFORMATION:

➢ **Power factor (PF)** is the ratio between true power expressed as **watts**, **kilo watts** or **kW** and the apparent power expressed as **volt-amps**, **VA** or **kVA**.

➢ Power factor is expressed as a percent that does not exceed 100 percent or a decimal.

➢ True power, is expressed as **watts**, a unit of work, **kW** or **kilowatts**; this condition occurs in AC circuits or loads that contain only resistance. This is why electric ranges, ovens, cooktops, dryers and water heaters are all rated in **watts** or **kW**. The current and the voltage will be "in-phase", meaning that the voltage and the current will reach their peak and zero values at the same time. This is what we call unity or a power factor of 100 percent.

➢ True power (**watts**) equals apparent power (**VA**) in an electrical circuit or load containing only resistance.

➢ True power (**watts**) is less than apparent power (**VA**) in a circuit or load containing inductance or capacitance, such as motors, transformers, HID and fluorescent lighting.

➢ The true power (**watts**) of a single-phase circuit or load that contains inductance or capacitance can be calculated by the use of the following formula:

Watts = volts x amperes x power factor

EXAMPLE – What is the true power, in watts, of a 10 ampere load supplied with 120 volts, having a power factor of 80 percent?

A. 1,000 watts
B. 1,200 watts

C. 2,400 watts

D. 960 watts

ANSWER – (D)   960 watts

Watts = volts x amperes x power factor

Watts = 120 volts x 10 amps x .8 = 960 watts

➢ The true power (watts) of a three-phase circuit or load that contains inductance or capacitance can be calculated by the use of the following formula:

Watts = volts x 1.732 x amperes x power factor

EXAMPLE – Determine the true power (watts) of a 7.5 ampere load with a power factor of 87 percent supplied from a three-phase, 208-volt source.

A. 1,375 watts

B. 2,350 watts

C. 2,700 watts

D. 3,132 watts

ANSWER – (B)   2,350 watts

Watts = volts x 1.732 x amperes x power factor

Watts = 208 volts x 1.732 x 7.5 amps x .87 = 2,350 watts

➢ In most **ac circuits** containing inductance or capacitance a phase shift exists, the current is **"out-of-phase"** with the voltage; the current and the voltage do not reach their peak and zero values at the same time. Apparent power (VA) is usually more than the power in watts when this condition occurs. Apparent power is calculated without considering the phase shift that may be present between total voltage and current in the circuit.

➢ Formulas used to determine the power factor are:

Power factor = $\dfrac{\text{watts}}{\text{VA}}$

Power factor = $\dfrac{\text{watts}}{\text{volt amps}}$

Power factor = $\dfrac{\text{kW x 1,000}}{\text{volt amps}}$

EXAMPLE - The power factor of a 5 kW load drawing 30 amperes of current when connected to a 208-volt, single-phase source is _____.

A. 92 percent

B. 46 percent

C. 80 percent

D. 83 percent
ANSWER – (C)   80 percent

$$PF = \frac{kW \times 1{,}000}{volt \times amperes}$$

$$PF = \frac{5\ kW \times 1{,}000}{208\ volts \times 30\ amps} = \frac{5{,}000}{6{,}240} = .80\ or\ 80\%$$

- Formulas used to determine the current of a single-phase electrical load or system when the voltage and power factor are known are:

$$I = \frac{watts}{volts \times PF}$$

$$I = \frac{kw \times 1{,}000}{volts \times PF}$$

EXAMPLE – A 300 watt industrial type HID luminaire (lighting fixture) has a power factor of 85 percent and is connected to a 120 volt branch circuit. The luminaire will draw _____ of current.

    A. 2.94 amperes
    B. 2.50 amperes
    C. 3.25 amperes
    D. 2.13 amperes

ANSWER – (A)   2.94 amperes

$$I = \frac{watts}{volts \times PF}$$

$$I = \frac{300\ watts}{120\ volts \times .85} = \frac{300}{102} = 2.94\ amperes$$

- Formulas used to determine the current of a three-phase load or system when the voltage and the power factor are known are:

$$I = \frac{watts}{volts \times 1.732 \times PF}$$

$$I = \frac{kw \times 1{,}000}{volts \times 1.732 \times PF}$$

EXAMPLE - A 5 kW load having a power factor of 90 percent will draw _____ when connected to a 208Y/120 volt, three-phase electrical system.

    A. 37.47 amperes
    B. 13.88 amperes

C. 17.87 amperes
D. 15.42 amperes

ANSWER – (D)   15.42 amperes

$$I = \frac{kW \times 1,000}{volts \times 1.732 \times PF}$$

$$I = \frac{5\ kW \times 1,000}{208\ volts \times 1.732 \times .9} = \frac{5,000}{324.2} = 15.42\ amperes$$

OHM'S LAW CIRCLE FORMULAS

RELATED INFORMATION:

> The Ohm's Law circle formula illustrates the relationship between **voltage**, **current** and **resistance**.

> The letter "**E**" represents electromotive force, or voltage.

> The letter "**I**" represents the intensity of the current.

> The letter "**R**" represents the friction opposite the flow of electrons in a conductor and is known as resistance; the unit of measurement is the ohm.

> In an alternating current circuit, factors that oppose current flow are conductor resistance, capacitive reactance, and inductive reactance. This total opposition to current flow is known as impedance and is also measured in ohms; the letter "**Z**" represents the impedance and may be substituted for the letter "**R**".

> The formula used to determine the current flow in an electrical circuit or load when the resistance and voltage are known is:

$$I = \frac{E}{R}$$

$$I = \frac{volts}{resistance}$$

EXAMPLE – A 120 volt circuit supplies an incandescent luminaire (lighting fixture) with a resistance of 200 ohms. Determine the current flow, in amperes, of the circuit.

A. 6.00 amperes
B. 0.60 amperes

C. 3.00 amperes
D. 1.60 amperes

ANSWER – (B)   0.60 amperes

$$I = \frac{volts}{resistance} = \frac{120\ volts}{200\ ohms} = 0.60\ amperes$$

➢ The formula used to determine the voltage or voltage drop in an electrical circuit when the current and resistance are known is:

E = I x R

E = current x resistance

EXAMPLE – Determine the voltage drop of two size 10 AWG copper conductors that supply a 16 ampere load located 100 feet from the voltage source.
Given: The total resistance of the two conductors is 0.25 ohms.

    A. 2.00 volts
    B. 0.40 volts
    C. 4.00 volts
    D. 40.00 volts

ANSWER – (C)   4.00 volts

E = I x R
E = 16 amperes x .25 ohms   = 4 volts

➢ The formula used to determine the resistance in an electrical circuit or load when the voltage and current are known is:

R = $\frac{E}{I}$

R = $\frac{voltage}{current}$

EXAMPLE – Determine the resistance of the heating elements of an electric baseboard heater that draws 8 amperes when supplied from a 120 volt source.

    A. 0.07 ohms
    B. 960 ohms
    C. 15 ohms
    D. 150 ohms

ANSWER – (C)   15 ohms

$$R = \frac{volts}{current} = \frac{120 \text{ volts}}{8 \text{ amperes}} = 15 \text{ ohms}$$

UNIT 1
SELF-ASSESSMENT QUIZ

1. One kVA is equal to _____.

    A. 100 VA
    B. 1,000 volts
    C. 1,000 VA
    D. 10,000 VA

2. 5,000 watts is equal to _____.

    A. 500 kW
    B. 5 kW
    C. 0.50 kW
    D. 50 kW

3. Where a 120-volt microwave oven is rated 1,200 watts, how much current, in amperes, will the microwave oven draw?

    A. 0.10 amperes
    B. 5 amperes
    C. 10 amperes
    D. 15 amperes

4. When an electric hair dryer draws six (6) amperes when connected to a 120 volt source, the rating of the hair dryer is _____ .

    A. 720 watts
    B. 750 watts
    C. 20 watts
    D. 200 watts

5. When a 240-volt, single-phase branch circuit has a current flow of 20 amperes, what is the resistance, in ohms, of this branch circuit?

    A. 3 ohms

B. 6 ohms
C. 9 ohms
D. 12 ohms

6.   When a 2 kW electric baseboard heater is connected to a 240-volt, single-phase circuit, the current flow in the circuit is _____.

   A. 4.15 amperes
   B. 8.33 amperes
   C. 12.50 amperes
   D. 16.66 amperes

7.   Determine the power consumed, in VA, by a lighting load that operates at 115 volts, draws eight amperes and has a power factor of 80 percent.

   A. 1,150 VA
   B. 960 VA
   C. 920 VA
   D. 736 VA

8.   A 150 ampere rated, 120/240-volt, single-phase residential service will have a volt-ampere rating of _____.

   A. 180,000 VA
   B. 90,000 VA
   C. 36,000 VA
   D. 72,000 VA

9.   A 15 kW, 208-volt, single-phase heat pump will have a full-load current rating   of _____.

   A. 72 amperes
   B. 46 amperes
   C. 66 amperes
   D. 33 amperes

10.   What is the power factor of a 6,500 watt load that draws 33 amperes of current when connected to a 240-volt, single-phase source?

   A. 1.21 percent
   B. 82.0 percent
   C. 68.0 percent
   D. 1.04 percent

11. Given: An electric baseboard heater has a total resistance of 22 ohms and is supplied with a 240-volt, single-phase power source. Determine the current.

    A. 10.9 amperes
    B. 21.8 amperes
    C. 0.09 amperes
    D. 1.01 amperes

12. The power factor of a 5 kW load drawing 30 amperes of current when connected to a 208-volt, single-phase source is _____.

    A. 92 percent
    B. 46 percent
    C. 80 percent
    D. 83 percent

13. A 200 ampere rated, 208Y/120-volt, three-phase, 4-wire commercial service will have a VA rating of _____.

    A. 360 VA
    B. 43,231 VA
    C. 41,600 VA
    D. 72,051 VA

14. Ohm's Law is a relationship between _____.

    A. current, voltage and amperes
    B. current, voltage and power
    C. voltage, current and resistance
    D. voltage, power and resistance

15. What is the rated secondary current of a 600 VA, single-phase transformer at unity power factor, that has a 200-volt input and a 15-volt secondary?

    A. 10 amperes
    B. 20 amperes
    C. 13 amperes
    D. 40 amperes

16. Determine the line current, in amperes, on a balanced three-phase electrical system with a load of 25 kVA per phase and a line voltage of 208Y/120-volts. Total power is 75 kVA.

   A. 87 amperes
   B. 144 amperes
   C. 208 amperes
   D. 360 amperes

17. If an industrial type HID luminaire (lighting fixture), rated at 300 watts, is connected to a 120-volt branch circuit and is drawing three amperes of current, the luminaire has a power factor of _____.

   A. 83 percent
   B. 93 percent
   C. 1.2 percent
   D. 79 percent

18. 5 horsepower is equal to _____.

   A. 5 kW
   B. 3,730 watts
   C. 5,000 watts
   D. 5 kVA

19. When eight (8) 400 watt metal halide luminaries (lighting fixtures), each have a power factor of .86, are connected to a 277-volt, single-phase lighting branch circuit, the full-load current (FLC) of the luminaires will be _____.

   A. 11.55 amperes
   B. 5.54 amperes
   C. 13.43 amperes
   D. 6.68 amperes

20. When a 400 ampere rated commercial service is supplied with a 480Y/277 volt, three-phase, 4-wire electrical system, the service has a rating of _____.

   A. 144.10 kVA
   B. 110.80 kVA

C. 192.00 kVA
D. 332.50 kVA

NOTES

UNIT 2

BRANCH CIRCUITS

Upon successfully completing this unit of study, the student will be familiar with the concept of sizing, rating and overcurrent protection of branch circuits as well as calculating the number required.

$$\# \text{ of CIRCUITS} = \frac{\text{LOAD VA}}{\text{CIRCUIT VA}}$$

UNIT 2

BRANCH CIRCUITS

RELATED INFORMATION:

➤ The definition of a **branch circuit** is the circuit conductors between the final overcurrent device (circuit breaker or fuse) protecting the circuit and the outlet(s). **[Article 100]** In other words, that portion of a wiring system that is beyond the final overcurrent device protecting the circuit and the outlet(s).

➤ The rating of a **branch circuit** is determined by the maximum ampere rating of the overcurrent protective device (circuit breaker or fuse) and **NOT** by the size of the conductors used for the branch-circuit. **[210.3]**

➤ In general, branch-circuit conductors shall have an allowable ampacity (current-carrying capacity) of **NOT** less than **125%** of the **continuous** load, plus **100%** of the **non-continuous** load to be served. **[210.19(A)(1)(a)]**

EXAMPLE – When a single branch-circuit serves a continuous load of 20 amperes and a non-continuous load of 10 amperes, the branch-circuit conductors are required to have an allowable current-carrying capacity of at least _____.

    A. 30.00 amperes
    B. 37.50 amperes
    C. 35.00 amperes
    D. 32.50 amperes

ANSWER – (C)   35.00 amperes

        20 amperes x 1.25 = 25 amperes
        10 amperes x 1.00 = 10 amperes
                  TOTAL = 35 amperes

➤ The definition of a **continuous** load is a load where the maximum current is expected to continue for **3 hours** or more. **[Article 100]**

➤ Examples of **continuous** loads are lighting loads for commercial and industrial occupancies that are expected to be operated for at least three (3) hours.

➤ Examples of **non-continuous** loads are general-purpose receptacle outlets provided for commercial, industrial, and residential occupancies and general-purpose lighting loads for residential occupancies.

➤ In general, overcurrent devices protecting branch-circuits shall have a rating of not less than **125%** of the **continuous** load to be served plus **100%** of the **non-continuous** load to be served. **[210.20(A)]** In other words, overcurrent devices protecting branch circuits are not to be loaded more than **80%** of their rated value when protecting **continuous** loads.

EXAMPLE - When a 100 ampere rated circuit breaker is used to protect a branch circuit serving a continuous load, the load shall not exceed _____.

      A. 80 amperes
      B. 100 amperes
      C. 125 amperes
      D. 115 amperes

ANSWER – (A)   80 amperes

        100 amperes x .80 = 80 amperes

➤ Note the exception to **210.20(A)**. If the overcurrent device protecting the circuit is **listed** for **continuous operation**, it shall be permitted to have a rating of **100%** of the continuous load(s) to be served. **Be advised**, circuit breakers are **NOT** listed for continuous operation, unless they have a rating of at least **400 amperes** or more.

➤ In general, branch-circuit loads shall be calculated as shown in **220.12**, **220.14**, and **220.16 [220.10]**

➤ In general, lighting loads are to be supplied by 15-and 20-ampere rated branch-circuits. **[210.23(A)]**

➤ Lighting loads for specific occupancies shall be based on the unit load per square foot depending on the type of occupancy as given on **Table 220.12**. **[220.12]**

Table 220.12 General Lighting Loads by Occupancy

Type of Occupancy	UNIT LOAD	
	Volt-Amperes per Square	Volt-Amperes per Square

	Meter	Foot
Armories and auditoriums	11	1
Banks	39[b]	3½[b]
Barber shops and beauty parlors	33	3
Churches	11	1
Clubs	22	2
Court rooms	22	2
Dwelling units[a]	33	3
Garages – commercial (storage)	6	½
Hospitals	22	2
Hotels and motels, including apartment houses without provision for cooking by tenants[a]	22	2
Industrial commercial (loft) buildings	22	2
Lodge rooms	17	1½
Office buildings	39[b]	3½[b]
Restaurants	22	2
Schools	33	3
Stores	33	3
Warehouses (storage)	3	¼
In any of the preceding occupancies except one-family dwellings and individual dwelling units of two-family and multifamily dwellings:		
Assembly halls and auditoriums	11	1
Halls, corridors, closets, stairways	6	½
Storage spaces	3	¼

[a]See 220.14(J) [b]See 220.14(K)

> General lighting loads are to be calculated from the outside dimensions of the building. **[220.12]**

> To determine the area, in square feet, of a building, simply multiply the length of the building times the width of the building.

EXAMPLE -   A building has outside dimensions of 100 feet in length and 75 feet in width. The building has a total area of _____.

        A. 750 square feet
        B. 175 square feet
        C. 7,500 square feet
        D. 1,750 square feet

ANSWER -   (C)   7,500 sq. ft.

        100 ft. x 75 ft. = 7,500 sq. ft.

➤   When calculating the area, in square feet, of a multi-story building, multiply the length of the building by the width of the building by the number of stories.

EXAMPLE -   A three (3) story building having outside dimensions of 100 feet by 75 feet has a total area of _____.

        A. 2,225 square feet
        B. 7,500 square feet
        C. 15,000 square feet
        D. 22,500 square feet

ANSWER -   (D)   22,500 sq. ft.

        100 ft. x 75 ft. x 3 (stories) = 22,500 sq. ft.

➤   When calculating lighting loads for **dwelling units** do **NOT** include open porches, garages or unfinished spaces not adaptable for future use. **[220.12]**

➤   Remember, in general, lighting loads for habitable spaces of dwelling units and guest rooms of hotels and motels are **not considered** as continuous use. But lighting loads of commercial and industrial occupancies **are considered** as continuous use.

➤   The formula used to determine the minimum number of general lighting branch-circuits required for a dwelling unit is:

Number of Circuits = $\dfrac{\text{load VA}}{\text{circuit VA}}$

EXAMPLE –   A dwelling unit having 2,000 sq. ft. of habitable space is required to have at least _____ 15-ampere, 120-volt general-purpose lighting branch-circuits.

A. two
B. three
C. four
D. five

ANSWER - (C)   four

$$\frac{2,000 \text{ sq. ft. x 3 VA}}{120 \text{ volts x 15 amperes}} = \frac{6,000 \text{ VA}}{1,800 \text{ VA}} = 3.3 = 4 \text{ circuits}$$

➤ When calculating branch-circuits, when your calculation is more than a whole number, ex. 3.3, you must go to the next whole number. In other words, you cannot install part of a circuit or circuit breaker.

➤ Apartment dwellings without provisions for cooking by tenants are to be calculated at the same value, **2 VA** per square foot, as hotels and motels when determining the minimum of general lighting branch-circuits required for the living units. **[Table 220.12]**

EXAMPLE - An apartment complex, without cooking facilities provided for the tenants, having 12,000 sq. ft. of living area, is required to have at least _____ 20 ampere, 120-volt general lighting branch-circuits, or at least _____ 15 ampere, 120-volt general lighting branch-circuits.

A. ten – ten
B. fourteen – fourteen
C. ten – thirteen
D. ten – fourteen

ANSWER – (D)   ten – fourteen

$$\frac{12,000 \text{ sq. ft. x 2 VA}}{120 \text{ volts x } \mathbf{20} \text{ amperes}} = \frac{24,000 \text{ VA}}{2,400 \text{ VA}} = 10 \text{ circuits}$$

$$\frac{12,000 \text{ sq. ft. x 2 VA}}{120 \text{ volts x } \mathbf{15} \text{ amperes}} = \frac{24,000 \text{ VA}}{1,800 \text{ VA}} = 13.3 = 14 \text{ circuits}$$

➤ A formula used to determine the minimum number of required general lighting branch-circuits for an office building, store, bank, restaurant, etc. is :

Number of Circuits = $\frac{\text{load VA x } \mathbf{125\%}}{\text{circuit VA}}$

EXAMPLE - A 10,000 sq. ft. restaurant is required to be provided with at least _____ 20-ampere, 120-volt general lighting branch-circuits.

A. eight

B. nine
C. ten
D. eleven

ANSWER - (D)   eleven

$$\frac{10,000 \times 2 \text{ VA} \times \textbf{125\%}}{120 \text{ volts} \times 20 \text{ amps}} - \frac{25,000 \text{ VA}}{2,400 \text{ VA}} - 10.4 = 11 \text{ circuits}$$

➢ Because the circuit breakers protecting the branch-circuits are not permitted to be loaded to more than **80 percent** of their rated value, **[210.20(A)]** we can also use this formula:

number of circuits = $\dfrac{\text{load VA}}{\text{circuit VA} \times \textbf{80\%}}$

number of circuits = $\dfrac{10,000 \times 2 \text{ VA}}{120 \times 20 \times \textbf{80\%}} = \dfrac{20,000 \text{ VA}}{1,920 \text{ VA}} = 10.4 = 11$ circuits

➢ Notice that **Table 220.12** reflects minimum requirements for general lighting loads. Many commercial, particularly mercantile, occupancies have luminaries (lighting fixtures) installed for display, specialty, enhancement or accent lighting in addition to the general lighting. These loads are required to be included when calculating lighting loads.

EXAMPLE -   A 15,000 sq. ft. retail store has 10,000 VA of accent lighting in addition to the general lighting. How many 120-volt, 20-ampere branch-circuits are required for the accent and general lighting loads?

    A. 30
    B. 24
    C. 36
    D. 32

ANSWER -   (A)   30 circuits

General ltg. circuits = $\dfrac{15,000 \times 3 \text{ VA}}{120 \times 20 \times 80\%} = \dfrac{45,000}{1,920} = 23.4 = 24$

Accent ltg. circuits = $\dfrac{10,000 \text{ VA}}{120 \times 20 \times 80\%} = \dfrac{10,000}{1,920} = 5.2 = 6$

24 + 6 = 30 circuits total

➢ When reviewing **Table 220.12** notice the subscript **(b)** opposite of banks and office buildings which refers you to **220.14(K)**. This article indicates when the number of general-purpose receptacle outlets to be installed in the building has not yet been determined, **one VA** per square foot is to be added to the calculation for the outlets. The NEC initiated this requirement because it is common practice for banks and office buildings to have future tenant spaces and the actual number of general-purpose receptacle outlets to be installed have not been determined prior to complete construction of the building.

➢ For non-dwelling units, receptacle outlets are to be calculated at a value of not less than **180 volt-amperes** for each single or duplex receptacle. **[220.14(I)]**

➢ The formula used to determine the maximum number of receptacle outlets permitted on a branch-circuit is:

$$\text{Number of Receptacles} = \frac{\text{circuit VA}}{180 \text{ VA}}$$

EXAMPLE - No more than _____ duplex receptacle outlets installed in a commercial establishment may be supplied from a single 20-ampere rated, 120-volt branch-circuit.

    A. ten
    B. twelve
    C. thirteen
    D. fourteen

ANSWER - (C) thirteen

$$\frac{120 \text{ volts x 20 amperes}}{180 \text{ VA}} = \frac{2,400}{180} = 13.3 = 13 \text{ receptacles}$$

➢ When determining the minimum number of required branch-circuits for general-purpose receptacle outlets when the specific number of receptacle outlets to be installed in a commercial building is known, this formula may be used:

$$\text{number of circuits} = \frac{180 \text{ VA x number of receptacles}}{\text{circuit VA}}$$

EXAMPLE - You are to install one hundred (100) duplex receptacle outlets in an existing office building. How many 20-ampere, 120-volt, branch-circuits will need to be added to supply the additional receptacles?

    A. twelve

B. ten
C. seven
D. eight

ANSWER - (D)   eight

$$\frac{180 \text{ VA x } 100}{120 \text{ volts x } 20 \text{ amps}} = \frac{18,000}{2,400} = 7.5 = 8 \text{ circuits}$$

➤ Article **220.14(G)** indicates two methods are permitted when calculating branch-circuits for show window lighting.
(1) 180 VA per receptacle outlet in compliance with **210.62**, which requires one receptacle per twelve linear feet of the show window.
(2) 200 volt-amps per linear foot of the show window.

The linear foot calculation method is the most commonly used method.   The following formula may be used:

$$\text{number of circuits} = \frac{200 \text{ VA x linear ft. x } \textbf{125\%}}{\text{circuit VA}}$$

EXAMPLE - A department store is to have seventy five (75) linear feet of show window space. Using the linear foot method of calculation, how many 20-ampere, 120-volt branch-circuits must be provided for the show window lighting?

A. eight
B. seven
C. six
D. five

ANSWER - (A)   eight

$$\frac{200 \text{ VA x } 75 \text{ ft. x } \textbf{125\%}}{20 \text{ amps x } 120 \text{ volts}} = \frac{18,750}{2,400} = 7.8 = 8 \text{ circuits}$$

➤ When calculating the number of required branch-circuits for multioutlet assemblies installed in commercial, industrial and educational locations, the calculation is to be based on the use of the supplied cord-connected equipment that is expected to be used at the same time. **[220.14(H)]**

➤ When calculating the required branch-circuits for fixed multioutlet assemblies where the cord-connected appliances are **unlikely** to be used simultaneously, you can use the following formula:

$$\text{number of circuits} = \frac{(\text{linear ft.}/5) \text{ x } 180 \text{ VA}}{\text{circuit VA}}$$

EXAMPLE - A small cabinet makers shop is to install fifty (50) feet of multioutlet assembly where the appliances to be used are unlikely to be operated simultaneously. Where 20-ampere, 120-volt branch-circuits are used to supply the assembly, what is the minimum required?

      A. one
      B. two
      C. three
      D. four

ANSWER - (A) one

$$\frac{(50/5) \times 180}{120 \text{ volts} \times 20 \text{ amps}} = \frac{(10) \times 180}{2,400} = \frac{1,800}{2,400} = .75 \text{ or 1 circuit}$$

> When calculating the branch-circuits required for fixed multioutlet assemblies where the cord-connected appliances are **likely** to be used simultaneously, the following formula may be used:

$$\text{number of circuits} = \frac{\text{linear ft.} \times 180 \text{ VA}}{\text{circuit VA}}$$

EXAMPLE - Seventy five (75) feet of fixed multioutlet assembly is to be wall-mounted in a retail outlet displaying television sets where most of the TV sets are operating simultaneously. How many 20-ampere, 120-volt branch-circuits are needed to supply this installation?

      A. two
      B. five
      C. six
      D. seven

ANSWER - (C) six

$$\frac{75 \text{ ft.} \times 180 \text{ VA}}{120 \text{ volts} \times 20 \text{ amps}} = \frac{13,500}{2,400} = 5.6 = 6 \text{ circuits}$$

> The definition of an individual branch-circuit is a branch-circuit that supplies only one utilization equipment. Examples of individual branch circuits would be branch-circuits supplying electric water heaters, dryers, ranges, cooktops, air conditioners, etc. **[Article 100]**

➢ For **other than** individual branch-circuits the rating of the circuits shall be 15, 20, 30, 40 and 50 amperes. **[210.3] Individual** branch circuits may also have ratings of the same size, in addition they may have ratings of 25, 35, 45 and 60 amperes or more. See **Article 240.6(A)** for the standard size ampere ratings of fuses and circuit breakers.

➢ When selecting ampere ratings of overcurrent protective devices, If the conductors being protected are **NOT** part of a multi-outlet branch circuit supplying receptacles for cord-and-plug-connected portable loads and the ampacity of the conductors do not correspond with the standard ampere rating of a fuse or circuit breaker and the next higher standard rating selected does **not exceed 800 amperes**, the next higher standard overcurrent device shall be permitted to be used. **[240.4(B)(1),(2)&(3)]**

➢ When selecting overcurrent protective devices where the overcurrent device is rated **over 800 amperes**, if the ampacity of the conductors do not correspond with the standard rating of a fuse or a circuit breaker you must go **down** to the next standard size fuse or circuit breaker. **[240.4(C)]**

➢ The overcurrent protection for small conductors, sizes 14 AWG through 10 AWG, shall be as listed in **240.4(D)**. Do not get overcurrent confused with ampacity.

➢ When sizing branch-circuits and overcurrent protection for appliances such as water heaters and cooktops, they are to be sized per **Article 422**. Branch-circuits for household cooking appliances shall be permitted to be in accordance with **Table 220.55**, which will be discussed later. **[422.10(A)]**

➢ Fixed storage-type water heaters with a capacity of 120 gallons or less shall be considered a continuous load when sizing branch-circuits. **[422.13]**

EXAMPLE - The branch-circuit conductors supplying a 5 kW, 240-volt, single-phase water heater, are required to have an ampacity of at least _____.

    A. 15.0 amperes
    B. 20.8 amperes
    C. 26.0 amperes
    D. 31.2 amperes

ANSWER - (C) 26.0 amperes

$$I = \frac{5 \text{ kW} \times 1{,}000}{240 \text{ volts}} = \frac{5{,}000}{240} = 20.8 \times \mathbf{125\%} = 26.04 \text{ amperes}$$

    *NOTE - To solve this problem you should refer to **422.13** and **422.10(A)**.

EXAMPLE - The MAXIMUM size circuit breaker that may be used to protect a 5 kW, 240-volt, single-phase electric water heater has a rating of _____.

      A. 20 amperes
      B. 25 amperes
      C. 30 amperes
      D. 35 amperes

ANSWER - (D)   35 amperes

$$I = \frac{5,000}{240} = 20.8 \text{ amps} \times 150\% = 31.2 \text{ amperes}$$

*NOTE - The next standard size circuit breaker has a rating of 35 amperes. To solve this problem you should refer to **422.11(E)(3)** and **240.6(A)**.

> When sizing branch-circuits and overcurrent protection for fixed electric space-heating equipment, they are to be sized in compliance with **Article 424**.

> Fixed electric space-heating equipment shall be considered as **continuous loads**. **[424.3(B)]**

EXAMPLE - The branch-circuit conductors supplying a 15 kW, 240 volt, single-phase fixed electric space-heater, are required to have an ampacity of at least _____.

      A. 42 amperes
      B. 52 amperes
      C. 63 amperes
      D. 78 amperes

ANSWER - (D)   78 amperes

$$I = \frac{15 \times 1,000}{240} = \frac{15,000}{240} = 62.5 \times \textbf{125\%} = 78 \text{ amperes}$$

> The following formula may be used to determine the minimum number of a required branch-circuits to supply fixed electric space-heating equipment:

number of circuits = load VA x **125%**

circuit VA

EXAMPLE - What is the minimum number of 20-ampere, 240-volt branch-circuits required for twelve (12) baseboard heaters, each rated 1,250 watts at 240-volts, single-phase?

        A. three
        B. four
        C. slx
        D. eight

ANSWER – (B)   four

$$\frac{1{,}250 \times 12 \times \mathbf{125\%}}{240 \text{ volts} \times 20 \text{ amps}} = \frac{18{,}750}{4{,}800} = 3.9 = 4 \text{ circuits}$$

UNIT 2
SELF-ASSESSMENT QUIZ

1. A continuous load is a load where the maximum current is expected to continue for _____ or more.

        A. 15 minutes
        B. one hour
        C. two hours
        D. three hours

2. Disregarding exceptions, branch-circuit conductors serving continuous loads are required to have an allowable ampacity of at LEAST _____ of the load(s) to be served.

        A. 80 percent
        B. 100 percent
        C. 125 percent

D. 150 percent

3. A six (6) story building having outside dimensions of 100 feet by 150 feet, has a total area of _____ .

    A. 10,000 sq. ft.
    B. 15,000 sq. ft.
    C. 90,000 sq. ft.
    D. 60,000 sq. ft.

4. Of the following listed, which one is NOT a standard rating for a circuit breaker?

    A. 50 amperes
    B. 75 amperes
    C. 90 amperes
    D. 110 amperes

5. In general, regardless of the conductor insulation, size 10 AWG copper conductors shall have overcurrent protection rated at NOT more than _____ .

    A. 30 amperes
    B. 25 amperes
    C. 35 amperes
    D. 20 amperes

6. The MINIMUM number of 120-volt, 15-ampere, general lighting branch-circuits required for a dwelling with 70 feet by 30 feet of livable space is _____.

    A. two
    B. three
    C. four
    D. five

7. When calculating the minimum number of required branch-circuits for general-purpose receptacles in a dwelling, how many VA per square foot is to be used for the calculation?

    A. none
    B. one VA
    C. two VA
    D. three VA

8. For other than dwelling units, receptacle outlets are to be calculated at a value of NOT less than _____ for each single or duplex receptacle.

    A. 100 VA
    B. 120 VA
    C. 150 VA
    D. 180 VA

9. What is the MAXIMUM continuous load, in VA, that a 240-volt, single-phase   branch-circuit may be protected with a 20-ampere rated circuit breaker?

    A. 2,400 VA
    B. 2,850 VA
    C. 3,840 VA
    D. 4,800 VA

10. Determine the MINIMUM number of 15-ampere, 120-volt general lighting   branch-circuits required for a dwelling having 2,600 sq. ft. of habitable space, a   garage that measures 20 feet by 30 feet, and a 1,300 sq. ft. basement that is   adaptable for future use.

    A. eight
    B. seven
    C. six
    D. five

11. A 240-volt, single-phase, 3,600 watt electric water heater is to be installed in a residential garage. What is the MAXIMUM size circuit breaker permitted for   overcurrent protection for the water heater?

    A. 15 amperes
    B. 20 amperes
    C. 30 amperes
    D. 25 amperes

12. An apartment complex, with cooking facilities provided for the tenants, having 16,000 sq. ft. of living area, is required to have at LEAST _____ 20-ampere,   120-volt general lighting branch-circuits.

    A. 18
    B. 27
    C. 20
    D. 14

13. A 6,000 sq. ft. bank is required to be provided with at LEAST _____ 20-ampere, 120-volt general lighting branch-circuits.

    A. 8
    B. 9
    C. 10
    D. 11

14. For a retail store, determine the MAXIMUM number of 120-volt fluorescent luminaries (lighting fixtures), each drawing 1.6 amperes may be supplied from a 20-ampere rated, 120-volt lighting branch-circuit.

      A. ten
      B. eight
      C. thirteen
      D. nine

15. For a commercial building, NO more than _____ single or duplex receptacles may be supplied from a 15-ampere, 120-volt branch-circuit.

      A. ten
      B. eleven
      C. twelve
      D. thirteen

16. Two hundred (200) feet of fixed multioutlet assembly is to be wall-mounted in a computer classroom where most of the computers are to be operating simultaneously. Determine the MINIMUM number of 20-ampere, 120-volt branch-circuits required to supply the multioutlet assembly.

      A. twelve
      B. fifteen
      C. thirteen
      D. eleven

17. The branch-circuit conductors supplying a 30 gallon fixed storage-type water heater, are required to have an ampacity of at LEAST _____ of the marked nameplate rating of the appliance.

      A. 80 percent
      B. 100 percent
      C. 125 percent
      D. 150 percent

18. Given: You are to install one hundred (100), 277-volt fluorescent luminaries (lighting fixtures) in a tenant space of a retail outlet mall. The lighting fixtures have a current rating of 0.75 amperes each. Determine the MINIMUM number of 20-ampere, 277-volt branch-circuits required to supply the luminaries.

      A. four

B. seven
C. six
D. five

19. A branch-circuit is to supply a continuous load of 160 amperes. The branch   circuit conductors are required to have an ampacity (current-carrying capacity)   of at LEAST _____.

A. 160 amperes
B. 200 amperes
C. 150 amperes
D. 128 amperes

20. The MAXIMUM ampere rating for a circuit breaker protecting a residential   central space electric heating unit rated at 18 kW at 240-volts, single-phase, is _____.

A. 75 amperes
B. 80 amperes
C. 90 amperes
D. 100 amperes

NOTES

UNIT 3

COOKING EQUIPMENT & APPLIANCE DEMAND LOADS

Upon successfully completing this study unit, the student will be familiar with the concept of calculating demand loads for household cooking equipment and appliances.

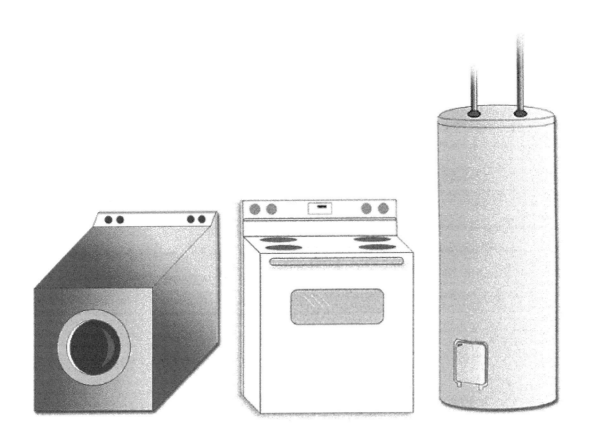

Unit 3

COOKING EQUIPMENT & APPLIANCE DEMAND LOADS

RELATED INFORMATION:

> The definition of **demand factor** is the ratio of the maximum demand of a system, or part of a system, to the total connected load of a system or the part of the system under consideration. **[Article 100]**

> The **demand load** of an electrical system or an electrical appliance is the MAXIMUM load of the system or appliance that may be required at a given time. In other words, **demand factors** are applied because all of the electrical loads are not used at the same time; all of the luminaires (lighting fixtures) will not be on at the same time, neither will all the receptacle outlets and appliances be fully loaded at the same time.

> A good example of this concept would be an electric range having a **connected load** rating of **12 kW**. The range-top has four heating elements, the oven has one heating element, another heating element is required for the broiler, and accessories such as timers and lights are included in the total connected load. Therefore, we can apply **demand factors** as shown in **Table 220.55** which reflects a **demand load** of **8 kW**, because we would not be using all of the heating elements and the accessories at their **MAXIMUM** value at any given time.

> **Table 220.55** and it's related notes are to be used to apply **demand factors** for household electric ranges, wall-mounted ovens, counter-mounted cooking units, and other household cooking appliances over **1¾ kW** rating. This table is to be used when applying **demand factors** when sizing services, feeders and branch circuits for dwelling units and instructional programs for educational institutions.

Table 220.55 Demand Factors and Loads for Household Electric Ranges, Wall-Mounted Ovens, Counter-Mounted Cooking Units, and Other Household Cooking Appliances over 1¾ kW Rating (Column C to be used in all cases except as otherwise permitted in Note 3).

Demand Factor (Percent) (See Notes)

Number of Appliances	Column A (Less than 3½ kW Rating)	Column B (3½ kW to 8¾ kW Rating)	Column C Maximum Demand (kW) (See Notes) (Not over 12 kW Rating)
1	80	80	8
2	75	65	11
3	70	55	14
4	66	50	17
5	62	45	20
6	59	43	21
7	56	40	22
8	53	36	23
9	51	35	24
10	49	34	25
11	47	32	26
12	45	32	27
13	43	32	28
14	41	32	29
15	40	32	30
16	39	28	31
17	38	28	32
18	37	28	33
19	36	28	34
20	35	28	35
21	34	26	36
22	33	26	37
23	32	26	38
24	31	26	39
25	30	26	40
26-30	30	24	15 kW + 1 kW for each range
31-40	30	22	
41-50	30	20	25 kW + ¾ kW for each range
51-60	30	18	
61 and over	30	16	

1. Over 12 kW through 27 kW ranges all of same rating. For ranges individually rated more than 12 kW but not more than 27 kW, the maximum demand in Column C shall be increased 5 percent for each additional kilowatt of rating or major fraction thereof by which the rating of individual ranges exceeds 12 kW.
2. Over 8¾ kW through 27 kW ranges of unequal ratings. For ranges individually rated more than 8¾ kW and of different ratings, but none exceeding 27 kW, an average value of rating shall be calculated by adding together the ratings of all ranges to obtain the total connected load (using 12 kW for any range rated less than 12 kW) and dividing by the total number of ranges. Then the maximum demand in Column C shall be increased 5 percent for each kilowatt or major fraction thereof by which this average value exceeds 12 kW.
3. Over 1¾ kW through 8¾ kW. In lieu of the method provided in Column C, it shall be permissible to add the nameplate ratings of all household cooking appliances rated more than 1¾ kW but not more than 8¾ kW and multiply the sum by the demand factors specified in Column A and Column B for the given number of appliances. Where the rating of cooking appliances falls under both Column A and Column B, the demand factors for each column shall be applied to the appliances for that column, and the results added together.
4. Branch-Circuit Load. It shall be permissible to calculate the branch-circuit load for one range in accordance with Table 220.55. The branch-circuit load for one wall-mounted oven or one counter-mounted cooking unit shall be the nameplate rating of the appliance. The branch-circuit load for a counter-mounted cooking unit and not more than two wall-mounted ovens, all supplied from a single branch circuit and located in the same room, shall be calculated by adding the nameplate rating of the individual appliances and treating this total as equivalent to one range.
5. This table also applies to household cooking appliances rated over 1¾ kW and used in instructional programs.

> Take notice that household electric ranges having a rating of **8.75 kW** or **more** are required to be supplied by at least a **40 ampere** rated branch circuit. **[210.19(A)(3)]** Also, **note 4** to **Table 220.55** states the branch circuit load for **one** wall-mounted oven or **one** counter-mounted cooking unit shall be the **nameplate rating** of the appliance. Therefore, demand factors are **not** to be applied when sizing branch circuits for these single cooking units.

> **Table 220.55** is separated into four columns. The first column shows the number of appliances. **Column A** is to be used when determining demand factors of cooking equipment of **less than 3½ kW rating** and is expressed in **percent**. **Column B** is used for equipment rated **3½ to 8¾ kW** and is also expressed in **percent**. **Column C** lists applicable demand factors for equipment rated **not over 12 kW** and is expressed in **kW**. When applying demand factors be sure you are in the correct column and on the right line, because the maximum demand changes in relationship with the number of appliances.

> As per **note 3**, When the rating of cooking appliances fall under **both** Column A and B, the demand factors for each column shall be applied for that column and the results added together.

EXAMPLE –   A small residential duplex has a 3 kW counter-mounted cooktop and a 4 kW wall-mounted oven installed in each unit. Determine the demand load, in kW, to be added to the ungrounded service-entrance conductors for the cooking equipment.

        A. 9.7 kW
        B. 14.0 kW
        C. 11.2 kW
        D. 10.5 kW

ANSWER -   (A)   9.7 kW

        Col. A – 3 kW + 3 kW = 6 kW x **75%** = 4.5 kW
        Col. B – 4 kW + 4 kW = 8 kW x **65%** = 5.2 kW
                            TOTAL = 9.7 kW demand

> When a single range having a rating of **3½ kW to 8¾ kW** is used as cooking equipment for households, we may use the demand factors shown in **Column B** when sizing branch-circuits, (**note 4**) feeders and service-entrance conductors.

EXAMPLE –   What is the demand load, in kW, for the branch-circuit conductors supplying an 8 kW residential electric range?

        A. 8.0 kW
        B. 6.4 kW
        C. 6.0 kW
        D. 7.2 kW

ANSWER –   (B)   6.4 kW

8 kW x 80% = 6.4 kW demand load

> Column C is to be used when applying demand factors for electric ranges of **not over 12 kW** rating.

EXAMPLE - Determine the demand load, in kW, to be added to the ungrounded service-entrance conductors for a 9.6 kW residential electric range.

      A. 9.6 kW
      B. 8.0 kW
      C. 10.0 kW
      D. 12.0 kW

ANSWER - (B) 8.0 kW

        Column C of Table 220.55 shows a demand of **8 kW** for one range not over 12 kW rating.

> When we have multiple ranges of **equal ratings** up to **12 kW** we are to also use **Column C**.

EXAMPLE - A ten (10) unit apartment complex is to have a 10 kW electric range installed in each unit. When sizing the ungrounded service-entrance conductors, the total demand load for the multiple ranges is _____.

      A. 30 kW
      B. 80 kW
      C. 25 kW
      D. 100 kW

ANSWER - (C) 25 kW

        Column C of Table 220.55 shows a demand of 25 kW for ten ranges of not over 12 kW rating.

> When applying maximum demand factors for ranges all of the **same rating over 12 kW through 27 kW**, we are to apply **note 1 and Column C** of **Table 220.55**, which states we are to increase the Column C demand value by **5%** for each kW that exceeds 12 kW.

EXAMPLE - What is the branch-circuit demand load, in amperes, for one 16 kW, 240 volt, single-phase residential electric range?

      A. 33 amperes

B. 50 amperes
C. 40 amperes
D. 67 amperes

ANSWER – (C)   40 amperes

16 kW – 12 kW = 4 kW x 5% – 20% increase in Column C
Col. C demand (1 range) = 8 kW x 120% = 9.6 kW demand

$$I = \frac{9.6 \text{ kW x } 1,000}{240 \text{ volts}} = \frac{9,600}{240} = 40 \text{ amperes}$$

> When applying demand factors for **multiple ranges**, all having the **same** nameplate rating of **more than 12 kW**, but **not more than 27 kW**, we are to also apply **note 1 and Column C** of **Table 220.55**.

EXAMPLE -   A four (4) unit residential town house has a 14 kW electric range installed in each unit. What is the demand load for the ranges, in kW, to be added to the ungrounded service-entrance conductors when sizing the service?

A. 56.0 kW
B. 44.8 kW
C. 28.0 kW
D. 18.7 kW

ANSWER -   (D)   18.7 kW

14 kW – 12 kW = 2 kW x 5% = 10% increase in Column C
Col. C demand (4 ranges) = 17 kW x 110% = 18.7 kW

> When applying maximum demand factors of ranges having **unequal ratings of 8¾ kW through 27 kW** we are to apply **note 2 and Column C** of **Table 220.55**.

EXAMPLE -   The vocational education department of a high school is to have three (3) electric ranges installed in a classroom; one 10 kW, one 11 kW and one 12 kW. The ranges are to be supplied by a 208 volt, single-phase feeder from a sub-panel. What is the demand load, in amperes, on the ungrounded feeder conductors?

A. 58 amperes
B. 67 amperes
C. 136 amperes
D. 142 amperes

ANSWER - (B)   67 amperes

In this situation you simply refer to Column C, which shows demand of 14 kW for three ranges, because not any of the ranges have a nameplate rating above 12 kW.

$$I = \frac{14 \text{ kW} \times 1,000}{208 \text{ volts}} = \frac{14,000}{208} = 67.3 \text{ amperes}$$

> When calculating demand factors for ranges of **unequal ratings** of **8¾ through 27 kW**, when the nameplate rating of any **range less than 12 kW** you are to use **12 kW** as a **minimum** and add the ratings together and divide by the number of ranges to obtain the average, then apply the same steps as per **note 1**. [**Note 2, Table 220.55**]

EXAMPLE -   Refer to the previous example. Another classroom in the high school is to install two electric ranges, one 16 kW and one 11 kW. Determine the demand load, in amperes, on the 208 volt, single-phase ungrounded feeder conductors.

A. 67 amperes
B. 76 amperes
C. 58 amperes
D. 63 amperes

ANSWER – (C)   58 amperes

$$12 \text{ kW (minimum)} + 16 \text{ kW} = \frac{28 \text{ kW}}{2 \text{ (ranges)}} = 14 \text{ kW average}$$

14 kW – 12 kW = 2 kW x **5%** = **10%** increase in Column C
Col. C demand (2 ranges) = 11 kW x **110%** = 12.1 kW demand

$$I = \frac{12.1 \text{ kW} \times 1,000}{208 \text{ volts}} = \frac{12,100}{208} = 58 \text{ amperes}$$

> **Note 4** of **Table 220.55** addresses **branch-circuits**; it states it is permissible to calculate the branch-circuit load for one range in accordance with **Table 220.55**, as we have shown. As mentioned before, the branch-circuit load for **one wall-mounted oven** or **one counter-mounted cooking unit** shall be the **nameplate rating** of the appliance. When sizing branch-circuit loads for a **single branch-circuit** supplying a counter-mounted cooking unit and not more than two (2) wall-mounted ovens, it is permissible to add the nameplate ratings of the appliances together and treat the result as one range.

EXAMPLE -   A 240-volt, single-phase branch-circuit (home run) is to supply one (1) 6 kW rated counter-mounted cooking unit and two (2) wall-mounted 4 kW rated ovens in a residential kitchen. What is the demand load, in amperes, on the branch-circuit for the appliances?

A. 22 amperes
B. 27 amperes
C. 33 amperes
D. 37 amperes

ANSWER -   (D)   37 amperes

6 kW + 4 kW + 4 kW = 14 kW connected load
14 kW – 12 kW = 2 kW x 5% = **10%** increase in Column C
Col. C demand (1 range) = 8 kW x 110% = 8.8 kW demand load

$$I = \frac{8.8 \text{ kW x } 1{,}000}{240 \text{ volts}} = \frac{8{,}800}{240} = 36.6 \text{ amperes}$$

➢ **Section 220.61(B)(1)** permits an additional demand factor of **70 percent** for the **neutral** (grounded) conductor, for a feeder or service supplying household electric ranges, wall-mounted ovens, counter mounted cooking units, and electric dryers after apply the applicable demand factors of **Table 220.55** for ranges and **Table 220.54** for dryers.

EXAMPLE - A four (4) unit apartment house is to have a 10.5 kW electric range installed in each unit. Determine the demand load, in kW, on the grounded (neutral) service-entrance conductor for the ranges.

A. 11.9 kW
B. 13.6 kW
C. 17.0 kW
D. 10.4 kW

ANSWER -   (A)   11.9 kW

Column C shows a demand of 17 kW for the demand on the ungrounded conductors for the four (4) electric ranges.

17 kW x **70%** = 11.9 kW neutral demand

➢ In a residential occupancy, a **75%** demand factor is permitted to be applied when **four(4) or more** fastened in place appliances such as water heaters, trash compactors, garage door openers, dishwashers, garbage disposers, sump pumps, attic fans, etc., are supplied from the same feeder or service. **[220.53]** **Note** this section does not apply to ranges, clothes dryers, space-heating and air-conditioning equipment.

EXAMPLE - A one-family dwelling unit is to have the following fastened in place appliances installed:

one – 1,200 VA dishwasher
one – 4,000 VA water heater
one – 1,150 VA garbage disposer
one -   700 VA attic fan
one – 1,920 VA garage door opener

The demand load, in VA, on the ungrounded service-entrance conductors for the listed appliances is _____.

A. 7,728 VA
B. 6,728 VA
C. 6,276 VA
D. 8,970 VA

ANSWER - (B)   6,728 VA

1,200 VA dishwasher
4,000 VA water heater
1,150 VA garbage disposer
   700 VA attic fan
1,920 VA garage door opener
8,970 VA connected load x **75%** = 6,728 VA demand

➢ In residential occupancies, demand factors may also be applied to electric clothes dryers; the use of demand factors in **Table 220.54** shall be permitted when sizing feeders and service entrance conductors. Each dryer shall be calculated at a **minimum of 5,000 watts (volt-amperes)** or the nameplate rating, whichever is larger. **[220.54]**

EXAMPLE - An eight (8) unit multifamily dwelling is to have the following electric clothes dryers installed in the laundry rooms of the tenants:

two – 4.5 kW rated
two – 5.5 kW rated
two – 6.0 kW rated
two – 6.5 kW rated

The demand load, in kW, to be added to the ungrounded feeder conductors for the listed electric dryers is _____.

A. 27.0 kW
B. 27.6 kW
C. 34.5 kW
D. 33.8 kW

ANSWER - (B)   27.6 kW

> two dryers @ 5.0 kW (minimum) = 10 kW
> two dryers @ 5.5 kW   = 11 kW
> two dryers @ 6.0 kW   = 12 kW
> two dryers @ 6.5 kW   = 13 kW
>   connected load   = 46 kW x **60%** = 27.6 kW

> ➤ An additional demand factor of **70 percent** is permitted for the **neutral** (grounded conductor) for a feeder or service supplying electric clothes dryers for dwelling units. **[220.61(B)(1)]**

EXAMPLE -   Refer to the previous example. The demand, in kW, on the grounded (neutral) conductor of the feeder conductors is _____.

> A. 32.20 kW
> B. 27.60 kW
> C. 19.32 kW
> D. 18.90 kW

ANSWER -   (C)   19.32 kW

> 27.6 kW (demand) load x **70%** (neutral demand) = 19.32 kW

> ➤ For commercial cooking related equipment, branch-circuits and overcurrent protection are sized according to the nameplate rating on the appliance. When sizing feeder and service conductors we may apply demand factors in accordance with **Table 220.56**. These demand factors shall not apply to space heating, ventilating or air-conditioning equipment. However, the feeder or service demand load is **not** permitted to be less than the sum of the **largest two** kitchen equipment loads. **[220.56]**

EXAMPLE -   A feeder is to supply the following cooking related equipment in the kitchen of a restaurant:

> oven   - 10 kW
> booster heater   - 15 kW
> dishwasher   - 2 kW
> garbage disposal - 1 kW
> water heater   - 6 kW
> steamer   - 4 kW

> What is the demand load on the ungrounded feeder conductors for the appliances?

> A. 38.0 kW
> B. 24.7 kW
> C. 26.6 kW
> D. 25.0 kW

ANSWER - (D)   25.0 kW

oven   - 10 kW
booster heater   - 15 kW
dishwasher   - 2 kW
garbage disposal -   1 kW
water heater   - 6 kW
steamer   - 4 kW
            Total = 38 kW (connected load)
                        X **65%** (demand)
                        = 24.7 kW **demand load**

But, the **two largest** loads are rated 10 kW and 15 kW which totals **25 kW**.

UNIT 3
SELF-ASSESSMENT QUIZ

1.   What is the demand load, in kW, on the ungrounded service-entrance conductors of a residence for one 8.5 kW rated electric range?

A. 6.8 kW
B. 8.0 kW
C. 8.5 kW
D. 10.6 kW

2. The demand factor for six (6) residential electric clothes dryers installed in a multifamily dwelling unit is _____.

    A. 70 percent
    B. 80 percent
    C. 60 percent
    D. 75 percent

3. A single-family dwelling has three (3) ovens, one rated 6 kW, one rated 8 kW and one rated 3.5 kW. The kitchen also has a counter-mounted cooktop rated at 6 kW and a broiler rated at 3.5 kW. The feeder demand will be _____ on the ungrounded conductors for the cooking equipment.

    A. 12.2 kW
    B. 18.6 kW
    C. 27.3 kW
    D. 30.1 kW

4. It shall be permissible to apply a demand factor of _____ to the nameplate rating of four (4) or more fastened in place storage-type electric water heaters in a multifamily dwelling, when calculating the demand load on the service entrance or feeder conductors.

    A. 50 percent
    B. 75 percent
    C. 80 percent
    D. 90 percent

5. When doing residential service and feeder calculations, electric clothes dryers are to be calculated at a MINIMUM of _____ watts (VA) or the nameplate rating, whichever is larger.

    A. 3,000
    B. 4,500
    C. 5,000
    D. 6,000

6. For residential electric ranges rated at 8.75 kW or more, the MINIMUM branch circuit rating shall be at LEAST _____.

    A. 30 amperes
    B. 40 amperes
    C. 50 amperes
    D. 60 amperes

7. Determine the demand load, in VA, on the service-entrance conductors of a one-family dwelling when the house has the following fastened in place electric appliances:

               water heater   - 4,800 VA
               dishwasher   - 1,200 VA
               garbage disposal - 1,150 VA
               trash compactor -   800 VA
               attic fan   - 1,200 VA

    A. 6,863 VA
    B. 9,150 VA
    C. 8,579 VA
    D. 11,438 VA

8. What is the branch-circuit demand load, in amperes, for one (1) 240-volt, single-phase, 6 kW wall-mounted oven located in a dwelling unit?

    A. 40 amperes
    B. 30 amperes
    C. 25 amperes
    D. 20 amperes

9. When doing dwelling unit service and feeder calculations, when a residence has an electric clothes dryer rated at 240-volts, 30 amperes, the demand load, in VA, to be applied to the ungrounded (line) conductors is _____.

    A. 3,500 VA
    B. 5,000 VA
    C. 6,000 VA
    D. 7,200 VA

10. Determine the demand load, in kW, to be added to the grounded (neutral) service-entrance conductor for one 10.5 kW residential electric range.

    A. 5.6 kW
    B. 8.0 kW
    C. 10.5 kW
    D. 12.0 kW

11. An 18 kW residential electric range has a demand load of _____ on the ungrounded (line) feeder and service-entrance conductors.

    A. 12.0 kW
    B. 10.4 kW
    C. 14.4 kW
    D. 12.6 kW

12. When sizing a branch-circuit for a 5 kW, 240-volt, single-phase commercial booster heater installed in the kitchen of a restaurant, the branch-circuit conductors are required to have the ability to carry at LEAST _____.

    A. 30 amperes
    B. 35 amperes
    C. 21 amperes
    D. 25 amperes

13. A twelve (12) unit apartment complex is to have a 9 kW electric range installed in each unit. When sizing the (line) ungrounded service-entrance conductors, the total demand load for the multiple ranges is _____.

    A. 99 kW
    B. 30 kW
    C. 36 kW
    D. 27 kW

14. A residential branch circuit is to supply two (2) wall-mounted ovens rated at 4.5 kW each and one (1) counter-mounted cooktop rated at 6 kW. The appliances are rated 240-volts, single-phase. The demand load on the branch-circuit conductors is _____.

    A. 32.4 amperes
    B. 38.3 amperes
    C. 42.1 amperes
    D. 43.8 amperes

15. The demand factor of an electrical system is the ratio of the maximum demand for a system to _____.

    A. the total connected load of the system.
    B. 125% of the total connected load of the system.
    C. 125% of the total connected continuous load of the system.
    D. 80% of the total connected non-continuous load plus 125% of the total connected continuous load of the system.

16. What is the service demand load, in kW, for six (6) storage type electric water heaters rated at 5 kW each, installed in a multifamily dwelling unit?

    A. 30.0 kW
    B. 24.0 kW
    C. 22.5 kW
    D. 26.0 kW

17. For dwelling units, the feeder and service neutral demand load for electric clothes dryers shall be calculated at _____ of the demand load as determined by Table 220.54.

    A. 100 percent
    B. 75 percent
    C. 80 percent
    D. 70 percent

18. What is the branch-circuit demand load, in amperes, for one 13.5 kW rated, 240-volt, single-phase residential electric range?

    A. 33 amperes
    B. 37 amperes
    C. 50 amperes
    D. 58 amperes

19. What is the demand load, in kW, for the feeder and service conductors for the following commercial kitchen equipment installed in a restaurant?

water heater	- 6.0 kW
dishwasher	- 2.0 kW
booster heater	- 7.5 kW
oven	- 6.0 kW
waste disposal	- 1.5 kW
mixer	- 2.5 kW

    A. 13 kW
    B. 17 kW
    C. 26 kW
    D. 19 kW

20. What is the demand load, in kW, on the grounded (neutral) service-entrance conductor for a multifamily dwelling when six (6) household electric ranges, each having a 9.5 kW rating, are installed?

    A. 15 kW
    B. 21 kW
    C. 26 kW
    D. 34 kW

UNIT 4

CONDUCTOR AMPACITY AND SIZING

Upon successfully completing this unit of study, the student will be familiar with the concept of determining the ampacity of conductors, application of correction factors, proper sizing, and insulation ratings of conductors.

$$\textbf{Required Ampacity } = \frac{\textbf{Load}}{\textbf{Correction Factors}}$$

UNIT 4

CONDUCTOR AMPACITY AND SIZING

RELATED INFORMATION:

- ➤ The definition of **ampacity** is the maximum current, in amperes, that a conductor can carry continuously under the conditions of use **without exceeding** its temperature rating. **[Article 100]** To get a better understanding of **ampacity**, perhaps we might consider it as **current-carrying capacity**, or the maximum amperage a conductor can carry without damaging the conductor and/or its insulation.

- ➤ When determining the ampacity of a conductor, or sizing a conductor, there are several factors needed to be taken into consideration; the ambient temperature, the type and temperature rating of the conductor insulation, the number of current-carrying conductors contained in the raceway or cable, the temperature rating of the terminations, characteristics of the load to be served, the environment the conductor will be subject to and voltage drop, which will be discussed later.

- ➤ **Table 310.104 (A)** lists the various types of insulated conductors, rated 600 volts, that includes maximum operating temperatures, application provisions and insulation characteristics. Some conductors are dual rated in regard to the location in which they are installed. For example, type **THHW** is rated **75 deg. C** for wet locations and **90 deg. C** for dry locations.

- ➤ **Table 310.15(B)(16)** lists the ampacity values for copper, aluminum or copper clad aluminum conductors, up to 2000 volts, with temperature ratings of 60 deg. C through 90 deg. C. This table is based on **not more than three** current-carrying conductors in a raceway, cable or directly buried in the earth at an ambient temperature (temperature surrounding the wire) of **30 deg. C or 86 deg. F**.

Table 310.15(B)(16) (formerly Table 310.16) Allowable Ampacities of Insulated Conductors Rated Up to and Including 2000 Volts, 60°C Through 90°C (140°F Through 194°F), Not More Than Three Current-Carrying Conductors in Raceway, Cable or Earth (Directly Buried), Based on Ambient Temperature of 30°C (86°F)*

Temperature Rating of Conductor (See Table 310.104(A)					
60°C (140°F)	75°C(167°F)	90°C(194°F)	60°C(140°F)	75°C (167°F)	90° (194°F)
Types TW, UF	Types RHW, THHW,THW, THWN,XHHW, USE, ZW	Types TBS, SA, SIS, FEP, FEPB, MI, RHH, RHW-2, THHN, THHW, THW-2, THWN-2, USE-2, XHH, XHHW, XHHW-2, ZW-2	Types TW, UF	Types RHW, THHW,THW THWN, XHHW, USE	Types TBS, SA, SIS, THHN, THHW, THW-2, THWN-2, RHH, RHW-2, USE-2, XHH, XHHW, XHHW-2, ZW-2
Size AWG or kcmil	COPPER		ALUMINUM OR COPPER-CLAD ALUMINUM			Size AWG or kcmil

Size AWG or kcmil	COPPER			ALUMINUM OR COPPER-CLAD ALUMINUM			Size AWG or kcmil
18	-	-	14	-	-	-	-
16	-	-	18	-	-	-	-
14**	15	20	25	-	-	-	-
12**	20	25	30	15	20	25	12**
10**	30	35	40	25	30	35	10**
8	40	50	55	35	40	45	8
6	55	65	75	40	50	55	6
4	70	85	95	55	65	75	4
3	85	100	115	65	75	85	3
2	95	115	130	75	90	100	2
1	110	130	145	85	100	115	1
1/0	125	150	170	100	120	135	1/0
2/0	145	175	195	115	135	150	2/0
3/0	165	200	225	130	155	175	3/0
4/0	195	230	260	150	180	205	4/0
250	215	255	290	170	205	230	250
300	240	285	320	195	230	260	300
350	260	310	350	210	250	280	350
400	280	335	380	225	270	305	400
500	320	380	430	260	310	350	500
600	350	420	475	285	340	385	600
700	385	460	520	315	375	425	700
750	400	475	535	320	385	435	750
800	410	490	555	330	395	445	800
900	435	520	585	355	425	480	900
1000	455	545	615	375	445	500	1000
1250	495	590	665	405	485	545	1250
1500	525	625	705	435	520	585	1500
1750	545	650	735	455	545	615	1750
2000	555	665	750	470	560	630	2000

* Refer to 310.15(B)(2) for the ampacity correction factors where the ambient temperature is other than 30°C (86°F).
*Refer to 240.4(D) for conductor overcurrent protection limitations.

> The body of **Table 310.15(B)(16)** lists ampacities of conductors used in areas where the ambient temperature is 30 deg. C or 86 deg. F, this is called **normal operating temperature**. The left half of the table is for **copper** conductors and the right half of the table is for **aluminum or copper clad aluminum** conductors.

➢ The temperature rating of a conductor is the maximum temperature, at any location along its length, that the conductor can withstand over a prolonged period of time without serious damage occurring. **[310.15(A)(3), INF. Note #1]**

➢ When conductors are subject to ambient temperatures above 86 deg. F, the resistance of the conductors are also increased proportionately. The greater the elevated ambient temperature, the greater the resistance. When the **resistance** of a conductor **increases** the **ampacity** of the conductor **decreases**. When this condition occurs, you must apply the appropriate temperature correction factors given in **Table 310.15(B)(2)(a).**

Table 310.15(B)(2)(a) Ambient Temperature Correction Factors Based on 30°C (86°F)				
For ambient temperatures other than 30°C (86°F), multiply the allowable ampacities specified in the ampacity table by the appropriate correction factor shown below.				
Ambient Temp. (°C)	Temperature Rating of Conductor			Ambient Temp. (°F)
	60° C	75°C	90° C	
10 or less	1.29	1.20	1.15	50 or less
11-15	1.22	1.15	1.12	51-59
16-20	1.15	1.11	1.08	60-68
21-25	1.08	1.05	1.04	69-77
26-30	1.00	1.00	1.00	78-86
31-35	0.91	0.94	0.96	87-95
36-40	0.82	0.88	0.91	96-104
41-45	0.71	0.82	0.87	105-113
46-50	0.58	0.75	0.82	114-122
51-55	0.41	0.67	0.76	123-131
56-60	-	0.58	0.71	132-140
61-65	-	0.47	0.65	141-149
66-70	-	0.33	0.58	150-158
71-75	-	-	0.50	159-167
76-80	-	-	0.41	168-176
81-85	-	-	0.29	177-185

EXAMPLE -   When a size 3 AWG copper conductor, with THW insulation, is installed in an area where the ambient temperature is 114 deg. F, the wire has an allowable ampacity of _____.

     A. 100 amperes
     B. 75 amperes
     C. 82 amperes
     D. 58 amperes

ANSWER -   (B)   75 amperes

     100 amperes x .75 = 75 amperes

     To solve this problem, first we locate the wire size on the left side of **Table 310.15(B)(16)** and look to the right under the copper THW column, with a temperature rating of 75°C, and note the ampacity of the wire is 100 amperes at normal operating temperature. Then, we apply the values as shown in **Table 310.15(B)(2)(a).** Look to the right side of the table where the ambient temperature is shown as °**F** and find the ambient temperature. Next, we follow that line to the left where the line intersects with the **75° C column** (temperature rating of conductor) to find our correction factor of **.75**, or 75%. Finally, to find the allowable ampacity of the conductor, multiply the two values together.

EXAMPLE -   When a size 1/0 AWG THWN aluminum conductor is installed in an ambient temperature of 45 deg. C, the conductor has an allowable ampacity of _____.

     A. 100 amperes
     B. 90 amperes
     C. 98 amperes
     D. 104 amperes

ANSWER -   (C)   98 amperes

     1/0 THWN aluminum ampacity before derating = 120 amperes
     120 amps x .82 (correction factor) = 98.4 amperes

     We use the same steps as before. First, we find the wire size which has an ampacity of 120 amperes. **[Tbl. 310.15(B)(16)]** Then, we find the ambient temperature, this time on the left portion of **Table 310.15(B)(2)(a)**, and go to the right under the THWN aluminum column (temperature rating of conductor) to find the correction factor of **.82**. Next, multiply the two values together.

➢ The temperature correction factors on **Table 310.15(B)(2)(a)** are to be applied when sizing conductors for a given load located in an area with an elevated ambient temperature. The following formula should be used:

$$\text{Required ampacity} = \frac{\text{load}}{\text{correction factor}}$$

EXAMPLE - Where a 100 ampere load is to be supplied with THWN copper conductors in an area where the ambient temperature will reach 110 deg. F, size _____ THWN conductors are required to serve the load.

      A. 1 AWG
      B. 2 AWG
      C. 3 AWG
      D. 1/0 AWG

ANSWER - (A)   1 AWG

$$\text{required ampacity} = \frac{100 \text{ amps}}{.82} = 122 \text{ amperes}$$

Table 310.15(B)(16) indicates size 1 AWG copper conductors with an ampacity of 130 amperes, should be selected. To cross reference:

130 amperes x .82 (correction factor) = 107 amperes

➢ Conductors are to be sized in accordance with the lowest temperature rating of the terminal, device or conductor of the circuit. **[110.14(C)]** In other words, conductors must be sized to the **lowest temperature rating** of the wire, circuit breaker, terminal or device.

➢ Conductors with temperature ratings higher than that of the terminations are permitted to be used for ampacity adjustment and/or correction. **[110.14(C)]** Today, most terminations are rated at **60 deg. C or 75 deg. C**. This permits us to use THHN conductors for derating purposes, but the conductor size is based on the lower terminal rating of the circuit breaker, equipment or device, not the 90 deg. C rating of the conductor insulation.

EXAMPLE - The load on a size 6 AWG THHN copper conductor is limited to _____ where connected to a circuit breaker with a termination rated at 60° C.

      A. 75 amperes
      B. 65 amperes
      C. 60 amperes
      D. 55 amperes

ANSWER -   (D)   55 amperes

Table 310.15(B)(16) lists the ampacity of size 6 AWG, copper,
60° C rated conductors to be 55 amperes.

EXAMPLE -   The load, in amperes, on a size 6 AWG THHN copper conductor is permitted to be no
more than _____ where connected to a fusible disconnect switch with terminals
rated at 75 deg. C.

A. 75 amperes
B. 65 amperes
C. 60 amperes
D. 55 amperes

ANSWER -   (B)   65 amperes

Table 310.15(B)(16) lists the ampacity of size 6 AWG copper
75 deg. C rated conductors to be 65 amperes.

➤   Many circuit breakers and disconnect switches now have dual ratings marked **60/75
deg. C**. Under this condition, for 60 deg. C conductors, derating and ampacity values
are to be based on the 60 deg. C terminal ratings; 75 deg. C and 90 deg. C conductors
derating and ampacity values may be based on either the 60 deg. C or 75 deg. C
terminal ratings.

➤   Many conductors now are dual rated such as **THWN/THHN**. The ampacity rating is
based on the THWN, 75 deg. C values, but the derating factor(s) may be based on the
THHN 90 deg. C values.

➤   The allowable **ampacity** of **Types NM**, **NMC** and **NMS** cable shall be in accordance
with the **60 deg. C** conductor temperature rating. The **90 deg. C** rating shall be
permitted to be used for **ampacity derating** purposes, provided the final ampacity
does not exceed that for a 60 deg. C rated conductor. **[334.80]**

EXAMPLE -   A size 12/2 AWG w/ground copper NM cable is to be installed in an attic of a dwelling
where the ambient temperature is 125 deg. F. Determine the ampacity of the cable.

A. 22.8 amperes
B. 14.5 amperes
C. 24.6 amperes
D. 17.4 amperes

ANSWER - (A)   22.8 amperes

        Ampacity of 12 AWG at 90 deg. C before derating = 30 amperes
        30 amperes x .76 (temperature correction) = 22.8 amperes

        Under this condition, the ampacity of 22.8 amperes is NOT permitted, because this value is more than the 20 ampere rating of the 12 AWG conductors at the 60 deg. C temperature rating.

EXAMPLE - A size 10/3 AWG w/ground copper NM cable is to be installed in the crawl space of a dwelling where the ambient temperature is 100 deg. F. Determine the ampacity of the cable.

    A. 24.6 amperes
    B. 36.4 amperes
    C. 32.3 amperes
    D. 30.0 amperes

ANSWER - (D)   30.0 amperes

        Ampacity of 10 AWG at 90 deg. C before derating = 40 amperes
        40 amperes x .91 (temp. correction) = 36.4 amperes

        Under this condition the ampacity of 36.4 amperes is also NOT permitted, because this value is more than the 30 ampere rating of 10 AWG conductors at the 60 deg. C rating.

➢ When there are more than three (3) current-carrying conductors in a raceway or cable, the ability of the conductors to dissipate heat is reduced. Therefore, when this condition exists in a raceway or cable longer than 24 inches the allowable ampacity of each conductor shall be reduced as shown in **Table 310.15(B)(3)(a)**.

EXAMPLE - What is the allowable ampacity of a size 1/0 AWG THW copper conductor installed in a conduit longer than 24 inches, when there are three (3) other current-carrying conductors contained in the same pipe?

    A. 150 amperes
    B. 120 amperes
    C. 105 amperes
    D. 140 amperes

ANSWER - (B)   120 amperes

        150 amperes x .8 (adjustment factor) = 120 amperes

First, find the ampacity of the conductor, before derating, as shown in **Table 310.15(B)(16)**. Then, apply the appropriate adjustment factor as shown in **Table 310.15(B)(3)(a).**

➤ When there are four (4) or more current-carrying conductors in a raceway or cable, longer than 24 inches, installed in an area with an elevated temperature, **both** the temperature correction and the adjustment factor for the number of current-carrying conductors must be applied.

EXAMPLE - Determine the allowable ampacity of a size 2 AWG THWN aluminum conductor installed in a 20 foot long conduit with seven (7) other current-carrying conductors of the same size and insulation, where the ambient temperature is 99 deg. F.

    A. 59 amperes
    B. 71 amperes
    C. 55 amperes
    D. 63 amperes

ANSWER - (C) 55 amperes

    Size 2 AWG THWN AL ampacity before derating = 90 amperes
    90 amperes x .88 (temp. correction) x .7 (adj. factor) = 55 amps

    First, find the ampacity of the conductor as shown in **Table 310.15(B)(16)** before derating. Then, apply the temperature correction factor. **[Table 310.15(B)(2)(a)]** Next, apply the adjustment factor for the multiple current-carrying conductors as shown in **Table 310.15(B)(3)(a),** and multiply the three values together.

➤ When sizing conductors for a given load in an area with an elevated ambient temperature, installed in a raceway or cable more than 24 inches in length, the following formula may be used when there are more than three current-carrying conductors in the raceway or cable.

$$\text{Required ampacity} = \frac{\text{Load}}{\text{temp. correction x adj. factor}}$$

EXAMPLE - A 100 ampere load is located in an environment where the temperature reaches 115 deg. F, and is to be supplied with four (4) 75 deg. C rated copper current-carrying conductors. Determine the proper size wire to serve the load. All terminations are rated at 75 deg. C.

    A. 1/0 AWG
    B. 2/0 AWG
    C. 1 AWG
    D. 3 AWG

ANSWER - (B)   2/0 AWG

$$\text{ampacity} = \frac{100 \text{ amperes (load)}}{.76 \text{ (temp.) x .8 (adj.)}} = \frac{100}{0.6} = 167 \text{ amperes}$$

*NOTE – Size 2/0 AWG copper conductors rated at 75 deg. C
with an ampacity of 175 amperes are required.

➤ Generally, where conductors or cables are installed in raceways exposed to direct sunlight on or above rooftops, the temperature values shown in **Table 310.15(B)(3)(c)** shall be added to the outdoor temperature and applied to the temperature correction factors in **Tables 310.15(B)(2)(a) and 310.15(B)(2)(b)**. **[310.15(B)(3)(c)]** The temperature adders must be applied up to a height of 36 inches above a rooftop. For example, when a conduit containing conductors rated at 75 deg. C is installed 3 inches above a rooftop and exposed to direct sunlight in an ambient temperature of 100 deg. F then, **40 degrees F** is to be added to the maximum ambient temperature. In this case, the value of **140 degrees F** must be used for the temperature correction factor adjustments from **Table 310.15(B)(2)(a)**.

Example - Determine the allowable ampacity of a size 10 AWG THWN copper conductor, installed in a conduit three (3) inches above a rooftop where the outdoor ambient temperature reaches 110 degrees F.

    A. 33.60 amperes
    B. 30.80 amperes
    C. 20. 30 amperes
    D. 11.55 amperes

Answer –   (D) 11.5 amperes

        outside ambient temperature =   110 ° F
        adder (3 in. above roof)   =   + 40 ° F
                        Total   =   150 ° F
    35 amperes x .33 (temperature correction) = 11.55 amperes

First, find the ampacity of the conductor as indicated in **Table 310.15(B)(16)** before derating. Then, locate the appropriate adder as shown in **Table 310.15(B)(3)(C)** and add this value to the ambient temperature. Next, find the correct temperature correction factor in **Table 310.15(B)(2)(a)** and multiple this value by the conductor ampacity value as given before derating.

➤ When considering current-carrying conductors, the neutral conductor is **not counted** when the neutral carries only the **unbalanced current** of the circuit; for example, 120/240 volt single-phase systems. **[310.15(B)(5)(a)]** The neutral does carry current, but is not required to be counted.

➢ The neutral **is considered** a current-carrying conductor on a 4-wire, 3-phase wye circuit where the major portion of the load consists of **nonlinear loads**. **[310.15(B)(5)(c)]** Examples of nonlinear loads are high intensity discharge (HID) lighting and fluorescent lighting, information technology equipment, computers, and data processing equipment.

➢ As per Section **310.15(B)(7)** for sizing **120/240-volt**, **3-wire**, **single-phase** service and feeder conductors rated 100 through 400 amperes, for one-family dwelling units and individual units of a multi-family dwelling, they are permitted to have an ampacity not less than 83 percent of the service or feeder rating.

EXAMPLE - A one-family dwelling is supplied with a 120/240-volt, single-phase electrical system from the local utility company and has a demand load of 200 amperes. What is the MINIMUM size THWN/THHN aluminum service-entrance conductors required?

       A. 250 kcmil
       B. 4/0 AWG
       C. 3/0 AWG
       D. 2/0 AWG

ANSWER - (B) 4/0 AWG

       200 amperes x .83 = 166 amperes

       Size 4/0 AWG THWN/THHN aluminum service-entrance conductors with an ampacity of 180 amperes should be selected from **Table 310.15(B)(16).**

➢ When single-insulated conductors are installed in free air, they can dissipate the heat caused by the current flowing in the conductors more readily than when installed in raceways. The conductors have a greater allowable ampacity therefore, **Table 310.15(B)(17)** may be applied in the same manner as previously referenced in this unit.

EXAMPLE - When ambient temperature is not a consideration, when installed in free air, a size 6 AWG THWN copper conductor has a MAXIMUM allowable ampacity of _____.

       A. 65 amperes
       B. 75 amperes
       C. 105 amperes
       D. 95 amperes

ANSWER - (D) 95 amperes

Table 310.15(B)(17) shows size 6 AWG THWN copper conductors to have an allowable ampacity of 95 amperes.

UNIT 4
SELF-ASSESSMENT QUIZ

1. A conduit having a length of fifty (50) feet contains nine (9) conductors. Six (6) of the conductors are considered to be current-carrying. What is the derating factor that must be applied to the ampacity of the current-carrying conductors?

    A. 80 percent
    B. 70 percent
    C. 60 percent
    D. 50 percent

2. Type XHHW insulated conductors may be used in _____.

    A. dry locations only
    B. wet locations only
    C. dry or damp locations only
    D. dry, damp or wet locations

3. A twenty five (25) feet run of electrical metallic tubing encloses three (3) current-carrying size 2 AWG THW copper conductors in an area where the ambient temperature is 125 deg. F. The correction factor that must be applied for the elevated ambient temperature is _____.

    A. 0.67
    B. 0.82
    C. 0.75
    D. 0.76

4. What is the MINIMUM size copper SE cable with Type XHHW insulation that may be used as ungrounded service-entrance conductors for a 150-ampere, 120/240 volt, single-phase residential service?

    A. 1/0 AWG
    B. 1 AWG
    C. 2 AWG

D. 3 AWG

5. When ambient temperature is not a factor, a size 8 AWG single copper conductor with Type FEPB insulation, installed in free air, will have a MAXIMUM allowable ampacity of _____.

   A. 80 amperes
   B. 55 amperes
   C. 45 amperes
   D. 83 amperes

6. What is the MAXIMUM allowable ampacity of a size 8 AWG THWN copper conductor installed in a conduit with two (2) other current-carrying conductors where the ambient temperature is 86 deg. F?

   A. 40 amperes
   B. 45 amperes
   C. 50 amperes
   D. 55 amperes

7. Three (3) size 1/0 AWG THW copper current-carrying conductors are contained within a raceway where the ambient temperature is 120 deg. F. What is the allowable ampacity of the individual conductors?

   A. 113 amperes
   B. 130 amperes
   C. 146 amperes
   D. 150 amperes

8. Determine the MAXIMUM allowable current-carrying capacity of a size 4 AWG copper conductor with THWN insulation installed in a conduit ten (10) feet in length with five (5) other current-carrying conductors.

   A. 60 amperes
   B. 52 amperes
   C. 85 amperes
   D. 68 amperes

9. You are to serve a 240-volt, single-phase, 3-wire, 200-ampere non-continuous load in an area where the expected ambient temperature is 110 deg. F. Using 75 deg. C rated aluminum conductors and considering terminations are rated at 75 deg. C, determine the MINIMUM size conductors required to supply the load.

A. 250 kcmil
B. 300 kcmil
C. 350 kcmil
D. 400 kcmil

10. When a 60 deg. C rated size 6 AWG copper conductor is terminated on a circuit breaker having a marked temperature rating of 60/75 deg. C, the conductor has an allowable ampacity of _____.

   A. 40 amperes
   B. 55 amperes
   C. 50 amperes
   D. 65 amperes

11. The allowable ampacity of a size 3/0 AWG THHN copper conductor installed in an environment with an ambient temperature of 50 deg. C is _____.

   A. 225 amperes
   B. 200 amperes
   C. 164 amperes
   D. 185 amperes

12. The allowable ampacity of size 2 AWG copper conductors with a dual rated insulation of THWN/THHN enclosed in a rigid metal conduct (RMC) when installed in a wet location is _____.

   A. 115 amperes
   B. 130 amperes
   C. 95 amperes
   D. 100 amperes

13. After all demand factors have been taken into consideration for a one-family dwelling, the demand load is determined to be 45,000 VA. The house is to be supplied with a 120/240-volt, single-phase underground installed electrical system. What MINIMUM size USE cable with aluminum conductors is required for the underground supplied service?

   A. 2/0 AWG
   B. 3/0 AWG
   C. 4/0 AWG
   D. 250 kcmil

14. When a conduit is installed 3½ inches above a rooftop and exposed to direct sunlight, a temperature adder of _____ is to be applied to the outdoor ambient temperature when determining the allowable ampacity of the conductors contained in the conduit.

   A. 60°F

B. 22°F
C. 30°C
D. 40°F

15. What MINIMUM size THHN copper conductors are required for a 240-volt, single-phase, 70 ampere branch circuit if the temperature on the circuit breaker and the equipment are listed for 75 deg. C when the demand load is 65 amperes?

   A. 10 AWG
   B. 8 AWG
   C. 6 AWG
   D. 4 AWG

16. The ampacity of eight (8) current-carrying size 10 AWG THW copper conductors enclosed in an electrical metallic tubing (EMT) 18 inches long is _____.

   A. 30 amperes
   B. 35 amperes
   C. 28 amperes
   D. 24 amperes

17. Under which, if any, of the following conditions is the neutral NOT to be counted as a current-carrying conductor?

   I. When it is only carrying the unbalanced current of a single-phase system.
   II. When it is the neutral of a 3-phase, wye connected system where the major portion of the load consists of nonlinear loads.

   A. I only
   B. II only
   C. both I and II
   D. neither I nor II

18. A conductor with _____ insulation has a different ampacity and temperature rating when used in a wet location compared to when used in a dry location.

   A. THWN
   B. THHN
   C. THW
   D. XHHW

19. A 3-phase, 4-wire, 208Y/120-volt feeder is to supply a panelboard of a department store with a 104 ampere continuous fluorescent lighting load. Where using 75 deg. C rated aluminum feeder conductors, determine the MINIMUM size required.

A. 250 kcmil
B. 4/0 AWG
C. 3/0 AWG
D. 2/0 AWG

20. Eight (8) 75 deg. C rated current-carrying branch circuit conductors are to be installed in a common raceway having a length of fifty (50) feet where located in an attic having an ambient temperature of 100 deg. F. Each conductor is to supply a continuous lighting load of 15 amperes and terminate on a 75 deg. C circuit breaker. Each conductor is required to have an ampacity of at least _____.

A. 21.3 amperes
B. 26.8 amperes
C. 30.4 amperes
D. 32.6 amperes

UNIT 5

BOX AND RACEWAY SIZING

Upon successfully completing this unit of study the student will be familiar with the concept of properly sizing electrical boxes and raceways.

Number of Wires Permitted =

$$\frac{\textbf{Allowable Fill}}{\textbf{Wire Size}}$$

UNIT 5

BOX AND RACEWAY SIZING

Outlet and Device Box Sizing

RELATED INFORMATION:

> ➤ Device and junction boxes are required to be of a sufficient size to house conductors and/or devices, clamps and support fittings without damaging the conductor's insulation. Therefore, when sizing boxes, conductors, clamps and support fittings are required to be counted in order to select the proper size box. **[314.16]**

> ➤ To properly size outlet boxes you must count the conductors within the box correctly. **Section 314.16(B)(1)** is to be used as a guideline to count the conductors as follows:

>> 1) Conductors that originate outside the box or that are spliced within the box are counted **one** for each conductor.

>> 2) Conductors unbroken within the box, less than 12 inches in length, that pass through the box without splicing or terminating are counted **one** for each conductor.

>> 3) Conductors 12 inches or longer that are looped and unbroken are counted as **two** for a single conductor.

>> 4) Conductors that originate within the box and do not leave the box such as, bonding jumpers and pigtails are **not counted**.

>> 5) Conductors from a domed luminaire (fixture) that terminate within the box are **not counted**.

> ➤ When sizing device and junction boxes, the insulation of the conductors are not required to be taken into consideration. The volume required for the individual conductors is expressed in **cubic inches** and/or **cubic centimeters**, no matter what the insulation characteristics of the conductor(s) is/are.

> ➤ To determine the volume, in cubic inches, of a box simply multiply the length times the width times the depth of the box.

EXAMPLE -   A box that measures 6 inches x 6 inches and is 4 inches deep has a volume of

_____.

A. 96 cubic inches
B. 144 cubic inches
C. 24 cubic inches
D. 36 cubic inches

ANSWER - (B)   144 cubic inches

6 in. x 6 in. x 4 in. = 144 cubic inches

➤ **Table 314.16(A)** may be used to determine the **MINIMUM** size outlet box required for a given number of conductors, or when determining the **MAXIMUM** number of conductors permitted in an outlet box when all of the conductors in the box are of the **same size**.

EXAMPLE - Determine the MAXIMUM number of size 12 AWG THWN conductors permitted in a 4 x 1½ in. square box.

A. seven
B. eight
C. nine
D. ten

ANSWER - (C)   nine

The right hand side of **Table 314.16(B)** under the **12** column shows nine conductors permitted in the box.

EXAMPLE - Of the following listed, which one of the boxes is the MINIMUM required to house three (3) size 12 AWG THWN/THHN conductors and three (3) size 12 AWG THW conductors?

A. 4 x 1½ in. octagon
B. 4 x 2¼ in. octagon
C. 4 x 1½ in. square
D. 4 x 2¼ in. square

ANSWER - (A)   4 x 1½ in. octagon

Table 314.16(B) permits six (6) size 12 AWG conductors in a 4 x 1½ in. octagon box.

➤ **Table 314.16(A)** shall apply where no fittings or devices, such as cable clamps, luminaire studs, hickeys, receptacles, switches or dimmers, are enclosed in the box. **Table 314.16(A)** does not take into consideration the fill requirements for these fittings or devices; where one or more of these items are contained in the box, the number of conductors permitted as shown in the table shall be reduced as follows:

1) **cable clamps** – One or more internal cable clamps present in the box are counted as **one** conductor, based on the **largest** conductor in the box. **[314.16(B)(2)]**

2) **support fittings** – One or more luminaire (fixture) studs and/or hickeys in the box are counted as **one** conductor for each type of fitting, based on the **largest** conductor in the box. **[314.16(B)(3)]**

3) **devices** – For each yoke or strap containing one or more device present in the box, they are to be counted as **two wires**, based on the **largest** conductor connected to the device. **[314.16(B)(4)]**

4) **equipment grounding conductors** – One or more equipment grounding conductors or bonding jumpers contained in a box are to be counted as **one** conductor, based on the **largest** equipment grounding conductor or bonding jumper in the box. **[314.16(B)(5)]** Where an **additional set** of isolated equipment grounding conductors are in the box, they are to be counted as **one** conductor, based on the **largest** equipment grounding conductor in the additional set.

➤ When doing box fill calculations we must take into consideration the volume taken up by all conductors, fittings and devices contained in the box to properly size the box.

EXAMPLE - A device box contains two (2) internal clamps, two (2) equipment grounding conductors, one (1) bonding jumper and one (1) duplex receptacle. The number of conductors permitted in the box is to be reduced by _____ conductors.

    A. three
    B. four
    C. five
    D. six

ANSWER - (B) four

clamps	= 1 wire
receptacle	= 2 wires
equip. grounding & bonding wires	= 1 wire
TOTAL	= 4 wires

➤ When calculating the proper size outlet box to be used when the conductors are of different sizes, you are to determine the volume of the conductors, in cubic inches, by applying **Table 314.16(B)**, and then size the box by using **Table 314.16(A)**.

EXAMPLE - Determine which one of the following listed outlet boxes is the MINIMUM size required to enclose the following conductors:

- six (6) size 12 AWG conductors
- two (2) size 14 AWG conductors
- one (1) size 14 AWG equipment grounding conductors

    A. 4 x 1½ in. octagon
    B. 4 x 1½ in. square
    C. 4 x 2¼ in. square
    D. 4¼ x 1½ in. square

ANSWER - (B)   4 x 1½ in. square

Size 12 AWG = 2.25 cu. in. x 6	=	13.5 cubic inches
Size 14 AWG = 2.00 cu. in. x 2	=	4.0 cubic inches
Size 14 AWG Equip. grounding x 1	=	2.0 cubic inches
		19.5 cubic inches

Table 314.16(A) requires a 4 x 1½ inch square box having a volume of 21 cubic inches.

Junction and Pull Box Sizing

RELATED INFORMATION:

> **Section 314.16** states when boxes enclosing conductors of size **4 AWG or larger** are used as pull or junction boxes, they are to comply with the provisions of **314.28**. Under this condition, pull and junction boxes are to be sized by the raceways entering the box(es) and not by the size of the conductors contained in the box.

> In straight pulls, the length of the box shall not be less than **eight times** the trade diameter of the largest raceway entering the box. **[314.28(A)(1)]**

EXAMPLE - Determine the MINIMUM length of a pull box that has a trade size 3½ inch conduit entering at each end, and containing conductors of size 250 kcmil, when a straight pull of the conductors is to be made.

    A. 21 inches
    B. 24 inches
    C. 28 inches
    D. 32 inches

ANSWER - (C)   28 inches

        3.5 in. (conduit) x 8 = 28 inches

> Where splices, angle or U-pulls are made, the distance between each raceway entry inside the box and opposite wall of the box shall not be less than **six (6) times** the trade size of the raceway in a row. **[314.28(A)(2)]** Then, you are to add the sum of the trade size diameter of any additional raceways entering the box. In other words, for angle or U-pulls, the proper size junction box can be determined by multiplying the largest raceway by six (6) and add any additional conduits.

EXAMPLE - A junction box is to be installed where the conductors are larger than size 4 AWG and an angle (90 deg.) pull of the conductors is to be made. Two (2) trade size 3 inch conduits are to enter the box from the top and two (2) trade size 3 inch conduits are to enter the box from the side. Determine the MINIMUM size pull box required.

        A. 36 in. x 36 in.
        B. 27 in. x 27 in.
        C. 24 in. x 24 in.
        D. 21 in. x 21 in.

ANSWER - (D)   21 in. x 21 in.

        Top to bottom – 3 in. (largest conduit) x 6 = 18 in. + 3 in. = 21 in.
        Side to side – 3 in. (largest conduit) x 6 = 18 in. + 3 in. = 21 in.

EXAMPLE - A pull box has one (1) trade size 2 inch conduit and one (1) trade size 1½ inch conduit entering the top and two (2) trade size 2 inch conduits on the left side. Where conductors are larger than 4 AWG and an angle (90 deg.) pull of the conductors is to be made, determine the MINIMUM distance required from the top wall to the bottom wall.

        A. 13½ inches
        B. 11 inches
        C. 12 inches
        D. 16 inches

ANSWER - (A)   13½ inches

        2 in. (largest conduit) x 6 = 12 + 1½ in. = 13½ inches

Conduit and Tubing Sizing

RELATED INFORMATION:

➢ When electrical conduit or tubing enclose conductors of the same size, with the same type of insulation, when the conduit or tubing is more than 24 inches in length, application of **Annex C**, **Tables C.1 through C.12(A)** is permitted to be used when determining the MAXIMUM number of conductors permitted. **[Chapter 9, Table 1]** This is the fastest and easiest method of determining the MAXIMUM number of conductors allowed in a standard trade size conduit or tubing.

➢ Located at the first part of **Annex C** there is a listing of the various types of standard electrical conduits. Use this table to find the particular type of conduit you are going to use when determining conduit fill.

EXAMPLE - Determine the MINIMUM trade size electrical metallic tubing (EMT), more than 24 inches in length, permitted to enclose twelve (12) size 10 AWG THWN conductors.

     A. 3/4 in.
     B. 1 in.
     C. 1¼ in.
     D. 1½ in.

ANSWER - (B) 1 inch

First locate **Table C.1** of **Annex C**. Next, refer to the type of insulation **(THWN)** of the conductors. Then, locate the wire size **(10 AWG)**, and you will find for twelve (12) size 10 AWG THWN conductors a trade size 1 inch EMT is required.

EXAMPLE - A trade size 1½ inch Schedule 40 PVC conduit, 25 feet in length, is permitted to enclose no more than _____ size 2 AWG XHHW compact aluminum conductors.

     A. six
     B. seven
     C. eight
     D. ten

ANSWER - (C) eight

First, locate **Table C.10(A)** of **Annex C**. Next, find the insulation type **(XHHW)** of the conductors. Then, locate the conduit size **(1½ in.)** and conductor size **(2 AWG)**, and you will find a trade size 1½ inch Schedule 40 PVC is permitted to enclose eight (8) size 2 AWG XHHW compact aluminum conductors.

➢ When conduit or tubing enclose conductors of different sizes and/or insulations, **Chapter 9**, **Tables 4, 5 and 5A**, with their related notes, are to be applied to determine the proper fill.

> **Table 1** of **Chapter 9** shows the permitted fill, in percent of conduit and tubing, when one, two or over two conductors are installed; for example, when more than two (2) conductors are installed in a conduit or tubing they shall be permitted to be filled to **40 percent** of their cross-sectional area.

> Where conduit or tubing nipples have a MAXIMUM length not to exceed 24 inches between boxes and enclosures, the nipples shall be permitted to be filled to **60 percent** of their total cross-sectional area.
> **[Chapter 9, Note 4]**

> **Table 4, Chapter 9** list the various types of conduit and tubing. Each type of conduit or tubing is shown as a separate table. At the top of each table is shown the internal diameter and the percent of fill. Under the percent of fill heading you will find the allowable fill of each size conduit or tubing expressed in square inches and millimeters. On the left side of the table the trade size and metric designator of the conduit or tubing are listed. To find the allowable fill of a specific conduit or tubing simply locate the conduit or tubing size and extend to the right under the proper **percent** of fill heading.

EXAMPLE - When more than two (2) conductors are installed in a trade size 2 inch electrical metallic tubing (EMT) longer than 24 inches, the EMT has an allowable fill of _____.

      A. 2.013 square inches
      B. 1.778 square inches
      C. 1.040 square inches
      D. 1.342 square inches

ANSWER - (D)   1.342 square inches

Under this condition the 2 in. EMT is permitted to have an allowable fill of 40 percent. **[Table 4, Chapter 9]**

EXAMPLE - When four (4) current-carrying conductors are installed in a trade size 2 inch electrical metallic tubing (EMT) nipple 18 inches long, the EMT has a MAXIMUM allowable fill of _____.

      A. 2.013 square inches
      B. 1.778 square inches
      C. 1.040 square inches
      D. 1.342 square inches

ANSWER - (A)   2.013 square inches

Under this condition the 2 in. EMT is permitted to have an allowable fill of 60 percent. **[Table 4, Chapter 9]**

> **Table 5**, **Chapter 9** shows the various sizes and insulations of conductors expressed in millimeters and square inches in accordance with appropriate diameter and area. In

most cases we relate to the **approximate area** in **square inches** on the right side of the table.

EXAMPLE -   A size 8 AWG THWN copper conductor has an approximate area of

_____.

        A. 0.0437 square inches
        B. 0.0366 square inches
        C. 0.0835 square inches
        D. 0.2160 square inches

ANSWER -   (B)   0.0366 square inches

First, we locate the insulation **(THWN)** of the conductor.
Then, the size **(8 AWG)**, and look to the extreme right side of the table to find the approximate area in square inches.
[Table 5, Chapter 9]

➤ **Table 5A**, **Chapter 9** shows the various sizes and insulations of **compact aluminum conductors** expressed in millimeters and square inches with approximate diameter and area, much like **Table 5 of Chapter 9**. This table is structured different than **Table 5** but, is easier to use because there is only four (4) types of conductor insulations listed. Again refer to the approximate area in square inches of the conductor when calculating raceway fill.

EXAMPLE -   What is the area, in square inches, of a size 3/0 AWG XHHW compact aluminum conductor.

        A. 0.590 square inches
        B. 0.2733 square inches
        C. 0.2290 square inches
        D. 0.1885 square inches

ANSWER -   (C)   0.2290 square inches

First, from **Table 5A of Chapter 9**, locate the insulation **(XHHW)** of the conductor.
Then, locate the wire size, **(3/0 AWG)**, and look under the **in.²** heading to find the area.

➤ Where equipment grounding or bonding conductors are installed in conduit or tubing, they shall be included when calculating the permitted fill. **[Chapter 9, Note 3]** If insulated, use the **Table 5** to find the approximate area; if bare find the area in square inches from **Table 8 of Chapter 9**, look under the heading of **in²**.

EXAMPLE - A size 8 AWG solid bare equipment grounding conductor has an area of _____.

      A. 0.128 square inches
      B. 0.146 square inches
      C. 0.017 square inches
      D. 0.013 square inches

ANSWER - (D) 0.013 square inches

First, locate the wire size and stranding properties from **Table 8 of Chapter 9**.
Next, extend to the right under the **in.²** heading to find the area.

> Conduits or tubing enclosing different size conductors and/or conductors having different insulations are sized by locating the area, in square inches, of each conductor per **Table 5**, **Table 5A** or **Table 8** and multiplying by the number of conductors. This total is used to select the proper size raceway using **Table 4** in **Chapter 9**.

EXAMPLE - Determine the MINIMUM trade size intermediate metal conduit (IMC)   permitted to enclose three (3) size 8 AWG XHHW copper branch-circuit   conductors and six (6) size 12 AWG THWN copper control-circuit   conductors. The IMC is to be fifty (50) feet in length.

      A. 1/2 in.
      B. 3/4 in.
      C. 1 in.
      D. 1¼ in.

ANSWER - (B) 3/4 in.

8 XHHW = .0437 sq. in. x 3 conductors = .1311 square inches
12 THWN = .0133 sq. in. x 6 conductors = .0798 square inches
TOTAL = .2109 square inches

A trade size 3/4 in. IMC having an allowable fill @ 40% of 0.235 square inches is the MINIMUM required.

EXAMPLE -   Determine the MINIMUM trade size, one (1) foot long, rigid metal   conduit (RMC) to enclose the following listed copper conductors.

- four (4) – 3/0 AWG THWN
- four (4) – 4/0 AWG THHN

    A. 3 in.
    B. 2 in.
    C. 3½ in.
    D. 2½ in.

ANSWER -   (D)   2½ inches

    3/0 THWN = .2679 x 4 conductors   = 1.0716 square inches
    4/0 THHN = .3237 x 4 conductors   = <u>1.2948 square inches</u>
    TOTAL = 2.3664 square inches

    A trade size 2½ in. RMC nipple having an allowable fill @ 60% of 2.919 square inches is the MINIMUM required.

➤   When determining the number of conductors, all of the same size, permitted in a conduit or tubing 24 inches or less in length, simply divide the allowable fill area of the conduit or tubing by the area of one (1) conductor.

EXAMPLE -   Determine the MAXIMUM number of size 2/0 AWG THHN copper conductors permitted to be installed in a trade size 2 in. electrical metallic tubing (EMT) 18 inches long.

    A. seven
    B. eight
    C. nine
    D. ten

ANSWER -   (C)   nine

    <u>2.013 sq. in.</u> (allowable fill) = 9.05 or 9 wires
    .2223 sq. in. (area of wire)

➤   When calculating the MAXIMUM number of conductors, all of the same size, permitted in a conduit or tubing, when the calculation results in a decimal of **0.8** or larger, an additional wire of the same size may be installed.   **[Chapter 9, Note 7]**

EXAMPLE - Determine the MAXIMUM number of size 1/0 AWG THWN copper conductors permitted to be installed in a trade size 1¼ in. rigid metal conduit (RMC) nipple.

>   A. four
>   B. five
>   C. six
>   D. seven

ANSWER - (B)   five

$$\frac{0.916 \text{ sq. in.} \text{ (allowable fill)}}{.1855 \text{ sq. in. (area of wire)}} = 4.9 \text{ or 5 wires}$$

Wireway and Gutter Sizing

RELATED INFORMATION:

> ➤ When calculating the number of conductors, all of the same size, permitted in a metal or nonmetallic wireway, or an auxiliary gutter, the fill shall not exceed **20 percent** of the interior cross-sectional area of the wireway or gutter where splices or taps are not made. **[366.22(A)&(B)]**, **[376.22(A)]** and **[378.22]** Use the same steps as before; first, find the allowable fill and divide by the area of one (1) conductor. Disregard the length of the wireway or gutter.

EXAMPLE - Determine the MAXIMUM number of size 4/0 AWG XHHW copper   conductors permitted to be installed in a 4 in. x 4 in. metal wireway.

>   A. ten
>   B. eleven
>   C. twenty
>   D. sixteen

ANSWER - (A)   ten

4 in. x 4 in. = 16 sq. in. x 20% = 3.2 sq. in. permitted fill

$$\frac{3.2 \text{ sq. in. (permitted fill)}}{.3197 \text{ sq. in. (area of wire)}} = 10 \text{ wires}$$

> ➤ When conductors are of different sizes and/or insulations, **wireways** and **gutters** can be properly sized by dividing the total area, in square inches, of the conductors by the **20 percent** permitted fill area, where splices or taps are not made. Or find the area, in square inches, of a specific wireway or gutter and multiply by **20 percent** to find the allowable fill. Using this method you may have to try more than one size gutter or wireway to find the proper size.

EXAMPLE -   A wireway is to contain the following listed conductors.

- three – size 250 kcmil THHN compact aluminum
- three – size 4/0 AWG THHN compact aluminum
- three – size 1/0 AWG THHN compact aluminum

Which one of the following listed wireways is the MINIMUM size required to house the conductors?

    A. 4 in. x 4 in.
    B. 6 in. x 6 in.
    C. 8 in. x 8 in.
    D. 12 in. x 12 in.

ANSWER -   (A)   4 in. x 4 in.

First, go to **Table 5A of Chapter 9** to determine the area of the conductors.

250 kcmil THHN compact AL = .3525 sq. in. x 3 = 1.0575 sq. in.
4/0 AWG THHN compact AL = .2780 sq. in. x 3 = 0.8340 sq. in.
1/0 AWG THHN compact AL = .1590 sq. in. x 3 = 0.4770 sq. in.
                                      TOTAL = 2.3685 sq. in.

$\dfrac{2.3685 \text{ (area of wires)}}{20\% \text{ (permitted fill)}}$ = 11.8425 sq. in. required area

A 4 in. x 4 in. wireway with an area of 16 square inches is required.

To cross-check:
4 in. x 4 in. = 16 sq. in. x 20% = 3.2 square inches allowable fill
This wireway having an allowable fill of 3.2 square inches may contain the conductors having an area of 2.3685 square inches.

UNIT 5
SELF-ASSESSMENT QUIZ

1. A 4 in. x 1½ in. octagon junction box with a flat blank cover may contain no more than _____ size 14 AWG conductors.

   A. six
   B. seven
   C. nine
   D. ten

2. A luminaire stud in a ceiling-mounted outlet box is considered an equivalent of _____ conductor(s).

   A. one
   B. two
   C. three
   D. none of these

3. When determining box fill, size 12 AWG THHN conductors are to be calculated at _____ for each conductor housed in the box.

   A. 1.75 cubic inches
   B. 2.00 cubic inches
   C. 2.25 cubic inches
   D. 2.50 cubic inches

4. For the purpose of determining conductor fill in a device box, a three-way switch is counted as equal to _____ conductor(s), based on the largest conductor connected to the switch.

   A. zero
   B. one
   C. two
   D. three

5. How many size 12/2 AWG with ground, nonmetallic sheathed cable(s) (NM) is/are permitted to be installed in a device box having a total volume of 18 cubic inches where a duplex receptacle outlet is in the box?

   A. one
   B. two
   C. three
   D. four

6. Determine the MINIMUM size trade size, fifty (50) foot long, intermediate metal conduit (IMC) permitted to enclose four (4), size 8 AWG THWN copper branch circuit conductors.

    A. ½ inch
    B. ¾ inch
    C. 1 inch
    D. 1¼ inches

7. A two-gang device box is to contain two (2) size 12/2 AWG with ground nonmetallic sheathed (NM) cables connected to a duplex receptacle and two (2), size 14/2 AWG with ground NM cables connected to a single-pole switch. The device box will contain four (4) internal clamps. The two-gang box is required to have a volume of at least _____.

    A. 36 cubic inches
    B. 34 cubic inches
    C. 30 cubic inches
    D. 28 cubic inches

8. A single-gang FS box is permitted to contain no more than _____ size 14 AWG THHN conductors.

    A. six
    B. seven
    C. eight
    D. nine

9. Two (2) size 12 AWG conductors are looped inside a junction box so that there is more than 12 inches of free conductor. The conductors are not spliced and do not terminate on devices. What volume, in cubic inches, must be counted for the looped conductors?

    A. 2.25 cubic inches
    B. 3.75 cubic inches
    C. 4.50 cubic inches
    D. 9.00 cubic inches

10. When a pull-box is to contain conductors of size 4 AWG or larger and a straight pull of the conductors is to be made, the length of the box shall not be less than _____ times the trade size of the largest raceway entering the box.

    A. six
    B. four
    C. eight
    D. none of these

11. Where a conduit or tubing more than 24 inches in length, contains more than two (2) conductors, the conduit or tubing is permitted an allowable fill of _____ of its cross-sectional area.

A. 40 percent
B. 60 percent
C. 53 percent
D. 75 percent

12. Where a conduit having a length of 24 inches or less is installed between a panelboard and a wireway, the conduit is permitted to be filled to no more than _____ of its cross-sectional area.

    A. 40 percent
    B. 60 percent
    C. 53 percent
    D. 75 percent

13. For the purpose of determining conductor fill in conduit, what is the total area, in square inches (in.²), of four (4) size 4/0 AWG THWN and three (3) size 3/0 AWG THWN copper conductors?

    A. 2.0985 square inches
    B. 1.8081 square inches
    C. 2.3664 square inches
    D. 2.4223 square inches

14. Determine the MAXIMUM number of size 300 kcmil RHW copper conductors, without outer coverings, permitted to be installed in an 18 inch long, trade size 4 inch, electrical metallic tubing (EMT) nipple.

    A. fourteen
    B. fifteen
    C. sixteen
    D. seventeen

15. A junction box is to be installed where size 4/0 AWG THWN conductors enclosed in trade size 2½ in. electrical metallic tubing (EMT) are to be spliced. One EMT enters the box from the top and one EMT enters the box from the side. The NEC® mandates a distance of not less than _____ be maintained between the conduits inside the box.

    A. 20 inches
    B. 12 inches
    C. 18 inches
    D. 15 inches

16. A pull box is to be installed where the conductors are larger than size 4 AWG and an angle (90°) pull of the conductors is to be made. Two (2) trade size 3 inch conduits are to enter the box from the top and one (1) trade size 3 inch conduit and one (1) trade size 2½ inch conduit are to enter the box from the side. The pull box is required to have dimensions of at LEAST _____.

A. 21 in. x 21 in.
B. 21 in. x 20½ in.
C. 18 in. x 18 in.
D. 24 in. x 24 in.

17. A fifty (50) ft. run of Schedule 40 PVC conduit is to contain the following copper conductors:

- four (4) size 1 AWG XHHW
- one (1) size 6 AWG bare

Determine the MINIMUM trade size PVC required per the NEC®.

A. 2 inches
B. 1½ inches
C. 1¼ inches
D. 1 inch

18. The fill shall not exceed _____ of the interior of the cross-sectional area of a metal wireway where splices or taps are not made.

A. 20 percent
B. 40 percent
C. 53 percent
D. 75 percent

19. Determine the MAXIMUM number of size 250 kcmil XHHW compact aluminum conductors permitted to be installed in a 4 in. x 4 in. six (6) ft. long metal wireway.

A. twenty
B. ten
C. eight
D. nine

20. A metal wireway is to contain the following listed copper conductors:

- eight (8) - size 500 kcmil THWN
- twenty-four (24) - size 2 AWG THWN

Which one of the following listed wireways is the MINIMUM size to house the conductors?

A. 10 in. x 10 in.
B. 6 in. x 6 in.
C. 8 in. x 8 in.
D. 12 in. x 12 in.

NOTES

UNIT 6

VOLTAGE DROP CALCULATIONS

Upon successfully completing this unit of study the student will be familiar with the concept and causes of voltage drop, as well as the means to prevent excessive voltage drop in three-phase and single-phase circuits.

$$VD = \frac{2 \times K \times I \times D}{CM}$$

UNIT 6

VOLTAGE DROP CALCULATIONS

RELATED INFORMATION:

> The conductors of an electrical system should be of sufficient size so that the voltage drop is not excessive. Typical results of excessive voltage drop are as follows:

1) luminaires (lighting fixtures) dimming when appliances or motors are turned on,
2) overheating of motors and appliances,
3) shortened life span of appliances such as computers, TVs, refrigerators and freezers,
4) nuisance tripping of circuit breakers,
5) delayed starting of high-intensity discharge lighting.

> The loss of voltage, known as voltage drop, is apparent in all electrical circuits due to the resistance of the circuit conductors. This loss of voltage varies with conductor material, conductor size, conductor length, ambient temperature and intensity of the current.

> The NEC® recommends the MAXIMUM voltage drop to be limited to 3 percent at the farthest outlet for branch circuits and 5 percent on both feeder and branch circuits to the farthest outlet. **[210.19(A)(1) IN#4]** and **[215.2(A)(3) IN#2]** In practical work, many engineers try to limit the voltage drop for lighting and power branch circuits to 2 percent and 4 percent for feeders.

> **The smaller the wire size, the greater the resistance** because, the small cross-sectional area of the conductor restricts the flow of electrons; thus, the greater the voltage drop. **The larger the wire size, the less the resistance** because, the larger cross-sectional area of the conductor permits the electrons to flow more freely; thus, the less voltage drop. So, the most practical way to limit voltage drop is increase the wire size. Although not always practical, voltage drop may be decreased by:

1) increasing the voltage, which reduces the intensity of the current,

2) change the conductor material say, from aluminum to copper which reduces the resistance,

3) move the load closer to its source voltage, which reduces the conductor resistance.

➤ A useful and common formula that may be used to determine the voltage drop in a single-phase circuit is:

$$VD = \frac{2 \times K \times I \times D}{CM}$$

Formula Definitions:

VD – Volts dropped from a circuit.

2 – Multiplying factor for single-phase circuits. The **2** represents the conductor length in a single-phase circuit.

K - Approximate resistivity of the conductor per mil foot at an operating temperature of 75°C/167°F. A mil foot is a wire one (1) foot long and one (1) mil in diameter. The approximate **K** value (constant) for copper wire is **12.9 ohms** and for aluminum wire is **21.2 ohms**.

I - Current or amperage draw of the load at 100 percent.

D - The distance, in feet, from the source voltage to the load.

CM - The area of the conductor expressed in **circular mils**, which can be found in **Chapter 9, Table 8**, which lists wire sizes from 18 AWG through 2,000 kcmil. For example, a size 10 AWG conductor has a cross-sectional area of 10,380 circular mils. For conductors of size 250 kcmil through size 2,000 kcmil, the cross-sectional area in circular mils can be determined by adding three (3) zeros to the kcmil size. For example, a size 300 kcmil conductor has a cross-sectional area of 300,000 circular mils.

EXAMPLE - A 120-volt, single-phase branch circuit, using size 12 AWG copper conductors, is supplying a 15 ampere load located sixty (60) feet from the panelboard. Determine the approximate voltage drop. (K = 12.9)

    A. 2 volts
    B. 4 volts
    C. 6 volts
    D. 8 volts

ANSWER - (B) 4 volts

CM = 6,530 (12 AWG)
K = 12.9 ohms (copper)
I = 15 amperes
D = 60 feet

$$VD = \frac{2 \times 12.9 \times 15 \times 60}{6,530} = \frac{23,220}{6,530} = 3.55 \text{ volts}$$

➤ A useful and common formula that may be used to determine the voltage drop in a **three-phase** circuit is:

$$VD = \frac{1.732 \times K \times I \times D}{CM}$$

➤ The multiplying factor for **three-phase** circuits is **1.732**. The square root of 3 represents the conductor length in a three-phase circuit. The only difference between the single-phase and the three-phase formulas is that "**1.732**" has replaced "2".

EXAMPLE - A 208Y/120-volt, three-phase feeder, using size 4 AWG aluminum conductors is to supply an 80 ampere load located one hundred (100) feet from the switchboard. Determine the approximate voltage drop.
(K = 21.2)

    A. 9.3 volts
    B. 5.0 volts
    C. 7.0 volts
    D. 9.0 volts

ANSWER - (C) 7.0 volts

CM = 41,740 (4 AWG)
K = 21.2 ohms (aluminum)
I = 80 amperes
D = 100 feet

$$VD = \frac{1.732 \times 21.2 \times 80 \times 100}{41,740} = \frac{293,747}{41,740} = 7.0 \text{ volts}$$

➤ As stated before, the size of the conductor affects voltage drop because of the resistance variables. Conductors are to be sized to prevent excessive voltage drop. A useful formula that may be used to size the conductors and prevent excessive voltage drop in a single-phase circuit is:

$$CM = \frac{2 \times K \times I \times D}{VD}$$

➤ When determining wire size, VD is the actual volts allowed to be dropped from the circuit. For example, the recommended voltage drop in a 240 volt, single-phase branch circuit is 3 percent; 3 percent of 240 volts is 7.2 volts. DO NOT enter 3 percent in the VD position in the formula, enter the value of the actual voltage permitted to be lost or dropped.

EXAMPLE - A 240-volt, single-phase, 52 ampere load is located two-hundred (200) feet from the panelboard. What MINIMUM size copper branch circuit   conductors should be used to supply this load when voltage drop is to be   limited to 3 percent? (K = 12.9)

        A. 8 AWG
        B. 6 AWG
        C. 4 AWG
        D. 2 AWG

ANSWER - (C)   4 AWG

$$VD = 240 \times 0.03 = 7.2 \text{ volts}$$
K = 12.9 ohms (copper)
I = 52 amperes
D = 200 feet

$$CM = \frac{2 \times 12.9 \times 52 \times 200}{7.2} = \frac{268,320}{7.2} = 37,267 \text{ CM}$$

In this situation, a size 4 AWG conductor with a circular mil area (CMA) of 41,740 CM is required because, a size 6 AWG conductor with a CMA of 26,240 CM would not limit the voltage drop to 3 percent.

➤ A useful formula that may be used to size conductors in a three-phase circuit to prevent excessive voltage drop is:

$$CM = \frac{1.732 \times K \times I \times D}{VD}$$

EXAMPLE - A 208Y/120-volt, 3-phase, 150 ampere load is located two hundred and fifty (250) feet from the main distribution switchboard. What MINIMUM size copper feeder conductors are required to supply the load when voltage drop is to be limited to 3 percent? (K = 12.9)

        A. 4/0 AWG
        B. 1/0 AWG
        C. 2/0 AWG
        D. 3/0 AWG

ANSWER - (D)   3/0 AWG

$$VD = 208 \times 0.03 = 6.24 \text{ volts}$$

K = 12.9 ohms (copper)
I = 150 amperes
D = 250 feet

$$CM = \frac{1.732 \times 12.9 \times 150 \times 250}{6.24} = \frac{83,786}{6.24} = 134,272 \text{ CM}$$

A size 3/0 AWG conductor with a CMA of 167,800 CM is required
to limit the voltage drop to 6.24 volts.

➢ Voltage drop can be limited in a circuit by limiting the length of the circuit conductors. The following formula can be used to determine the approximate distance circuit conductors may be installed to prevent excessive voltage drop in a single-phase circuit.

$$D = \frac{CM \times VD}{2 \times K \times I}$$

EXAMPLE - What is the approximate MAXIMUM distance a 120-volt, single-phase, 1,800 VA load, supplied with size 12 AWG copper branch circuit conductors can be located from the panelboard, when the permitted voltage drop is to be not more than three percent?

    A. 60 feet
    B. 75 feet
    C. 90 feet
    D. 120 feet

ANSWER - (A) 60 feet

CM = 6,530 (12 AWG)
VD = 120 volts x .03 = 3.6 volts
K = 12.9 ohms
$$I = \frac{VA}{volts} = \frac{1,800 \text{ VA}}{120 \text{ volts}} = 15 \text{ amperes}$$

$$D = \frac{6,530 \times 3.6}{2 \times 12.9 \times 15} = \frac{23,508}{387} = 60.7 \text{ feet}$$

➢ When determining the approximate distance circuit conductors may be installed in three-phase circuits to prevent excessive voltage drop, the following formula can be used:

$$D = \frac{CM \times VD}{1.732 \times K \times I}$$

EXAMPLE - A transformer having a 208Y/120-volt, 3-phase secondary is to supply a panelboard with a 130 ampere demand load. The feeder conductors are size 1/0 AWG THWN copper. What is the MAXIMUM approximate distance the panelboard can be located from the transformer so that the voltage drop does not exceed three percent?

A. 125 feet
B. 65 feet
C. 225 feet
D. 200 feet

ANSWER - (C)   225 feet

        CM = 105,600 (1/0 AWG)
        VD = 208 volts x .03 = 6.24 volts
        K = 12.9 ohms
        I = 130 amperes

$$D = \frac{105{,}600 \times 6.24}{1.732 \times 12.9 \times 130} = \frac{658{,}944}{2{,}905} = 227 \text{ feet}$$

> Another way of limiting voltage drop is to limit the intensity of the current on the conductors. Perhaps, you may have an existing installation and if additional loads are added, this may cause excessive voltage drop on the feeder conductors. The following formula can be used to determine the MAXIMUM load permitted when limiting voltage drop on single-phase circuits:

$$I = \frac{CM \times VD}{2 \times K \times D}$$

EXAMPLE - A 240-volt, single-phase feeder with size 2/0 AWG THWN aluminum conductors is supplying an existing panelboard located 260 feet from the main switchboard. What is the MAXIMUM load that can be placed on the panelboard so that the voltage drop is limited to three percent?

        A. 143 amperes
        B. 175 amperes
        C. 122 amperes
        D. 87 amperes

ANSWER - (D)   87 amperes

        CM = 133,100 CM (2/0 AWG)
        VD = 240 volts x .03 = 7.2 volts
        K = 21.2 ohms (aluminum)
        D = 260 feet

$$I = \frac{133{,}100 \times 7.2}{2 \times 21.2 \times 260} = \frac{958{,}320}{11{,}024} = 86.9 \text{ amperes}$$

➢ The following formula can be used to determine the MAXIMUM load permitted when limiting the voltage drop on three-phase circuits:

$$I = \frac{CM \times VD}{1.732 \times K \times D}$$

EXAMPLE - An existing 208Y/120-volt, three-phase, 4-wire, panelboard is supplied with size 2 AWG THW copper feeder conductors from the main switchboard. The panelboard is located three-hundred (300) feet from the main switchboard. What is the MAXIMUM load, in amperes, the conductors can carry without exceeding a three percent voltage drop?

    A. 62 amperes
    B. 54 amperes
    C. 38 amperes
    D. 79 amperes

ANSWER - (A) 62 amperes

    CM = 66,360 (2 AWG)
    VD = 208 x .03 = 6.24 volts
    K = 12.9 ohms (copper)
    D = 300 feet

$$I = \frac{66{,}360 \times 6.24}{1.732 \times 12.9 \times 300} = \frac{414{,}086}{6{,}703} = 61.77 \text{ amperes}$$

➢ Another method of determining the voltage drop of the conductors for **single-phase circuits only** is to apply the Ohm's Law Method, using the following formula:

VD = I x R

FORMULA DEFINITIONS:

    VD = Volts dropped from a circuit
    I = Intensity of the current, or the load, in amperes, at 100 percent.
    R = Total conductor resistance, which can be found in **Chapter 9**, **Table 8** of the NEC®, under the ohm/KFT column. Using this

method, you must take into consideration the **total length** of both the conductors to find total resistance.

EXAMPLE - Two (2) size 12 AWG THWN/THHN 120-volt, single-phase, copper branch circuit conductors are to supply a 15 ampere load located one-hundred (100) feet from the panelboard. Determine the approximate voltage drop.

    A. 3 volts
    B. 6 volts
    C. 9 volts
    D. 12 volts

ANSWER - (B) 6 volts

    R = 1.98 ohms per 1,000 feet **(Chapter 9, Table 8)**

$$R = \frac{1.98}{1,000} = 0.00198 \text{ ohms per ft.} \times 200 \text{ ft} = .396 \text{ ohms total}$$

    I = 15 amperes

    VD = 15 amps x .396 ohms = 5.94 volts

EXAMPLE - A 240-volt, single-phase branch circuit is to supply a 32 ampere load with size 8 AWG THWN copper conductors. The load is one-hundred and fifty (150) feet from the panelboard; determine the voltage drop.

    A. 4 volts
    B. 15 volts
    C. 7.5 volts
    D. 6 volts

ANSWER - (C) 7.5 volts

    R = .778 ohms per 1,000 feet **(Chapter 9, Table 8)**

$$R = \frac{.788}{1,000} = 0.000788 \text{ ohms per ft.} \times 300 \text{ ft.} = .2334 \text{ ohms total}$$

    VD = 32 amps x .2334 ohms = 7.46 volts

UNIT 6
SELF-ASSESSMENT QUIZ

1. Voltage drop can be limited in a circuit by:

    I. increasing the conductor size.
    II. reducing the load.

      A. I only
      B. II only
      C. either I or II
      D. neither I nor II

2. The NEC® recommends the voltage drop on 120-volt branch circuits to be limited to _____.

      A. 3.6 volts
      B. 3 volts
      C. 6 volts
      D. 4.5 volts

3. The cross-sectional area of a conductor is expressed in _____.

      A. mils
      B. square inches
      C. cubic inches
      D. circular mils

4. The resistance of a conductor is determined by the _____.

      A. conductors cross-sectional area
      B. material type
      C. length of the conductor
      D. all of these

5. A size 6 AWG copper conductor has a cross-sectional area of _____.

      A. 24,640 CM
      B. 26,240 CM
      C. 16,510 CM
      D. 41,740 CM

6. A common formula that can be used to determine the voltage drop on the conductors of a single-phase circuit is:

A. VD = $\dfrac{1.732 \times K \times I \times D}{CM}$

B. VD = $\dfrac{2 \times K \times I \times CM}{D}$

C. VD = $\dfrac{CM \times D}{2 \times K \times I}$

D. VD = $\dfrac{2 \times K \times I \times D}{CM}$

7. A 240-volt, single-phase branch circuit, using size 8 AWG copper conductors, is to supply a 32 ampere load located eighty (80) feet from the panelboard. Determine the approximate voltage drop. (K=12.9)

    A. 2 volts
    B. 4 volts
    C. 6 volts
    D. 8 volts

8. Determine the voltage drop on the conductors of a control circuit given the following:

    • current = 5 amperes
    • total conductor length = 300 feet
    • conductor resistance = 4 ohms per 1,000 feet

    A. 0.02 volts
    B. 0.12 volts
    C. 6.00 volts
    D. 1.20 volts

9. A 10,800 VA, 240-volt, single-phase load is located two-hundred (200) feet from the panelboard and is supplied with size 6 AWG THWN copper conductors. Determine the approximate voltage drop on the circuit. (K=12.9)

    A. 9 volts
    B. 5 volts
    C. 12 volts
    D. 18 volts

10. A size 1 AWG aluminum USE feeder cable is to supply a 100 ampere, 120/240 volt, single-phase load located one hundred and forty (140) feet from the panelboard. Determine the approximate voltage drop on this feeder circuit. (K=21.2)

A. 14 volts
B. 7 volts
C. 4 volts
D. 9 volts

11. A 208Y/120-volt, three-phase feeder, using size 300 kcmil copper conductors is to supply a 275 ampere demand load located one hundred and twenty-five (125) feet from the switchboard. Determine the approximate voltage drop on this feeder circuit. (K=12.9)

    A. 2.50 volts
    B. 5.00 volts
    C. 6.75 volts
    D. 4.50 volts

12. A 240-volt, single-phase 114 ampere load is located one hundred and sixty (160) feet from the panelboard. What MINIMUM size copper branch circuit conductors should be used to supply this load when voltage drop is to be limited to 3 percent? (K=12.9)

    A. 1/0 AWG
    B. 1 AWG
    C. 3 AWG
    D. 2 AWG

13. A three-phase, 208Y/120-volt forty (40) ampere continuous load is to be located three hundred (300) feet from the panelboard. Determine the MINIMUM size copper branch circuit conductors required to serve the load. Assume the voltage drop is to be limited to not more than 3 percent. (K=12.9)

    A. 4 AWG
    B. 3 AWG
    C. 2 AWG
    D. 1 AWG

14. A three-phase 208Y/120-volt feeder, consisting of aluminum conductors, is to supply a panelboard with a 36 kVA continuous load. If the voltage drop is to be limited to six (6) volts, and the panelboard is located two hundred (200) feet from the voltage source, what MINIMUM size conductors are required? (K=21.2)

    A. 2/0 AWG

B. 3/0 AWG
C. 4/0 AWG
D. 250 kcmil

15. Determine the approximate MAXIMUM distance a 240-volt, single-phase 32 ampere load, supplied with a size 8 AWG copper branch circuit conductors can be located from the panelboard, when the voltage drop is to be limited to 3 percent. (K=12.9)

   A. 140 feet
   B. 170 feet
   C. 70 feet
   D. 60 feet

NOTES

UNIT 7

AC MOTOR CALCULATIONS

Upon successfully completing this unit of study the student will be familiar with the concept of properly sizing conductors, overcurrent protection, overload protection, and disconnects for AC electric motors.

UNIT 7

AC MOTOR CALCULATIONS

RELATED INFORMATION:

> ➤ In general, when sizing the conductors, disconnecting means and overcurrent protection for **continuous-duty** ac motors, the full-load current values of the motor(s) given in **Tables 430.247** through **430.250** shall be used, instead of the actual current rating marked on the motor nameplate. **[430.6(A)(1)]** Note this rule does not apply for motors built for low speeds (less than 1,200 RPM) or high torque which may have higher full-load currents and multispeed motors which will have full-load current varying with the speed. For these motors the current values given on the motor(s) nameplate shall be used instead of the NEC® tables.

> ➤ **All** motors shall be considered to be for **continuous-duty** unless the nature of the apparatus it drives is such that the motor cannot operate continuously with load under any condition of use. **[430.33]** Examples of motors **not** considered as continuous duty are motors operating elevators, cranes and assembly line machines.

> ➤ In general, in order to properly size branch circuit conductors supplying a single continuous duty motor you are to comply with **430.22** which requires the conductors to have an ampacity of at least **125 percent** of the motor's full-load current (FLC) rating as determined in the related tables in the NEC®. The actual conductor sizes are to be selected from **Tables 310.15(B)(16)** or from **Table 400.5(A)**. The conductors are to be sized according to the temperature ratings (60°C or 75°C) of the equipment terminations.

EXAMPLE - Determine the MINIMUM size THHN copper conductors required to supply a 3 hp, 240-volt, single-phase continuous-duty motor when all terminations have a rating of 75°C.

        A. 14 AWG
        B. 12 AWG
        C. 10 AWG
        D. 8 AWG

ANSWER - (B)   12 AWG

        motor FLC = 17 amperes **[Table 430.248]**
        17 amperes x 125% **[430.22]** = 21.25 amperes

Size 12 AWG THHN is rated at 25 amperes at 75°C
[Table 310.15(B)(16)]

➢ Conductors that supply a motor used in a short-time, intermittent, or varying duty application are permitted to have an ampacity of not less than the percentage values shown on **Table 430.22(E)**, based the full-load current rating indicated on the **motor's nameplate**.

EXAMPLE - Conductors supplying a 40 hp, 480-volt, three-phase, 5 minute rated elevator motor with an ampere rating of 50 amperes marked on the nameplate, shall have an ampacity of at least _____.

      A. 42.5 amperes
      B. 45.9 amperes
      C. 62.5 amperes
      D. 67.5 amperes

ANSWER - (A) 42.5 amperes

      motor FLA = 50 amperes x 85% **[Table 430.22(E)]** = 42.5 amps

➢ In general, conductors that supply more than one continuous-duty motor on a single circuit and/or motor(s) and other load(s), are required to have an ampacity of not less than **125 percent** of the full-load current rating of the **highest** rated motor in the group plus **100 percent** of the full-load current ratings of all the **remaining motors** in the group, also the ampacity required for the other load(s).**[430.24]**

EXAMPLE - Determine the MINIMUM size THWN/THHN copper feeder conductors required to supply two (2) induction type, 208-volt, three-phase, continuous-duty motors; one (1) 10 hp and one (1) 15 hp. Consider all terminations are rated 75°C.

      A. 6 AWG
      B. 4 AWG
      C. 3 AWG
      D. 2 AWG

ANSWER - (C) 3 AWG

      10 hp FLC = 30.8 amps **[Tbl. 430.250]** x 100% = 30.80 amperes
      15 HP FLC = 46.2 amps **[Tbl. 430.250]** x 125% = <u>57.75 amperes</u>

88.55 amperes

Size 3 AWG THWN is rated at 100 amperes. **[Table 310.15(B)(16)]**

➤ Each motor and its accessories is required to have branch circuit, short-circuit and ground fault protection by the use of overcurrent protective devices such as fuses or circuit breakers. The overcurrent protective devices are to be sized no larger than the percentage values given in **Table 430.52**. **[430.52(C)(1)]** Where the values for overcurrent protection determined from **Table 430.52** does not correspond with the standard sizes or ratings as listed per **240.6(A)** the next higher standard overcurrent protection device is permitted to be used.
[430.52(C)(1), Ex 1] This is known as **initial sizing**.

EXAMPLE - Determine the MAXIMUM initial rating of nontime delay fuses to be used for branch-circuit, short-circuit and ground-fault protection for a 5 hp, 230-volt, three-phase, squirrel cage, continuous-duty motor.

      A. 40 amperes
      B. 45 amperes
      C. 50 amperes
      D. 60 amperes

ANSWER - (C) 50 amperes

      5 hp FLC = 15.2 amperes **[Table 430.250]**
      15.2 amperes x 300% = 45.6 amperes **[Table 430.52]**

      Since 45.6 amperes is not a standard rating for nontime delay fuses, as per **430.52(C)(1) Ex. 1**, you are permitted to go up to   the next standard size fuse which is rated at 50 amperes.

➤ When sizing overcurrent protection for motors, the selected rating or setting, if adjustable, should be as low as possible for MAXIMUM protection. However, if the motor is under severe starting conditions, the rating or setting designated in **Table 450.52** or as permitted by **430.52(C)(1) Ex. 1** is not large enough for the starting current of the motor, you are permitted to go up to a higher value as allowed by **430.52(C)(1) Ex. 2**. This is known as **MAXIMUM** or **absolute MAXIMUM** sizing.

EXAMPLE - Determine the absolute MAXIMUM standard size time-delay fuses permitted for short-circuit, branch-circuit and ground-fault protection for a 40 hp, 480-volt, three-phase, induction type, continuous-duty motor.

      A. 100 amperes
      B. 110 amperes
      C. 115 amperes
      D. 125 amperes

ANSWER - (B) 110 amperes

        40 hp FLC = 52 amperes **[Table 430.250]**
        52 amperes x 225% = 117 amperes **[430.52(C)(1)Ex.2(b)]**

        Since you are NOT permitted to exceed 225% of the FLC of the motor, you must go down to the next smaller standard size fuse as listed in **240.6(A).**

➢ In general, to properly size the overcurrent protection device for **feeder** conductors supplying two or more motors, the rules as specified in **430.62(A)** are to be applied which states, the protective device is to be sized by:

  (1) not greater than the largest overcurrent protection device provided for any motor in the group,

  (2) plus the sum of the full-load currents of the other motors of the group.

        When sizing **feeder** overcurrent protection for motors, when the value you select does not correspond with a standard rating as listed per **240.6(A)** you are NOT permitted to go up to the next standard size, you must go **down**.

EXAMPLE - What standard size time-delay fuses are required for the feeder overcurrent protection of a feeder supplying four (4), 15 hp, 480-volt, three-phase, continuous-duty induction-type motors, each protected with 40 ampere rated time-delay fuses?

    A. 100 amperes
    B. 110 amperes
    C. 125 amperes
    D. 150 amperes

ANSWER - (A) 100 amperes

        15 hp FLC = 21 amperes **[Table 430.250]**

        40 A (largest OCP in group) + 21 A + 21 A + 21 A = 103 amps

        You are required to go down to 100 ampere rated fuses. **[240.6(A)]**

➢ In addition to overcurrent protection, most continuous-duty electric motors rated more than 1 hp and motors automatically started having a rating of 1 hp or less, are required to be protected from harmful **overloads**. **[430.32(A)]** To properly size the overload protective devices, they shall be selected to trip at no more than the percentage values of the motors nameplate rating given in **430.32(A)(1)**, **(MINIMUM)** or **430.32(C)**, **(MAXIMUM)** instead of the full-load current values from Tables 430.248, 430.249 and 430.250. Today, many manufacturers have adjustable overloads installed in motor controllers or starters for protecting the motor against overloads, which are harmful to it.

➢ The ampere trip setting value of the separate overloads is based upon **service factor** and **temperature rise** of the motor, as indicated on the motor **nameplate**. The running overload protection may range from **115%** to **125% (MINIMUM)** **[430.32(A)(1)]** to no more than **140% (MAXIMUM) [430.32(C)]** of the motor's ampere **nameplate** rating. The service factor indicated on the nameplate usually ranges from **1.00** to **1.30**. For example, if a motor has a service factor rating of 1.15 this means that the motor can operate up to **115%** of its rating without undue harm where the ambient temperature is not more than 104°F or 40°C. The temperature rise indicated on the motors nameplate relates to the heating effect of the motor when it is running properly in relation to the ambient temperature. The higher the temperature rise indicated on the nameplate the hotter the motor runs. For example, a motor with a 40°C temperature rise means, under normal operating conditions the motor should not get warmer than 40°C or 104°F. If too great a load is put on the motor or the ambient temperature is elevated, the motor will become excessively hot, causing probable injury to the insulation of the windings.

EXAMPLE - What is the MINIMUM size running overload protection, in amperes, required for a 2 hp, 208-volt, single-phase, squirrel cage motor with a temperature rise of 42°C and a FLA of 12 amperes indicated on the nameplate?

    A. 13.20 amperes
    B. 15.18 amperes
    C. 15.00 amperes
    D. 13.80 amperes

ANSWER - (D)   13.80 amperes

    2 hp FLA (nameplate) = 12 amperes

    12 amps x 115% (all other motors) = 13.8 amps **[430.32(A)(1)]**

EXAMPLE - Refer to the previous example. Assume the ampere rating you have selected is not sufficient to start the motor and trips. Determine the MAXIMUM size overload protection permitted.

    A. 15.00 amperes
    B. 15.60 amperes
    C. 16.80 amperes

D. 17.16 amperes

ANSWER - (B)   15.60 amperes

   2 hp FLA (nameplate) = 12 amperes

   12 amps x 130% (all other motors) = 15.60 amps **[430.32(C)]**

➤ Some motors are provided with a **thermal protector integral** with the motor, located inside the motor housing, for overload protection. **[430.32(A)(2)]** Under this condition, the ultimate trip setting, in amperes, shall not exceed the percentage values as expressed in **430.32(A)(2)**, multiplied by the motor's full-load current as given in **Table 430.248**, **Table 430.249** or **Table 430.250**.

EXAMPLE -   Determine the MAXIMUM current setting permitted for overload protection for a motor that has a thermal protector integral with the motor, given the following:

   • 1 hp – squirrel cage
   • single-phase, 120-volts

   A. 24.96 amperes
   B. 20.80 amperes
   C. 22.40 amperes
   D. 27.20 amperes

ANSWER - (A)   24.96 amperes

   1 hp FLC = 16 amperes **[Table 430.248]**

   16 amperes x 156% **[430.32(A)(2)]** = 24.96 amperes

➤ In general, each motor must be provided with some form of approved manual **disconnecting means**. The disconnecting means is required to have an ampere rating of not less than **115 percent** of the full-load current rating of the motor as determined in **Table 430.248** through **430.250.[430.110(A)]** For motors rated 2 hp through 100 hp the disconnecting means may be a general-use switch, rated in horsepower, a circuit breaker, or a manual motor controller when marked **"Suitable as Motor Disconnect"**. **[430.109(A)(6)]**

EXAMPLE -   When an inverse time circuit breaker is used as a disconnecting means only for a 7½ hp, single-phase, 240-volt, ac motor, the circuit breaker must have a standard ampacity rating of at LEAST _____.

   A. 40 amperes
   B. 50 amperes
   C. 100 amperes
   D. 46 amperes

ANSWER -   (B)   50 amperes

        7½ hp FLA = 40 amperes **[Table 430.248]**

        40 amperes x 115% = 46 amperes **[430.110A]**

        As per **240.6(A),** the next standard size circuit breaker has a rating of 50 amperes.

> For stationary ac motors of 2 hp or less and 300 volts or less the disconnecting means is permitted to be an ac general-use snap switch where the motor full-load current rating is not more than **80 percent** of the ampere rating of the switch. **[430.109(C)(2)]**

EXAMPLE -   A 20 ampere rated ac general-use snap switch is permitted for use as a disconnecting means for a 120-volt, single-phase, ac motor when the motor has a rating of 2 hp or less and a full-load current rating of _____ or less.

    A. 20 amperes
    B. 16 amperes
    C. 12 amperes
    D. 25 amperes

ANSWER -   (B)   16 amperes

        20 amperes (switch rating) x 80% = 16 amperes
        [430.109(C)(2)]

UNIT 7
SELF-ASSESSMENT QUIZ

1. In general, when sizing the conductors, disconnecting means or overcurrent protection for a continuous-duty ac motor, they are to be sized based on the _____.

    A. starting current of the motor
    B. locked rotor current of the motor
    C. motors stopping current
    D. running current of the motor at usual speed

2. For continuous-duty motors, the motor nameplate ampere rating is used to determine the size of the _____ for motors.

    A. disconnecting means
    B. branch-circuit conductors
    C. short-circuit protection
    D. overload protection

3. Branch-circuit conductors that supply a single, continuous-duty ac motor shall have an ampacity of not less than _____ of the full-load current of the motor.

    A. 80 percent
    B. 100 percent
    C. 125 percent
    D. 150 percent

4. When determining the required ampacity of the branch-circuit conductors to supply a three-phase, continuous-duty motor, the full-load current values of the motor given on _____ shall be used.

    A. Table 430.250 of the NEC®
    B. Table 430.52 of the NEC®
    C. Table 430.248 of the NEC®
    D. the motor's nameplate

5. When determining the initial standard size, time-delay fuses required for branch-circuit, short-circuit and ground-fault protection of a single-phase, 240 volt, ac motor, the fuses

shall have a rating of _____ of the full-load current of the motor. When the value determined does not correspond to a standard ampere rating, the next higher standard rating shall be permitted.

A. 175 percent
B. 150 percent
C. 225 percent
D. 300 percent

6. Motors with a service factor of not less than 1.15 indicated on the nameplate, shall have the overload protection sized at _____ of the full-load ampere rating of the motor when modifications of the value selected in not necessary.

A. 115 percent
B. 125 percent
C. 130 percent
D. 140 percent

7. The full-load running current of a 3 hp, 208-volt, single-phase, continuous-duty, ac motor is _____.

A. 10.6 amperes
B. 13.2 amperes
C. 18.7 amperes
D. 19.6 amperes

8. Branch-circuit conductors supplying a three-phase, 208-volt, 10 hp continuous duty, induction-type, Design B motor, are required to have an ampacity of at LEAST _____.

A. 30.80 amperes
B. 35.42 amperes
C. 38.50 amperes
D. 46.20 amperes

9. Determine the MINIMUM ampere rating for an adjustable trip overload protective device responsive to motor current, used to protect a 20 hp, 230 volt, three-phase, induction type, ac motor with temperature rise of 48°C and a full-load ampere rating of 54 amperes indicated on the nameplate.

A. 54.0 amperes
B. 62.1 amperes
C. 70.2 amperes
D. 75.6 amperes

10. Refer to the previous question. If the trip setting you selected was not adequate to start the motor and trips, determine the MAXIMUM ampere setting of the adjustable overload protective device as permitted by the NEC®.

A. 62.1 amperes
B. 67.5 amperes
C. 70.2 amperes
D. 75.6 amperes

11. Determine the MINIMUM size Type SO cord permitted to supply a 40 hp, 460 volt, three-phase, continuous-duty, wound rotor ac motor installed in an area with an ambient temperature of 86°F.

   A. 2 AWG
   B. 4 AWG
   C. 6 AWG
   D. 8 AWG

12. The branch-circuit conductors supplying a 7½ hp, 240-volt, single-phase, continuous-duty ac motor must be at least size _____ copper conductors, when the conductors and all terminations are rated for 75°C and ambient temperature is not a consideration.

   A. 4 AWG
   B. 10 AWG
   C. 6 AWG
   D. 8 AWG

13. Where an ac motor has a thermal protector integral with the motor, determine the MAXIMUM current setting permitted for overload protection for a 2 hp, 120-volt, single-phase motor having a FLA of 22.5 amperes indicated on the nameplate.

   A. 35.1 amperes
   B. 31.5 amperes
   C. 37.4 amperes
   D. 33.6 amperes

14. Determine the MINIMUM size THWN/THHN copper conductors required to supply three (3) induction-type, 480-volt, three-phase, continuous-duty motors; one (1) 10 hp, one (1) 15 hp and one (1) 20 hp. Consider all terminations are rated for 75°C.

   A. 6 AWG
   B. 4 AWG
   C. 3 AWG
   D. 2 AWG

15. The MAXIMUM standard initial rating of time-delay fuses provided for the branch circuit, short-circuit and ground-fault protection required for a 7½ hp 240-volt, single-phase continuous-duty motor have a rating of _____.

   A. 50 amperes
   B. 60 amperes

C. 70 amperes
D. 80 amperes

16. Assume the motor in the previous question is under heavy load when starting and the fuses blow. Determine the absolute MAXIMUM standard rating permitted for overcurrent protection for the motor.

    A. 100 amperes
    B. 90 amperes
    C. 80 amperes
    D. 70 amperes

17. If the motor in question 15 is provided with an inverse time circuit breaker as overcurrent protection, the initial standard rating of the circuit breaker would be _____.

    A. 70 amperes
    B. 80 amperes
    C. 90 amperes
    D. 100 amperes

18. In general, a general-use fused switch used as a disconnecting means for a 25 hp, 480-volt, three-phase motor with a FLA of 32 amperes indicated on the nameplate, must have an ampere rating of at LEAST _____.

    A. 39 amperes
    B. 50 amperes
    C. 56 amperes
    D. 79 amperes

19. What MAXIMUM standard size time-delay fuses are required for the feeder overcurrent protection of a feeder supplying two (2) 20 hp, 480-volt, three-phase continuous-duty induction-type motors, each protected with 50 ampere rated time-delay fuses, and two (2) 30 hp, 480-volt, three-phase continuous duty induction-type motors, each protected with 70 ampere rated time-delay fuses?

    A. 200 amperes
    B. 125 amperes
    C. 150 amperes
    D. 175 amperes

20. What MINIMUM size THWN/THHN copper branch-circuit conductors are required to supply a continuous-duty, induction-type, 15 hp, 208-volt, three-phase motor, when installed in an area with an ambient temperature of 120°F? Consider all terminations are rated 75°C.

    A. 6 AWG
    B. 4 AWG
    C. 8 AWG
    D. 3 AWG

NOTES

UNIT 8

SINGLE-FAMILY DWELLING SERVICE CALCULATIONS

After completing this unit of study, the successful student will be familiar with the concept of properly sizing services for one-family dwellings.

UNIT 8

SINGLE-FAMILY DWELLING SERVICE CALCULATIONS

RELATED INFORMATION:

- A single-family dwelling is considered a building consisting solely of one dwelling unit with living and sleeping quarters and having permanent provisions for cooking, cleaning, and laundering.

- In order to properly size services for dwelling units you are to comply with the requirements as set forth in **Article 220** of the NEC® and additional Articles such as **210, 230** and **240** that may also apply. As indicated in **Section 310.15(B)(7)**, for sizing residential **120/240-volt, 3-wire, single phase** ungrounded (line) service conductors rated **100 through 400 amperes,** they are permitted to have an ampacity not less than **83 percent** of the service rating. For example, if the dwelling unit has a service rating of 150 amperes, the service-entrance conductors are permitted to have a rating of 125 amperes. 150 amperes x .83 = 124.5 amperes

- The NEC® recognizes two (2) methods when calculating dwelling services, the **general method**, also known as the **standard method** and the **optional method**. The standard method starts at **220.12** and the optional method starts at **220.80.** Generally, the optional method is easier to use because you simply add the nameplate values of the utilization equipment together and apply only one demand factor. With the general method, there are several demand factors applied. With either method the most common service provided for a one-family dwelling unit is 120/240-volts, single-phase.

- When using either calculation method, the **MINIMUM** size service for a one-family dwelling is required to be rated **100 amperes** because the ampacity for the ungrounded conductors shall not be less than the rating of the service disconnecting means **[230.42(B)]** and the service disconnecting means shall have a rating of not less than **100 amperes. [230.79(C)]**

- **Annex D** of the NEC® shows examples of both calculation methods and the steps and procedures to be used. We will follow these examples and steps to learn how to properly size services for one-family dwellings. First, we will look at the general (standard) method of calculation. You will find a completed example of this form using the standard method of calculation on page 123 of this text.

General Calculation Method

Step 1 - Determine the total connected load, in VA, of the general lighting and general-purpose receptacles by applying **Table 220.12**. Use the outside dimension of the house but, do not include garages, open porches and enclosed areas not adaptable for future use. **[220.12]**

EXAMPLE - What is the total connected load, in VA, for the general lighting and general-use receptacles of a one-family dwelling having 30 feet by 60 feet of livable space?

    A. 2,100 VA
    B. 3,600 VA
    C. 5,400 VA
    D. 6,300 VA

ANSWER - (C) 5,400 VA

    First, find the area, in square feet, of the livable space, then multiply by the value given in **Table 220.12**.

    30 ft. x 60 ft. = 1,800 sq. ft. x 3 VA **[Table 220.12]** = 5,400 VA

Step 2 - Find the total connected load of the small appliance and laundry branch circuits. A MINIMUM of **two (2)** small appliance branch circuits are required **[210.11(C)(1)]** and they shall be calculated at **1,500 VA** per circuit. **[220.52(A)]** A MINIMUM of **one (1)** branch circuit is required to supply the laundry **[210.11(C)(2)]** and shall be calculated at **1,500 VA** per circuit. **[220.52(B)]**

EXAMPLE - What is the MINIMUM total connected load, in VA, for the small appliance and laundry loads in a single-family dwelling?

    A. 4,500 VA
    B. 3,000 VA
    C. 6,000 VA
    D. 1,500 VA

ANSWER - (A) 4,500 VA

    2 small appl. circuits @ 1,500 VA each = 3,000 VA
    1 laundry circuit @ 1,500 VA   = 1,500 VA
                TOTAL = 4,500 VA

Step 3 - Apply the demand factors specified in **Table 220.42** for the general-purpose lighting and receptacle loads, plus the loads required for the small appliance and laundry branch circuits. **[220.42]**

EXAMPLE - What is the demand load, in VA, for a dwelling unit having a 5,400 VA total connected lighting load and a 4,500 VA connected load for small appliance and laundry branch-circuits?

    A. 9,900 VA
    B. 5,415 VA
    C. 6,780 VA
    D. 3,465 VA

ANSWER - (B) 5,415 VA

    5,400 VA (ltg.) + 4,500 VA (laund. & sm. appl.) = 9,900 VA total

    1st 3,000 VA @ 100% **[Table 220.42]**   = 3,000 VA
    9,900 VA – 3,000 VA = 6,900 VA (remainder) x 35% = 2,415 VA
                     DEMAND LOAD = 5,415 VA

Step 4 - Apply a demand factor of **75 percent** of the nameplate rating of **four (4)** or more fastened in place appliances.

    *NOTE – This rule does **not apply** for electric ranges, clothes dryers, space heating or air-conditioning equipment. **[220.53]**

EXAMPLE - A one-family dwelling is to have the following fastened in place appliances:

    garbage disposal –   864 VA
    dishwasher –   1,100 VA
    trash compactor –   1,188 VA
    water heater –   4,500 VA
    attic fan –   750 VA
    swimming pool pump – 1,250 VA
Where using the standard method of calculation for dwelling units, determine the demand load.

    A. 7,652 VA
    B. 9,652 VA
    C. 6,757 VA
    D. 7,239 VA

ANSWER - (D) 7,239 VA

```
garbage disposal  -    864 VA
dishwasher        -  1,100 VA
trash compactor   –  1,188 VA
water heater      –  4,500 VA
attic fan         -    750 VA
pump              -  1,250 VA
        TOTAL =  9,652 VA (connected load)
            x     75%
                 7,239 VA (demand load)
```

Step 5 - Determine the electric clothes dryer demand load, using **5,000 watts (volt – amperes)** as a MINIMUM or the nameplate rating, **whichever is larger**, for each dryer served. **[220.54]** You are permitted to use the demand factors shown in **Table 220.54**. A demand of **70 percent** of this value may be applied to the **neutral** (grounded) conductor. **[220.61(B)(1)]**

EXAMPLE - When a one-family dwelling is to have only one (1) 4,500 VA electric clothes dryer installed, the demand load will be _____ on the ungrounded service-entrance conductors and _____ on the grounded (neutral) conductor.

    A. 4,500 VA – 3,500 VA
    B. 3,500 VA – 4,500 VA
    C. 4,500 VA – 5,000 VA
    D. 5,000 VA – 3,500 VA

ANSWER - (D)   5,000 VA – 3,500 VA

        5,000 VA MINIMUM ungrounded conductors **[220.54]**
        5,000 VA x 70% = 3,500 VA neutral conductor **[220.61(B)(1)]**

Step 6 - Determine the demand load for the cooking appliances in accordance with **Table 220.55. [220.55]** This is explained in **Unit 3** of this book. A further demand of **70 percent** of the demand load on the ungrounded conductors may be applied to the **neutral** (grounded) conductor. **[220.61(B)(1)]**

EXAMPLE - A 12 kW electric range installed in a one-family dwelling will have a demand load of _____ on the ungrounded service-entrance conductors and a demand load of _____ on the grounded neutral conductor.

    A. 8,000 VA – 5,600 VA
    B. 12,000 VA – 8,400 VA
    C. 12,000 VA – 8,000 VA
    D. 8,000 VA – 3,920 VA

ANSWER - (A)   8,000 VA – 5,600 VA

        ungrounded conductors demand – 8 kW = 8,000 VA

[Table 220.55, Col. C]
grounded conductor – 8,000 VA x 70% = 5,600 VA
[220.61(B)(1)]

Step 7 - Determine the demand load for the fixed electric space heating or air-conditioning load; you are permitted to **omit the smaller** of the two because these loads are considered noncoincident loads, meaning, they are unlikely to be in use simultaneously. **[220.60]**

EXAMPLE - A one-family dwelling unit to be constructed will have a 10 kW (kVA), 240-volt, single-phase, fixed electric space heating unit and a 32 ampere, 240-volt, single-phase air-conditioning unit. When calculating the total load on the dwelling unit, what is the demand that should be applied to the service-entrance conductors?

   A. 10,000 VA
   B. 10,800 VA
   C. 9,600 VA
   D. 19,600 VA

ANSWER - (A)   10,000 VA

   First, compare the two loads.

   A/C unit -   P = I x E   P = 32 amperes x 240 volts = 7,680 VA
   Heating unit -   10 kW = 10 kW x 1,000 = 10,000 VA

   *NOTE – The heating unit is the larger of the loads, this value should be applied.

Step 8 - Add an additional **25 percent** of the full-load current of the **largest motor** in the dwelling. **[220.50]** Generally, the largest motor in the house is the air-conditioning unit.

EXAMPLE - A one-family dwelling will have the following motor loads installed:

   garbage disposal – 864 VA
   trash compactor – 1,188 VA
   attic fan – 750 VA
   pump motor – 1,250 VA

   When applying the largest motor rule for residential service calculations, how many VA should be added?

   A. 1,013 VA
   B. 1,563 VA
   C. 1,266 VA
   D. 313 VA

ANSWER -   (D)   313 VA

Largest motor (pump) 1,250 VA x 25% = 313 VA

Step 9 -   Add together the values determined from steps 3-8 to find the required volt-amperes. Next, apply the current formula **(I=P/E)** to determine the demand load. Then, multiply the current value by **83%** and size the service-entrance conductors using **Table 310.15(B)(16)**. Use **Table 250.66** for sizing the grounding electrode conductor.

EXAMPLE -   After all demand factors have been taken into consideration for a one-family dwelling unit, a demand load of 35,967 VA is determined. What MINIMUM size THWN aluminum ungrounded service-entrance conductors are required when the house is to have a 120/240-volt, single-phase, electrical system?

A. 1 AWG
B. 1/0 AWG
C. 2/0 AWG
D. 3/0 AWG

ANSWER -   (C)   2/0 AWG

First, find the load in amperes and multiply by 83%.

$$I = \frac{P}{E} = \frac{35,967}{240 \text{ volts}} = 150 \text{ amperes} \times 83\% = 124.5 \text{ amperes}$$

Table 310.15(B)(16) indicates size 2/0 AWG aluminum conductors having an ampacity of 135 amperes should be selected.

STANDARD CALCULATION: ONE-FAMILY DWELLING

1. GENERAL LIGHTING & RECEPTACLES: *Table 220.12*
_____ sq. ft. x 3 VA =   _____ VA

2. SMALL APPLIANCES 220.52(A) & LAUNDRY 220.52(B)
1,500 VA x _____ circuits =   _____ VA

3. APPLY DEMAND FACTORS: *Table 220.42*
Total of gen. ltg. & small appl.   _____ VA
First 3000 VA x 100%   =   3,000 VA
Next _____ VA x 35%   =   _____ VA **LINE**   **NEUTRAL**
Remaining _____ VA x 25% =   _____ VA
Total   _____ VA _____ VA _____VA

Copyright © 2014

4. FIXED APPLIANCES: 220.53

Water Heater =	_____ VA	
Disposal =	_____ VA	
Compactor =	_____ VA	
Dishwasher =	_____ VA	
_____ =	_____ VA	
_____ =	_____ VA	
_____ =	_____ VA	
Total	_____ VA (x 75% if 4 or more)=	_____ VA _____ VA

5. DRYER: 220.54; Table 220.54

_____ VA = _____ VA x 70%=_____ VA

6. COOKING EQUIPMENT: Table 220.55 & Notes
Col A _____ VA x _____% = _____ VA
Col B _____ VA x _____% = _____ VA
Col C _____ VA = _____ VA
Total _____ VA _____ VA x 70%=_____ VA

7. HEATING or A/C (largest): 220.60
Heating unit = _____ VA x 100% =_____ VA
A/C unit = _____ VA x 100% =_____ VA
Heat pump = _____ VA x 100% =_____ VA
Largest Load _____ VA

8. LARGEST MOTOR: 220.14(C)
_____ VA x 25% = _____ VA _____ VA

9. TOTAL [___] VA [___] VA
Line   I = _____ VA = _____ amperes
        240 volts
Neutral I = _____ VA = _____ amperes
         240 volts

Conductors are permitted to be sized @ 83% of the demand load if 120/240-volts, single-phase and not greater than 400 amperes.

STANDARD CALCULATION: ONE-FAMILY DWELLING

1. GENERAL LIGHTING & RECEPTACLES: Table 220.12
1,800 sq. ft. x 3 VA = 5,400 VA

2. SMALL APPLIANCES 220.52(A) & LAUNDRY 220.52(B)
1,500 VA x 3 circuits = 4,500 VA

3. APPLY DEMAND FACTORS: Table 220.42   LINE   NEUTRAL
Total of gen. ltg. & small appl. 9,900 VA
First 3000 VA x 100% = 3,000 VA
Next 6,900 VA x 35% = 2,415 VA
Remaining -0- VA x 25% = -0- VA
Total   5,415 VA   5,415 VA   5,415 VA

4. FIXED APPLIANCES: 220.53

Water Heater =	4,500 VA			
Disposal =	864 VA			
Compactor =	1,188 VA			
Dishwasher =	1,110 VA			
Attic fan =	750 VA			
Pump =	1,250 VA			
-0- =	-0- VA			
Total	9,652 VA (x 75% if 4 or more)=		7,239 VA	7,239 VA

5. DRYER: 220.54; Table 220.54

5,000 VA =	5,000 VA x 70%=	3,500 VA

6. COOKING EQUIPMENT: Table 220.55 & Notes

Col A -0- VA x -0- % =	-0- VA		
Col B -0- VA x -0- % =	-0- VA		
Col C 8,000 VA =	8,000 VA		
Total	8,000 VA	8,000 VA x 70%=	5,600 VA

7. HEATING or A/C (largest): 220.60

Heating unit = 10,000 VA x 100% = 10,000 VA	
A/C unit = 7,680 VA x 100% = 7,680 VA	
Heat pump = -0- VA x 100% = -0- VA	
Largest Load	10,000 VA

8. LARGEST MOTOR: 220.14(C)

1,250 VA x 25% =	313 VA	313 VA

9. TOTAL

	35,967 VA	22,067 VA
Line I = 35,967 VA = 150 amperes		
240 volts		
Neutral I = 22,067 VA = 92 amperes		
240 volts		

Conductors are permitted to be sized @ 83% of the demand load if 120/240-volts, single-phase and not greater than 400 amperes.

Optional Calculation Method

> In general, the **optional calculation method** for dwelling units provides an easier and less complex method than the standard (general) method for computing the total demand load for service-entrance conductors. The optional calculation method is reserved for dwelling units served by a single service with a connected load of **100 amperes or greater. [220.82(A)]** Therefore, since most one-family homes currently being constructed have a connected load of 100 amperes or more, this calculation method is frequently used. You will find a completed example of this form of calculation method on page 130 of this text.

> When using the **optional calculation method**, the calculated load shall not be less than **100 percent** of the **first 10 kW**, plus **40 percent** of the remainder of the **"general loads"**, including, general lighting and receptacles, laundry and small

appliance branch circuits and nameplate VA rating of all fastened in place motors and appliances, plus the larger of the air-conditioner or heating load. **[220.82(A)]** The following steps may be applied when using the optional calculation method for dwellings.

Step 1 - Compare the heating and air-conditioning loads. As per **220.82(C)**, include the **largest** of the following:

1. 100 percent of the nameplate rating(s) of the air-conditioning equipment.
2. 100 percent of the nameplate rating(s) of the heat pump(s) only.
3. 100 percent of the nameplate ratings of electric thermal storage and other heating systems where the usual load is expected to be continuous.

4. 100 percent of the nameplate rating(s) of the heat pump compressor and 65 percent of the supplemental electric heating for central electric space heating systems. If the heat pumps compressor is interlocked with the supplementary heat in a manner that both cannot be operated at the same time, the heat pump does not need to be added.

5. 65 percent of the nameplate rating(s) of electric space heating, if there are less than four (4) units having separate controls.

6. 40 percent of the nameplate rating(s) of electric space heating, if there are four (4) or more units with separate controls.

EXAMPLE - A one-family dwelling is to have the following heating and air-conditioning equipment:

two (2) 10 kW (kVA) electric space heating systems
two (2) 240-volt, single-phase, 50 ampere rated air-conditioners

When using the optional method of calculation for one-family dwellings, what demand, in VA, should be applied to the ungrounded service-entrance conductors for the heating or air-conditioning loads?

A. 20,000 VA
B. 24,000 VA
C. 15,600 VA
D. 13,000 VA

ANSWER - (B) 24,000 VA

Space heaters **[220.82(C)(5)]**
10 kVA + 10 kVA = 20 kVA x 1,000 = 20,000 VA

20,000 VA x 65% = 13,000 VA

A/C Equipment **[220.82(C)(1)]**
50 amps + 50 amps = 100 amperes x 240 volts = 24,000 VA

The A/C equipment with a computed load of 24,000 VA is to be used for this calculation.

Step 2 - Determine the connected load, in VA, of the general lighting and general-use receptacles; calculated from the outside dimensions of the dwelling using 3 VA per square foot. Do not include open porches, garages or unused or unfinished spaces not adapted for future use. **[220.82(B)(1)]**

EXAMPLE - Before demand factors are taken into consideration, determine the connected load, in VA, for the general lighting and general-use receptacles for a one-family dwelling having 5,000 square feet of livable space, a 600 square foot garage and a 350 square foot open porch.

    A. 15,000 VA
    B. 17,500 VA
    C. 17,850 VA
    D. 5,000 VA

ANSWER - (A) 15,000 VA

    5,000 sq. ft. x 3 VA **[220.82(B)(1)]** = 15,000 VA

Step 3 - Find the total connected load of the small appliance and laundry branch circuits; each circuit is to be calculated at **1,500 VA each**. **[220.82(B)(2)]** A MINIMUM of two (2) small-appliance branch circuits are required **[210.11(C)(1)]** and a MINIMUM of one (1) laundry branch circuit is required. **[210.11(C)(2)]**

EXAMPLE - A one-family dwelling is to have three (3) small-appliance branch circuits and one (1) laundry branch circuit installed. Before demand factors are taken into consideration, what is the total connected load of these circuits?

    A. 1,500 VA
    B. 3,000 VA
    C. 4,500 VA
    D. 6,000 VA

ANSWER - (D) 6,000 VA

    Small appliance circuits 3 x 1,500 VA = 4,500 VA **[220.52(A)]**
    Laundry circuit   1 x 1,500 VA = 1,500 VA **[220.52(B)]**
            TOTAL Connected Load = 6,000 VA

Step 4 - Find the total connected load of all fastened in place appliances, such as electric ranges, cooktops, ovens, clothes dryers and water heaters. This total is to be based on the nameplate rating of the appliances. **[220.82(B)(3)]** Also include the nameplate ratings of all motors, such as attic fans, sump pumps and water well and swimming pool pumps. **[220.82(B)(4)]**

EXAMPLE - A single family dwelling is to have the following fastened in place appliances and motors:

one – 12 kVA electric range
one – 6 kVA electric clothes dryer
one – 1,250 VA dishwasher
one – 1,176 VA trash compactor
one – 1,656 VA garbage disposer
one – 6,000 VA water heater
one – 1,176 VA attic fan
one – 1,250 VA microwave oven

What is the total connected load of this utilization equipment?

A. 26,508 VA
B. 30,508 VA
C. 25,508 VA
D. 26,805 VA

ANSWER - (B) 30,508 VA

range - 12 kVA x 1,000	= 12,000 VA
clothes dryer - 6 kVA x 1,000	= 6,000 VA
dishwasher	= 1,250 VA
trash compactor	= 1,176 VA
garbage disposer	= 1,656 VA
water heater	= 6,000 VA
attic fan	= 1,176 VA
microwave oven	= 1,250 VA
TOTAL Connected Load	= 30,508 VA

Step 5 - Total the **"general load"** as determined in steps 2, 3 and 4, then apply the demand factors as per **220.82(B)**, **100 percent** of the **first 10 kVA (10,000 VA)**, plus **40 percent** of the remainder.

EXAMPLE - Using the optional calculation method for one-family dwellings, determine the demand load on the ungrounded service-entrance conductors for a dwelling that has the following total connected general loads:

General lighting and receptacles   - 15,000 VA
Small appliance and laundry circuits   - 6,000 VA
Fastened in place appliances and motors - 30,500 VA

Copyright © 2014

A. 51,500 VA
B. 25,000 VA
C. 26,600 VA
D. 25,600 VA

ANSWER - (C) 26,600 VA

General lighting and receptacles   - 15,000 VA
Small appliance and laundry circuits   -   6,000 VA
Fastened in place appliances and motors   - 30,500 VA
TOTAL General Load   = 51,500 VA

1st 10,000 VA @ 100%   - 10,000 VA
Remainder (total – 10,000) = 41,500 VA @ 40% - 16,600 VA
DEMAND LOAD   = 26,600 VA

Step 6 - Add together the values determined from steps 1 and 5 to find the required volt-amperes. Next, apply the current formula **(I=P/E)** to determine the demand load. Then, multiply the current value by **83%** and size the service-entrance conductors using **Table 310.15(B)(16)**. Use **Table 250.66** for sizing the grounding electrode conductor.

EXAMPLE - When applying the optional method of calculation for a one-family dwelling, after all demand factors have been considered, a demand load of 50,600 VA is determined. Using standard overcurrent protective devices, determine the MAXIMUM ampere rating of the service overcurrent protective device and the MINIMUM size of 75ºC aluminum ungrounded service-entrance conductors required. The electrical system is 120/240-volts, single-phase.

A. 200 amperes OCP – 4/0 AWG aluminum conductors
B. 250 amperes OCP – 4/0 AWG aluminum conductors
C. 250 amperes OCP – 250 kcmil aluminum conductors
D. 225 amperes OCP – 4/0 AWG aluminum conductors

ANSWER - (D) 225 amperes – 4/0 AWG aluminum conductors

First, find the load in amperes.

$$I = \frac{P}{E} = \frac{50,600 \text{ VA}}{240 \text{ volts}} = 210.8 \text{ amperes (demand load)}$$

This value does not correspond with the standard ampere rating of an overcurrent protective device. Therefore, as per 2**40.4(B)**, the next higher standard overcurrent device is permitted to be used. **Section 240.6(A)** indicates a **225 ampere** rating is the next higher standard OCP rating.

To find the required ampacity of the conductors:

210.8 amperes **x 83% = 175 amperes**

Size 4/0 AWG 75ºC aluminum conductors with an ampacity of 180 amperes should be selected from **[Table 310.15(B)(16)]**.

OPTIONAL CALCULATION: ONE-FAMILY DWELLING

1. HEATING or A/C: *220.82(C)(1-6)*

Heating units (3 or less) = _____ VA x 65%	= _____ VA		
Heating units (4 or more) = _____ VA x 40%	= _____ VA		
A/C unit = _____ VA x 100%	= _____ VA		
Heat pump = _____ VA x 100%	= _____ VA	**LINE**	
Largest Load	= _____ VA		
Total	= _____ VA	_____ VA	

2. GENERAL LIGHTING: *220.82(B)(1)*   **NEUTRAL**

_____ sq. ft. x 3 VA per sq. ft.   = _____ VA   _____ VA

3. SMALL APPLIANCE & LAUNDRY LOADS: *220.82(B)(2)*

1,500 VA x _____ circuits   _____ VA   _____ VA

4. FIXED APPLIANCES & MOTORS: *220.82(B)(3)&(4)*

Dishwasher	=	_____ VA		_____ VA
Disposal	=	_____ VA		_____ VA
Compactor	=	_____ VA		_____ VA
Water heater	=	_____ VA		_____ VA
Range	=	_____ VA	@ 70%	_____ VA

Cooktop	=		_____ VA	@ 70%	_____ VA
Oven	=		_____ VA	@ 70%	_____ VA
Dryer	=		_____ VA	@ 70%	_____ VA
_____	=		_____ VA		_____ VA
_____	=		_____ VA		_____ VA
_____	=		_____ VA		_____ VA
		Total =	_____ VA		_____ VA

---

5. APPLY DEMAND FACTORS: *220.82(B)*

First 10,000 VA x 100% =   10,000 VA

Remaining _____ VA x 40% =   _____ VA

Total   _____ VA   _____ VA _____ VA

---

6. TOTAL   [_____] VA [_____] VA

LINE $I = \dfrac{\text{VA}}{240 \text{ volts}}$ = _____ amperes

NEUTRAL $I = \dfrac{\text{VA}}{240 \text{ volts}}$ = _____ amperes

Conductors are permitted to be sized @ 83% of the demand load if 120/240-volts, single-phase, or 100% if 208Y/120-volts, three-phase, or the load is greater than 400 amperes.

OPTIONAL CALCULATION: ONE-FAMILY DWELLING

1. HEATING or A/C: *220.82(C)(1-6)*

Heating units (3 or less) = _20,000_ VA x 65%	= _13,000_ VA	
Heating units (4 or more) = _____ VA x 40%	= _____ VA	
A/C unit = _24,000_ VA x 100%	= _24,000_ VA	
Heat pump = _____ VA x 100%	= _____ VA	**LINE**
Largest Load	= _24,000_ VA	
Total	= _24,000_ VA	_24,000_ VA

---

2. GENERAL LIGHTING: *220.82(B)(1)*   **NEUTRAL**

_5,000_ sq. ft. x 3 VA per sq. ft.   = _15,000_ VA   _15,000_ VA

---

3. SMALL APPLIANCE & LAUNDRY LOADS: *220.82(B)(2)*

1,500 VA x __4__ circuits   = _6,000_ VA   _6,000_ VA

---

4. FIXED APPLIANCES & MOTORS: *220.82(B)(3)&(4)*

Dishwasher	=	_1,250_ VA	_1,250_ VA
Disposal	=	_1,656_ VA	_1,656_ VA

Compactor	=	1,176 VA			1,176 VA
Water heater	=	6,000 VA			6,000 VA
Range	=	12,000 VA	@ 70%		8,400 VA
Cooktop	=	-0- VA	@ 70%		-0- VA
Oven	=	-0- VA	@ 70%		-0- VA
Dryer	=	6,000 VA	@ 70%		4,200 VA
Attic fan	=	1,176 VA			1,176 VA
Microwave	=	1,250 VA			1,250 VA
_____	=	_____ VA			_____ VA
		Total = 51,508 VA			_____ VA

5. APPLY DEMAND FACTORS: *220.82(B)*

First 10,000 VA x 100% =   10,000 VA

Remaining 41,508 VA x 40% =   16,603 VA

Total   26,603 VA   26,603 VA   46,108 VA

6. TOTAL   50,603 VA   46,108 VA

LINE $I = \dfrac{50,603 \text{ VA}}{240 \text{ volts}} = $ 211 amperes

NEUTRAL $I = \dfrac{46,108 \text{ VA}}{240 \text{ volts}} = $ 192 amperes

Conductors are to be sized per Table 310.15(B)(7) if 120/240 volts, single-phase, or Table 310.15(B)(16) if 208Y/120 volts, three-phase, or the load is greater than 400 amperes.

UNIT 8
SELF-ASSESSMENT QUIZ

1. The ungrounded service-entrance conductors for a one-family dwelling are required to have an ampacity of at LEAST _____.

     A. 60 amperes
     B. 100 amperes
     C. 75 amperes
     D. 150 amperes

2. When calculating the general lighting and general-use receptacle load for a dwelling unit, the _____ dimension of the dwelling is to be used.

I. outside
II. inside

  A. I only
  B. II only
  C. either I or II
  D. neither I or II

3. When sizing service-entrance conductors for a dwelling, a unit load of _____ shall be used for calculating the general lighting and general-use receptacle load.

  A. 3 VA per cubic foot
  B. 3.5 VA per square foot
  C. 3 VA per square foot
  D. 4 VA per square foot

4. What is the MINIMUM size copper SE cable with type THHW insulation that may be used as ungrounded service-entrance conductors for a 150-ampere rated 120/240-volt, 3-wire, single-phase residential service?

  A. 1/0 AWG
  B. 1 AWG
  C. 2 AWG
  D. 3 AWG

5. When calculating the total load for a one-family dwelling, what is the MINIMUM load, in VA, that must be added for the two (2), required small appliance branch circuits?

  A. 1,200 VA
  B. 2,400 VA
  C. 1,500 VA
  D. 3,000 VA

6. It shall be permissible to apply a demand factor of _____ to the nameplate rating load of four (4) or more fastened-in-place appliances when using the general method of calculation for dwellings.

  A. 75 percent
  B. 60 percent
  C. 50 percent
  D. 25 percent

7. When calculating the service for a dwelling, electric clothes dryers are to be calculated at a MINIMUM of _____ watts (VA) or the nameplate rating, which ever is larger.

    A. 3,000
    B. 4,500
    C. 5,000
    D. 6,000

8. A demand factor of _____ may be applied to the neutral loads of 240-volt, single-phase, electric clothes dryers and cooking equipment when doing residential service calculations.

    A. 75 percent
    B. 70 percent
    C. 60 percent
    D. 50 percent

9. Using the standard method of calculation for a single-family dwelling, determine the demand load, in VA, on the ungrounded service-entrance conductors when the residence has the following fixed appliances installed:

Water heater	- 4.5 kW	– 240 volts
Dishwasher	- 1,250 VA	– 120 volts
Garbage disposer	- 3/4 HP	– 120 volts
Trash compactor	- 1/2 HP	– 120 volts
Attic fan	- 1/3 HP	– 120 volts

    A. 7,085 VA
    B. 7,460 VA
    C. 9,446 VA
    D. 6,612 VA

10. When using the standard method of calculation for a one-family dwelling unit, determine the neutral demand load, in VA, for a 9 kW, 240-volt, single-phase electric range.

    A. 6,300 VA
    B. 6,750 VA
    C. 8,400 VA
    D. 5,600 VA

11. Determine the demand, in VA, on the ungrounded (line) service-entrance conductors for a 30 ampere, 240-volt, single-phase electric clothes dryer when using the standard method of calculation for a one-family dwelling.

    A. 5,000 VA
    B. 5,040 VA
    C. 7,200 VA
    D. 3,500 VA

12. What is the total connected load, in VA, for the general lighting and general-use receptacles, of a one-family residence having 35 feet by 75 feet of livable space?

    A. 2,625 VA
    B. 5,250 VA
    C. 9,188 VA
    D. 7,875 VA

13. When applying the standard calculation method for dwelling units, a demand load of _____ is to be applied to the first 3,000 VA of the general lighting and receptacle loads.

    A. 100 percent
    B. 80 percent
    C. 70 percent
    D. 35 percent

14. A single-family dwelling to be built will have 2,500 square feet of livable space, a 500 square foot garage, a 200 square foot open porch, a 1,250 square foot unfinished basement (adaptable for future use), three (3) small-appliance branch circuits and one (1) branch circuit for the laundry room. Determine the demand load, in VA, on the ungrounded (line) service-entrance conductors for the general lighting and receptacle loads using the standard method of calculation for a one-family dwelling.

    A. 12,000 VA
    B. 6,150 VA
    C. 17,250 VA
    D. 7,988 VA

15. When applying the optional method of calculation for a one-family dwelling, the air conditioning load, if used, is assessed at _____ of the nameplate rating(s) of the unit(s).

    A. 100 percent

B. 125 percent
C. 80 percent
D. 70 percent

16. When applying the optional method of calculation for a one-family dwelling, when the electric space equipment load is used, and if there are less than four (4) separately controlled units, the load is assessed at _____ of the nameplate rating(s) of the unit(s).

   A. 100 percent
   B. 80 percent
   C. 70 percent
   D. 65 percent

17. What is the demand load, in VA, on the ungrounded (line) service-entrance conductors for one (1) 10 kW electric range when using the optional method of calculation for a one-family residence?

   A. 8,000 VA
   B. 9,000 VA
   C. 10,000 VA
   D. 12,000 VA

18. Refer to the previous question. Determine the demand load, in VA, on the neutral (ungrounded) service-entrance conductor for the range.

   A. 10,000 VA
   B. 7,000 VA
   C. 8,000 VA
   D. 5,000 VA

19. When using the optional method of calculation for a one-family dwelling, the first _____ of the "general loads" shall be calculated at not less than 100 percent plus 40 percent of the remainder.

   A. 3,000 VA
   B. 1,000 VA
   C. 8 kVA
   D. 10 kVA

20. A one-family dwelling unit to be constructed will have the following total connected general loads:

- General lighting and receptacles = 17,500 VA
- Small appliance and laundry circuits = 7,500 VA
- Fastened in place appliances and motors = 40,500 VA

What is the demand load, in VA, on the ungrounded service-entrance conductors for the above referenced loads? (Use the optional method of calculation.)

A. 65,500 VA
B. 32,200 VA
C. 26,200 VA
D. 62,500 VA

NOTES

UNIT 9

MULTI-FAMILY DWELLING SERVICE CALCULATIONS

After successfully completing this unit of study, the student will have the ability to properly size services for multiple-family dwelling units.

UNIT 9

MULTI-FAMILY DWELLING SERVICE CALCULATIONS

RELATED INFORMATION:

> ➤ A multi-family dwelling unit is considered a building containing three or more dwelling units; examples are apartments, condominiums, and town houses.

> ➤ Many similarities exist between multi-family dwelling service calculations and one-family dwelling service calculations. Both can be calculated using the **standard (general) method** as well as the **optional method**. I suggest you become familiar with one-family dwelling calculations before attempting multi-family dwelling calculations.

> ➤ For multi-family dwellings the service-entrance conductor sizes are to be selected from **Table 310.15(B)(16).** The neutral load is permitted to be determined per **Section 220.61**. The rule in **Section 310.15(B)(7)(a)** that permits a reduction in the ampacity of service conductors, is reserved for one-family dwellings and individual units in a two-family or multifamily dwelling.

> ➤ **Annex D** of the NEC® shows examples of both calculation methods and the steps and procedures to be used. We will follow these examples and steps to learn to properly size services for multi-family dwellings. First, we will look at the general (standard) method of calculation. You will find a completed example of the general (standard) method of calculation on page 145 of this text.

General Calculation Method

Step 1 -   Determine the total connected load, in VA, of the general lighting and general-use receptacles. Simply multiply the number of units by the square footage of one unit, when they are all the same size, and multiply by **3 VA** per Table **220.12**. Do not include open porches, garages, and enclosed areas not adaptable for future use. **[220.12]**

EXAMPLE -   What is the total connected load, in VA, for the general lighting and general-use receptacles for a six (6) unit multi-family dwelling, when each apartment is 750 square feet?

A. 2,250 VA
B. 4,500 VA
C. 13,500 VA
D. 15,300 VA

ANSWER –   (C)   13,500 VA

First, find the area, in square feet, of the habitable spaces.

6 units X 750 sq.ft. = 4,500 sq.ft.

Next, multiply by 3 VA **[Table 220.12]**

4,500 sq.ft. X 3 VA = 13,500 VA

Step 2 -   Find the total connected load of the small appliance and laundry branch circuits. A minimum of **two (2)** small appliance branch circuits are required per unit **[210.11(C)(1)]** and they shall be calculated at **1,500 VA** per circuit. **[220.52(A)].** A minimum of **one (1)** branch circuit calculated at **1,500 VA** is required to supply the laundry of each unit having a laundry. **[210.11(C)(2)]** & **[220.52(B)].** When the multi-family dwelling unit has a common laundry facility provided on the premises and available to all building occupants, this is considered a "house load" and the laundry load can be omitted in this step.

EXAMPLE -   What is the minimum total connected load, in VA, for the small appliance and laundry loads for a six (6) unit multi-family dwelling, having laundry facilities in each unit?

A. 27,000 VA
B. 18,000 VA
C. 12,000 VA
D. 9,000 VA

ANSWER -   (A)   27,000 VA

2 small appl. circuits @ 1,500 VA X 6 units = 18,000 VA
1 laundry circuit @ 1,500 VA X 6 units   = 9,000 VA
                                    Total = 27,000 VA

Step 3 - Apply the demand factors specified in **Table 220.42** for the general purpose lighting and receptacle loads, plus the loads required for the small appliance and laundry branch circuits. **[220.42]**

EXAMPLE - What is the demand load, in VA, for a multi-family dwelling unit having a total connected general-purpose receptacle and lighting load of 13,500 VA and a total connected small appliance and laundry branch circuit load of 27,000 VA? (Use general method of calculation.)

    A. 13,125 VA
    B. 16,125 VA
    C. 37,500 VA
    D. 40,500 VA

ANSWER - (B) 16,125 VA

    General purpose lighting & receptacles = 13,500 VA
    Laundry & small appliances   = 27,000 VA
                 Total Connected Load = 40,500 VA

    1st 3,000 VA @ 100% **[Table 220.42]** =   3,000 VA
    40,500 VA – 3,000 VA = 37,500 VA
    37,500 VA (Remainder) X 35%   = 13,125 VA
                       Demand Load = 16,125 VA

Step 4 - Apply a demand factor of **75%** of the nameplate rating of **four (4)** or more fastened in place appliances. Examples include, water heater, dishwasher, trash compactor, garbage disposal, etc. **[220.53]** Note that this rule **does not apply** for electric ranges, clothes dryers, space heating or air conditioning equipment.

EXAMPLE - Using the standard (general) method of calculation for dwellings, determine the demand load, in VA, of a six (6) unit multi-family dwelling unit having the following fixed appliances installed in each unit:

    dishwasher   - 1,100 VA
    water heater   - 3,500 VA
    garbage disposal - 850 VA

    A. 32,700 VA
    B. 23,700 VA
    C. 22,890 VA
    D. 24,525 VA

ANSWER -   (D)   24,525 VA

Dishwasher   - 1,100 VA X 6 = 6,600 VA
Water Heater   - 3,500 VA X 6 = 21,000 VA
Garbage Disposal   - 850 VA X 6 = 5,100 VA
                Total Connected Load = 32,700 VA
                                     X 75% (demand)
                       Demand Load = 24,525 VA

Step 5 -   Determine the electric clothes dryer demand load, using **5,000 watts** (volt amperes) as the minimum or the nameplate rating, **whichever is larger**, for each dryer served. **[220.54]** Apply the demand factors listed in **Table 220.54**. A further demand of **70 percent** of this value may be applied to the **neutral** (grounded) conductor. **[220.61(B)(1)]**

EXAMPLE -   When the standard (general) method of calculation for dwellings is applied, if a six (6) unit apartment building having a 3.5 kW electric clothes dryer in each unit, the demand load, in VA, on the ungrounded service-entrance conductors is _____.

A. 15,750 VA
B. 21,000 VA
C. 22,500 VA
D. 30,000 VA

ANSWER -   (C)   22,500 VA

5,000 VA (minimum) x 6 = 30,000 VA
Demand **[Table 220.54]**   x   75 %
                          22,500 VA

STEP 6 -   Determine the demand load for the cooking appliances in accordance with **Table 220.55 [220.55]**. This is explained in **Unit 3** of this book. A further demand of **70 percent** of the demand load on the ungrounded conductors may be applied to the **neutral** (grounded) conductor. **[220.61(B)(1)]**

EXAMPLE -   An 8 kW electric range installed in each unit of a six (6) unit apartment building will have a demand load of _____ on the ungrounded service-entrance conductors and demand load of _____ on the grounded (neutral) conductor, when the standard method of calculation for dwellings is applied.

A. 43,000 VA – 30,100 VA
B. 20,640 VA – 14,448 VA
C. 48,000 VA – 33,600 VA
D. 43,000 VA – 32,250 VA

ANSWER -   (B)   20,640 VA – 14,448 VA

ungrounded conductor – **[Table 220.55, Column B.]**
8 kW x 6 units x 43% = 20.64 kW
20.64 kW x 1,000 = 20,640 VA

grounded conductor – **[220.61(B)(1)]**

20,640 VA x 70% = 14,448 VA

STEP 7 -   Determine the demand load for the fixed electric space heating or air
conditioning load; the smaller of the two is permitted to be omitted,
because these loads are considered noncoincident loads, meaning they
are unlikely to be used at the same time. **[220.60]**

EXAMPLE -   A six (6) unit apartment building to be constructed will have a 3 kW
(kVA), 240-volt, single-phase, fixed electric space heating unit and a
17 ampere, single-phase, 240-volt, air conditioning unit, installed in
each dwelling unit. When using the standard (general) method of
calculation for dwellings, what is the demand, in VA, that should be
applied to the service-entrance conductors?

A. 24,480 VA
B. 18,000 VA
C.   7,080 VA
D. 42,840 VA

ANSWER -   (A)   24,480 VA

First compare the two loads.
A/C unit – P = I x E   P= 17 amps x 240 volts = 4,080 VA
Heating unit – 3 kW x 1,000 = 3,000 VA

4,080 VA (larger) x 6 units = 24,480 VA

STEP 8 -   Add the values determined from steps 3 – 7 together to find the
required volt ampere rating of the service. Next, apply the current
formula **(I = P ÷ E)**, and size the service-entrance conductors using
Table 310.15(B)(16).

EXAMPLE -   After all demand factors have been taken into consideration for a multi-family dwelling unit, a demand load of 108,270 VA is determined for the ungrounded service-entrance conductors. What minimum size THWN copper ungrounded conductors are required for the dwelling service? (120/240-volt, 3-wire, single-phase electrical system.)

A. 400 kcmil
B. 500 kcmil
C. 600 kcmil
D. 700 kcmil

ANSWER -   (D)   700 kcmil

First, find the load in amperes.

$I = P \div E$

$I = \dfrac{108{,}270 \text{ VA}}{240 \text{ volts}} = 451.125$

Table 310.15(B)(16) is to be used for sizing the conductors. Size 700 kcmil conductors with an ampacity of 460 amperes should be selected.

STANDARD CALCULATION: MULTI-FAMILY DWELLING

1. GENERAL LIGHTING & RECEPTACLES: *Table 220.12*

_____ sq. ft. x 3 VA =   _____ VA

2. SMALL APPLIANCES 220.52(A) & LAUNDRY 220.52(B)

1,500 VA x _____ circuits =   _____ VA

3. APPLY DEMAND FACTORS: *Table 220.42*

Total of gen. ltg. & small appl.	_____ VA			
First 3000 VA x 100% =	3,000 VA			
Next _____ VA x 35% =	_____ VA	**LINE**	**NEUTRAL**	
Remaining _____ VA x 25% =	_____ VA			
Total =	_____ VA	_____ VA	_____ VA	

4. FIXED APPLIANCES: 220.53

Water Heater   _____ VA x _____ units = _____ VA
Disposal   _____ VA x _____ units = _____ VA
Compactor   _____ VA x _____ units = _____ VA
Dishwasher   _____ VA x _____ units = _____ VA
_____   _____ VA x _____ units = _____ VA
_____   _____ VA x _____ units = _____ VA
_____   _____ VA x _____ units = _____ VA

Total =   (x 75% if 4 or more) _____ VA = _____ VA   _____ VA

5. CLOTHES DRYERS: 220.54; *Table 220.54*

_____ VA x _____ units = _____ VA x _____ % = _____ VA x 70% = _____ VA

6. COOKING EQUIPMENT: *Table 220.54 & Notes*

Col A _____ VA x _____ units x _____ % = _____ VA
Col B _____ VA x _____ units x _____ % = _____ VA
Col C _____ VA x _____ units   = _____ VA
Total =   _____ VA   _____ VA x 70% = _____ VA

7. HEATING or A/C at 100% (largest): 220.60

Heating unit = _____ VA x _____ units = _____ VA
A/C unit   = _____ VA x _____ units = _____ VA
Heat pump   = _____ VA x _____ units = _____ VA
Largest Load   = _____ VA

8. TOTAL   [____] VA   [____] VA

Line   I = _____ VA = _____ amperes
                240 volts

Neutral   I = _____ VA = _____ amperes
                240 volts

Conductors are to be sized per Table 310.15(B)(16).

STANDARD CALCULATION: MULTI-FAMILY DWELLING

1. GENERAL LIGHTING & RECEPTACLES: *Table 220.12*
    4,500 sq. ft. x 3 VA =   13,500 VA

2. SMALL APPLIANCES *220.52(A)* & LAUNDRY *220.52(B)*
    1,500 VA x __18__ circuits =   27,000 VA

3. APPLY DEMAND FACTORS: *Table 220.42*

				LINE	NEUTRAL
Total of gen. ltg. & small appl.	40,500 VA				
First 3000 VA x 100%	=	3,000 VA			
Next 37,500 VA x 35%	=	13,125 VA			
Remaining _____ VA x 25% =		_____ VA			
Total		16,125 VA	16,125 VA	16,125 VA	

4. FIXED APPLIANCES: *220.53*
Water Heater	3,500 VA x __6__ units = 21,000 VA
Disposal	850 VA x __6__ units = 5,100 VA
Compactor	_____ VA x _____ units = _____ VA
Dishwasher	1,100 VA x __6__ units = 6,600 VA
_____	_____ VA x _____ units = _____ VA
_____	_____ VA x _____ units = _____ VA
_____	_____ VA x _____ units = _____ VA

Total   (x 75% if 4 or more) 32,700 VA =   24,525 VA   24,525 VA

5. CLOTHES DRYERS: *220.54*; *Table 220.54*
    5,000 VA x __6__ units = 30,000 VA x __75__ %   22,500 VA x 70%=   15,750 VA

6. COOKING EQUIPMENT: *Table 220.54* & Notes
    Col A _____ VA x _____ units x _____ % = _____ VA
    Col B 8,000 VA x __6__ units x __43__ % =   20,640 VA
    Col C _____ VA x _____ units   = _____ VA
    Total   =   20,640 VA   20,640 VA x 70%= 14,448 VA

7. HEATING or A/C at 100% (largest): *220.60*
    Heating unit = 3,000 VA x _____ units = _____ VA
    A/C unit   = 4,080 VA x __6__ units = 24,480 VA
    Heat pump   = _____ VA x _____ units = _____ VA
    Largest Load   =   24,480 VA

8. TOTAL   108,270 VA   70,848 VA

Line $I = \dfrac{108,270 \text{ VA}}{240 \text{ volts}} = 451$ amperes

                            220.61(B)(2)

Neutral $I = \dfrac{70,848 \text{ VA}}{240 \text{ volts}} = 295$ amperes – First 200 amps @ 100%   = 200 amperes

                                  Next 95 amps @70%   =   67 amperes

                                     TOTAL NEUTRAL = 267 amperes

Conductors are to be sized per Table 310.15(B)(16).

➢ When calculating the service size for multi-family dwellings, the **optional calculation method** is commonly applied, because it is an easier and less complex calculation method than the general (standard) method; less steps are used and it results in a smaller service size. The optional method is specifically designed for dwelling units having an electrical load of greater than 100 amperes. **[220.82(A)]** You will find a completed example of this calculation method on page 152 of this text.

➢ In general, the optional calculation method for multi-family dwellings may be applied when all of the following conditions are met: **[220.84(A)]**

1. No dwelling unit is supplied by more than one feeder.

2. Each dwelling unit is equipped with electric cooking equipment.

3. Each dwelling unit is equipped with either electric space heating or air conditioning, or both.

➢ The following steps may be applied when using the optional calculation method for multi-family dwellings. Notice the first two steps are the same for both calculation methods.

STEP 1 - Determine the total connected load, in VA, of the general lighting and general-use receptacle. Simply multiply the number of units by the square footage of all units of the same size and multiply by 3 VA per square foot. **[220.84(C)(1)]** Do not include open porches, balconies, and garages.

EXAMPLE - What is the connected load, in VA, for the general lighting and general-use receptacles for an eight (8) unit multi-family dwelling, when each apartment has 840 square feet of livable space?

A. 20,160 VA
B. 10,080 VA
C. 16,020 VA
D. 6,720 VA

ANSWER -   (A)   20,160 VA

First, find the total area in square feet.

8 units x 840 sq. ft. = 6,720 sq. ft.

Next, multiply by 3 VA **[220.84(C)(1)]**

6,720 sq. ft. x 3 VA = 20,160 VA

STEP 2 -   Find the connected load of the small appliances and laundry branch circuits. **[220.84(C)(2)]** Each unit is required to have at least **two (2)** small appliance branch circuits, **[210.11(C)(1)]** and **one (1)** laundry branch circuit, **[210.11(C)(2)]** and they shall be calculated at **1,500** VA per circuit. **[220.52(A)&(B)]**

EXAMPLE -   Determine the minimum connected load, in VA, for the small appliance and laundry loads for an eight (8) unit apartment building having a laundry facility in each unit.

A. 24,000 VA
B. 36,000 VA
C. 42,000 VA
D. 12,000 VA

ANSWER-   (B)   36,000 VA

2 small appl. circuits @ 1,500 VA x 8 units = 24,000 VA
1 laundry circuit @ 1,500 va x 8 units   = 12,000 VA
                                  TOTAL   36,000 VA

STEP 3 -   Calculate the connected load, at the nameplate rating, of all fastened in place appliances, such as electric ranges, cooktops, ovens, clothes, dryers, dishwashers, garbage disposers, and water heaters. **[220.84(C)(3)]**

EXAMPLE -   An eight (8) unit apartment building is to have the following fastened
             in place appliances installed in each unit.

             water heater   – 3.6 kW   – 240 volts
             electric range   – 8   kW – 240 volts
             dishwasher   – 1.1 kW – 120 volts
             garbage disposal   – 850 VA   – 120 volts
             clothes dryer   – 3.5 kW – 240 volts

             Determine the total connected load, in VA, for the appliances.

             A. 17,050 VA
             B. 102,300 VA
             C. 136,400 VA
             D. 51,150 VA

ANSWER -   (C)   136,400 VA

             water heater   - 3,600 VA x 8 units = 28,800 VA
             electric range   - 8,000 VA x 8 units = 64,000 VA
             dishwasher   - 1,100 VA x 8 units = 8,800 VA
             garbage disposal   -   850 VA x 8 units = 6,800 VA
             clothes dryer   - 3,500 VA x 8 units = 28,000 VA
                                        TOTAL   136,400 VA

STEP 4 -   Calculate the connected load of the larger of the air-conditioning or
               space heating equipment. Omit the smaller. **[220.84(C)(5)]**

EXAMPLE -   An eight(8) unit apartment building to be constructed will have a 3.5
             kW (kVA), 240 volt, single-phase, fixed electric space heating unit and
             a 17 ampere, single-phase, 240-volt air-conditioning unit installed in
             each dwelling unit. When applying the optional method of calculation
             for multi-family dwellings for services and feeders, what MINIMUM
             value, in VA, is permitted to be used?

             A. 60,640 VA
             B. 28,000 VA
             C. 24,480 VA
             D. 32,640 VA

ANSWER -   (D)   32,640 VA

             First, compare the two loads.
             A/C unit – P = I x E   P= 17 amps x 240 volts = 4,080 VA
             Heating unit – 3.5 kW x 1,000 = 3,500 VA

             4,080 (larger) x 8 units = 32,640 VA

STEP 5 - Add steps 1 through 4 to determine the total connected VA load of the dwelling units and apply the demand factors as per **Table 220.84**.

EXAMPLE - An eight (8) unit apartment building has the following total connected loads:

general lighting & receptacles	– 20,160 VA
small appliances & laundry circuits	– 36,000 VA
Fixed appliances	- 136,400 VA
A/C- heating equipment	– 32,640 VA

Use the optional method of calculation for multi-family dwellings, and determine the demand load, in VA, on the ungrounded service-entrance conductors.

A. 96,836 VA
B. 222,500 VA
C. 225,500 VA
D. 99,088 VA

ANSWER - (A)   93,836 VA

```
   20,160 VA
   36,000 VA
  136,400 VA
   32,640 VA
  225,200 VA    (connected load)
      x 43%      Table 220.84
   96,836 VA    (demand load)
```

STEP 6 - Add the "house loads" at the nameplate rating of the equipment. When the multi-family dwelling has a common laundry facility provided on the premises and available to all building occupants, this is considered a commercial occupancy and dwelling demand factors are **not** to be applied. If there are no "house loads," this step is omitted.

STEP 7 - Add the values determined from steps 5 and 6 (if any) together to find the required volt ampere rating of the service. Next, apply the current formula **(I = P ÷ E)** and size the service-entrance conductors using **Table 310.15(B)(16)**. The neutral load is determined per **220.61**.

EXAMPLE -   After all demand factors have been taken into consideration for a
             multi-family dwelling, a demand load of 96,836 VA is determined for
             the ungrounded service-entrance conductors. What minimum size
             THWN/THHN copper ungrounded conductors are required for the
             service? (120/240-volts, single-phase electrical system)

             A. 500 kcmil
             B. 600 kcmil
             C. 700 kcmil
             D. 750 kcmil

ANSWER -   (B)   600 kcmil

             First, find the load in amperes.

             $I = P \div E$

             $I = \dfrac{96,836 \text{ VA}}{240 \text{ volts}} = 403$ amperes

             Select 75°C rated conductors from **Table 310.15(B)(16).**
             Size 600 kcmil conductors with an ampacity of 420 amperes should be
             selected.

OPTIONAL CALCULATION: MULTI-FAMILY DWELLING

1. GENERAL LIGHTING & RECEPTACLES: *220.84(C)(1)*

	Line	Neutral
_____ sq. ft. x 3 VA =	(___) VA	(_____) VA

2. SMALL APPLIANCES & LAUNDRY *220.84(C)(2)*

	Line	Neutral
Small Appl. 1,500 VA x _____ circuits x _____ units=	_____ VA	_____ VA
Laundry 1,500 VA x _____ circuits x _____ units=	_____ VA	_____ VA
Total =	(_____) VA	(_____) VA

3. FIXED APPLIANCES: *220.84(C)(3)*

		Line	Neutral
Water Heater	_____ VA x _____ units =	_____ VA	_____ VA
Disposal	_____ VA x _____ units =	_____ VA	_____ VA
Compactor	_____ VA x _____ units =	_____ VA	_____ VA
Dishwasher	_____ VA x _____ units =	_____ VA	_____ VA
Range	_____ VA x _____ units =	_____ VA x 70%	_____ VA
Cooktop	_____ VA x _____ units =	_____ VA x 70%	_____ VA
Oven	_____ VA x _____ units =	_____ VA x 70%	_____ VA
Dryer	_____ VA x _____ units =	_____ VA x 70%	_____ VA
_____	_____ VA x _____ units =	_____ VA	_____ VA
_____	_____ VA x _____ units =	_____ VA	_____ VA
Total =		(_____) VA	(_____) VA

4. HEATING or A/C at 100% (largest): *220.84(C)(5)*

		Line	Neutral
Heating unit = _____ VA x _____ units = _____ VA			
A/C unit = _____ VA x _____ units = _____ VA			
Heat pump = _____ VA x _____ units = _____ VA			
Largest Load = _____ VA x _____ units = _____ VA		(_____) VA	(_____) VA

5. APPLY DEMAND FACTORS: *Table 220.84 Total of steps 1 -4*

	Line	Neutral
LINE _____ VA x _____ % =	[_____] VA	
NEUTRAL _____ VA x _____ % =		[_____] VA

6. HOUSE LOADS: *220.84(B)*

	Line	Neutral
Lighting _____ VA	_____ VA	_____ VA
Receptacles _____ VA	_____ VA	_____ VA
Motors _____ VA	_____ VA	_____ VA
_____ _____ VA	_____ VA	_____ VA
_____ _____ VA	_____ VA	_____ VA
Total =	[____] VA	[____] VA

7. TOTAL of STEPS 5 & 6

	Line	Neutral
	[____] VA	[____] VA

Line   I = _____ VA = _____ amperes
                240 volts

Neutral   I = _____ VA = _____ amperes
                240 volts

Conductors are to be sized per Table 310.15(B)(16).

OPTIONAL CALCULATION: MULTI-FAMILY DWELLING

	Line	Neutral
1. GENERAL LIGHTING & RECEPTACLES: 220.84(C)(1)		
6,720 sq. ft. x 3 VA =	(20,160) VA	(20,160) VA

				Line	Neutral
2. SMALL APPLIANCES & LAUNDRY 220.84(C)(2)					
Small Appl. 1,500 VA x __2__ circuits x __8__ units=				24,000 VA	24,000 VA
Laundry 1,500 VA x __1__ circuits x __8__ units=				12,000 VA	12,000 VA
Total =				(36,000) VA	(36,000) VA

3. FIXED APPLIANCES: 220.84(C)(3)

			Line	Neutral
Water Heater	3,600 VA x __8__ units =		28,800 VA	28,800 VA
Disposal	850 VA x __8__ units =		6,800 VA	6,800 VA
Compactor	_____ VA x _____ units =		_____ VA	_____ VA
Dishwasher	1,100 VA x __8__ units =		8,800 VA	8,800 VA
Range	8,000 VA x __8__ units =		64,000 VA x 70%	44,800 VA
Cooktop	_____ VA x _____ units =		_____ VA x 70%	_____ VA
Oven	_____ VA x _____ units =		_____ VA x 70%	_____ VA
Dryer	3,500 VA x __8__ units =		28,000 VA x 70%	19,600 VA
_____	_____ VA x _____ units =		_____ VA	_____ VA
_____	_____ VA x _____ units =		_____ VA	_____ VA
Total =			(136,400) VA	(108,800) VA

4. HEATING or A/C at 100% (largest): 220.84(C)(5)

			Line	Neutral
Heating unit = 3,500 VA x _____ units= _____ VA				
A/C unit = 4,080 VA x __8__ units =32,640 VA				
Heat pump = _____ VA x _____ units = _____ VA				
Largest Load = 4,080 VA x __8__ units =32,640 VA			(32,640) VA	(0) VA

5. APPLY DEMAND FACTORS: Table 220.84 Total of steps 1 -4

		Line	Neutral
LINE	225,200 VA x 43 % =	[96,836] VA	
NEUTRAL	164,960 VA x 43 % =		[70,933] VA

6. HOUSE LOADS: 220.84(B)

Lighting	_____ VA	_____ VA	_____ VA
Receptacles	_____ VA	_____ VA	_____ VA
Motors	_____ VA	_____ VA	_____ VA
_____	_____ VA	_____ VA	_____ VA
_____	_____ VA	_____ VA	_____ VA
Total =		[_____] VA	[_____] VA

7. TOTAL of STEPS 5 & 6

		_____ VA	70,933 VA
Line	I = 96,836 VA = 403 amperes		
	240 volts	**220.61(B)(2)**	
Neutral	I = 70,933 VA = 296 amperes – First 200 amps @100% = 200 amperes		
	240 volts	Next 96 amps @ 70% = 67 amperes	
		TOTAL NEUTRAL = 267 amperes	

Conductors are to be sized per Table 310.15(B)(16).

UNIT 9
SELF-ASSESSMENT QUIZ

1. When calculating the service entrance conductors supplying multi-family dwellings, the actual conductor sizes are to be selected from Table _____ of the NEC®.

    A. 310.15(B)(7)
    B. 310.15(B)(16)
    C. 220.61
    D. 310.15(B)(2)(a)

2. Each unit of a multi-family dwelling is required to have at LEAST _____ small appliance branch circuit(s) rated at _____ each.

    A. one -1,500 VA
    B. one – 2,400 VA
    C. three – 1,500 VA
    D. two – 1,500 VA

3. When applying the general method of calculation for multi-family dwellings, a demand factor of _____ may be applied to the nameplate rating of four (4) or more fastened in place appliances.

    A. 75 percent
    B. 60 percent
    C. 80 percent
    D. 50 percent

4. When sizing feeder and service-entrance conductors for a multi-family dwelling and the general method of calculation is used, before demand factors are applied electric clothes dryers are to be calculated at a MINIMUM of _____.

    A. the nameplate rating of the dryer
    B. 5,000 watts each
    C. 4,000 watts each
    D. 3,500 watts each

5. Feeder or service-entrance conductors supplying household cooking equipment and electric clothes dryers shall be permitted to have an additional demand factor of _____ applied to the neutral (grounded) conductor after the initial demand factors have been applied to the grounded conductors.

    A. 50 percent
    B. 60 percent
    C. 75 percent
    D. 70 percent

6. When sizing feeders and services for multi-family dwellings, that portion of the neutral (grounded) load that is in excess of 200 amperes an additional demand factor _____ of may be applied.

    A. 50 percent
    B. 60 percent
    C. 70 percent
    D. 75 percent

7. For sizing feeders and services, the optional calculation method is specifically designed for dwelling units having an electrical load of at LEAST greater than _____.

    A. 100 amperes
    B. 200 amperes
    C. 300 amperes
    D. 400 amperes

8. In general, when sizing feeders and services for multi-family dwellings, the optional calculation method may be applied when _____.

    I. no dwelling is supplied by more than one feeder.
    II. each dwelling is equipped with either electric space heating or air conditioning, or both.

    A. I only
    B. II only
    C. either I or II
    D. both I and II

9. When calculating services and/or feeders supplying multi-family dwellings, when determining the load to be used for the heating and air-conditioning equipment the _____ is required to be applied.

    A. air-conditioning load only
    B. heating load only
    C. sum of the two loads
    D. larger of the two

10. Determine the total area, in square feet of an apartment building having four (4) units of 900 sq. ft. each and six (6) units of 1,100 sq. ft. each.

    A. 9,800 sq. ft.
    B. 10,200 sq. ft.
    C. 10,000 sq. ft.
    D. 12,200 sq. ft.

11. Use the general method of calculation for multi-family dwellings and determine the general lighting, small appliance and laundry minimum demand load for an apartment building consisting of twenty (20) units, each having a living area of 840 sq. ft., when the laundry facilities are provided on the premises and available to all tenants.

    A. 50,400 VA
    B. 40,950 VA
    C. 110,400 VA
    D. 49,800 VA

12. In a 16 unit multi-family dwelling, each unit is provided with a garbage disposal (864 VA), a dishwasher (1,250 VA) and a water heater (3,600 VA). Apply the general (standard) method of calculation for dwellings, and determine the service demand for the fixed appliances.

    A. 91,424 VA
    B. 63,997 VA
    C. 68,568 VA
    D. 73,139 VA

13. Each unit in a 10 unit apartment building contains a 4 kW rated electric clothes dryer. Apply the general (standard) method of calculation and determine the demand load, in VA, on the ungrounded service-entrance conductors.

    A. 37,500 VA
    B. 27,500 VA
    C. 25,000 VA
    D. 20,000 VA

14. In a 12 unit apartment building, six (6) units are provided with a 8 kW electric range in each unit and six (6) units are provided with a 9 kW electric range in each unit. Apply the general (standard) method of calculations for dwellings and determine the demand load, in VA, on the ungrounded service-entrance conductors.

    A. 27,000 VA
    B. 41,640 VA
    C. 32,640 VA
    D. 102,000 VA

15. If an apartment building, with cooking facilities provided in each dwelling unit, has a general lighting and general use receptacle, laundry and small appliance connected load of 200.2 kW, what is the demand load, in VA, on the ungrounded service-entrance conductors? (Apply the general (standard) method of calculation.)

A. 64,000 VA
B. 64,750 VA
C. 65,300 VA
D. 70,080 VA

16. Each unit of a 14 unit multi-family dwelling has a habitable area of 1,250 sq. ft. Using the optional method of calculation for multi-family dwellings, what is the demand load, in VA, that must be applied to the service-entrance conductors for the general lighting and general-use receptacles, laundry and small appliance circuits?

A. 46,200 VA
B. 37,800 VA
C. 54,000 VA
D. 115,500 VA

17. Using the optional calculation method for multi-family dwellings, determine the demand load, in VA, that must be applied to the ungrounded service-entrance conductors for a 14 unit apartment building having a 4 kW electric clothes dryer in each unit.

A. 22,400 VA
B. 28,000 VA
C. 32,500 VA
D. 56,000 VA

18. Using the optional calculation method for multi-family dwellings, determine the demand load, in VA, that must be applied to the neutral (grounded) service-entrance conductors for a 14 unit apartment building provided with a 8 kW, 240-volt, single-phase electric range in each unit.

A. 112,000 VA
B. 44,800 VA
C. 35,840 VA
D. 31,360 VA

19. A 16 unit apartment building has the following 240-volt, single-phase heating and air-conditioning equipment installed in each apartment?

   * A/C unit – 3 hp
   * Heating unit – 5 kW
   * Circulating Motor – ½ hp (common for both htg. & A/C.)

Use the optional calculation method for multi-family dwellings and determine the demand load, in VA, on the ungrounded service-entrance conductors for the above listed equipment.

A. 31,200 VA
B. 38,538 VA
C. 35,383 VA
D. 32,797 VA

20. What MINIMUM size THWN/THHN copper ungrounded service-entrance conductors are required for a multi-family dwelling building provided with a 120/240-volt, single-phase service, when the building has a demand load of 90 kW on the service?

A. 400 kcmil
B. 500 kcmil
C. 600 kcmil
D. 700 kcmil

NOTES

UNIT 10

COMMERCIAL LOAD CALCULATIONS

Upon successfully completing this unit of study, the student will be familiar with the concept of properly sizing overcurrent protection, branch circuit, feeder, and service conductors for commercial occupancies.

UNIT 10

COMMERCIAL LOAD CALCULATIONS

RELATED INFORMATION:

➤ Examples of commercial occupancies are office buildings, banks, retail stores, restaurants, warehouses, laundries, mobile home and recreational vehicle (RV) parks, automobile dealerships, sporting facilities, motels, etc.

➤ The loads in commercial locations are diversified and are to be calculated based upon the type of occupancy, how the loads are to be used in the electrical system, and the requirements of the equipment to be supplied. A good example of a commercial occupancy with diverse loads would be a motel or hotel. The sleeping rooms are calculated much like residential occupancies but the lobby, hallways, meeting rooms, restaurant, and area lighting are considered commercial locations. Let's look at some of the requirements that apply to commercial occupancies.

➤ Most of the lighting for commercial locations is to be considered a **continuous load**. Examples of exceptions to this statement would be the sleeping rooms of hotels and motels, which will be addressed later in this unit, and temporary commercial storage facilities and warehouses. The definition of a **continuous load** is a load where the maximum current is expected to continue for **3 hours** or more. **[Article 100]**

➤ In general, branch circuit conductors shall have an allowable ampacity (current carrying capacity) of NOT less than **125%** of the **continuous load**, plus **100%** of the **non-continuous** load to be served. **[210.19(A)(1)(a)]**

EXAMPLE -   A branch circuit conductor supplying a continuous load of 24 amperes, must have an ampacity of at least _____.

A. 24 amperes
B. 30 amperes
C. 19 amperes
D. 36 amperes

ANSWER -   (B)   30 amperes

24 amperes x 125% = 30 amperes

➢ In general, overcurrent devices (fuses and circuit breakers) protecting branch circuits, shall have a rating of not less that **125%** of the **continuous load** to be served plus **100%** of the **non-continuous** load to be served. **[210.20(A)]** Another way to look at it is, fuses and circuit breakers protecting branch circuits are not permitted to be loaded more than **80%** of their rated value when protecting **continuous loads**.

EXAMPLE -   When a 30 ampere rated circuit breaker is used to protect a branch circuit supplying a continuous load, the load shall not exceed_____.

A. 30 amperes
B. 38 amperes
C. 24 amperes
D. 36 amperes

ANSWER -   (C)   24 amperes

30 amperes x 80% = 24 amperes

➢ If the overcurrent device is listed for **continuous operation**, it shall be permitted to have a rating of **100%** of the **continuous load(s)** to be supplied. **[210.20(A)EX.]** But, circuit breakers are **NOT** listed for continuous operation, unless they have a rating of at least **400 amperes** or more. The NEC® does not address this issue.

➢ This continuous load requirement also applies to feeders **[215.2(A)(1)]** & **[215.3]** and services. **[230.42(A)(1)&(2)]**

Lighting Loads

➢ In general, 15- or 20-ampere rated branch circuits are used to supply lighting loads. **[210.23(A)]**

➤ General lighting loads for specific occupancies shall be based on the unit load per square feet depending on the type of occupancy as shown on Table **220.12**, and calculated from the outside dimensions of the building. **[220.12]** This is a **MINIMUM** requirement.

➤ Most commercial occupancies now contain fluorescent and/or HID lighting systems. When the occupancies contain lighting systems of this category, the **larger** of either the area load of the VA per square foot of the facility, or the total connected load of the ampere ratings of the ballast or transformers of the luminaries (lighting fixtures) shall be used to size branch circuit, feeder, and service-entrance conductors. **[220.18(B)]**

EXAMPLE -   A retail department store having dimensions of 100 feet by 150 feet is to be constructed. The store will have three-hundred (300) fluorescent luminaires (lighting fixtures) installed for general lighting. Each luminaire will contain two (2), 120-volt ballasts that draw 0.75 amperes each. Determine the demand load, in VA, that must be applied to the service-entrance conductors for the general lighting.

    A. 45,000 VA
    B. 54,000 VA
    C. 56,250 VA
    D. 67,500 VA

ANSWER -   (D)   67,500 VA

Compare the two methods and use the larger value.

Table 220.12
150 ft. x 100 ft. = 15,000 sq. ft.

15,000 sq. ft. x 3 VA = 45,000 VA
  (continuous load)   x 125%
                        56,250 VA

220.18(B)
300 (fixt.) x 2 (ballast) x 120 volts x .75 amps = 54,000 VA
                        (continuous load)   x 125%
                                              67,500 VA

➤ Show window lighting for retail stores is commonly calculated at 200 volt-amperes per linear foot of show window. **[220.43(A)]** Such lighting is usually considered a **continuous load** because it is normally operated continuously for three (3) hours or more. Multiply **200 VA** per linear foot times **125%** to determine the load in VA.

EXAMPLE -   A retail store is to have 125 feet of show window lighting, which will be operated continuously during the business day. Determine the demand load in VA.

A. 31,250 VA
B. 25,000 VA
C. 28,125 VA
D. 12,500 VA

ANSWER -   (A)   31,250 VA

200 VA x 125 ft. x 125% = 31,250 VA

➤ When calculating the number of branch circuits required for lighting systems or receptacles, you can use the following formula:

$$\text{Number of circuits} = \frac{\text{Load VA}}{\text{circuit VA}}$$

EXAMPLE -   The total demand load for the show window lighting of a retail store is determined to be 31,250 VA. Determine the MINIMUM number of 120 volt, 20 ampere branch circuits required to supply the show window lighting.

A. ten
B. twelve
C. thirteen
D. none of these

ANSWER -   (C)   thirteen

$$\text{\# of circuits} = \frac{31,250 \text{ VA}}{120 \text{ volts x } 20 \text{ amps}} = \frac{31,250 \text{ VA}}{2,400 \text{ VA}} = 13 \text{ circuits}$$

➤ In addition to the general lighting, many commercial occupancies, particularly retail stores, have track lighting mounted for display or accent lighting. Again, commercial lighting systems are usually considered as continuous use. For track lighting in non-dwelling occupancies a load of **150 volt-amperes** shall be included for every **two (2) feet** of track. **[220.43(B)]** Multiply **150 VA** per linear foot times **125%** and divide by **two (2)** to determine the load in VA.

EXAMPLE -   A retail store is to have eighty (80) feet of accent track lighting
             installed and will be in use continuously during business
             hours. For the purpose of sizing branch-circuits, feeders and service-
             entrance conductors, determine the load in VA.

             A. 15,000 VA
             B. 10,000 VA
             C. 12,500 VA
             D. 7,500 VA

ANSWER -   (D)   7,500 VA

             $$\frac{150 \text{ VA} \times 80 \text{ ft.} \times 125\%}{2} = \frac{15,000}{2} = 7,500 \text{ VA}$$

   ➤ The general lighting and general-use receptacles for the guest
      rooms and suites of hotels and motels are permitted to be
      calculated by applying a demand load of **2 VA** per square foot
      [Table 220.12] and is permitted to be reduced by applying the
      demand factors as shown in **Table 220.42**. Even though this is a
      commercial occupancy, loads of this category are not considered as
      continuous use.

EXAMPLE -   Determine the general lighting and general-use receptacle demand
             load, in VA, for the guest rooms of a twenty-four (24) unit motel. Each
             guest room has 600 square feet of living area.

             A. 14,400 VA
             B. 13,520 VA
             C. 21,600 VA
             D. 28,800 VA

ANSWER -   (B)   13,520 VA

             24 units x 600 x 2 VA **[Table 220.12]** = 28,800 VA

             First 20,000 VA at 50% = 10,000 VA **[Table 220.42]**
             8,800 VA   at 40% =   3,520 VA
                     Demand Load = 13,520 VA

Electric Sign Loads

   ➤ The NEC® requires each commercial occupancy with grade level
      access to pedestrians to be provided with at least one (1) outlet for
      an exterior electric sign or outline lighting system. The outlet(s)
      is/are to be supplied by a branch-circuit rated at least 20 amperes.
      [600.5(A)]

➤ The branch-circuits that supply electric signs with incandescent and fluorescent lighting are not to exceed 20 amperes. **[600.5(B)(1)]**

➤ When calculating feeder and service-entrance conductors, each electric sign branch-circuit is to be calculated at a MINIMUM of **1,200 VA**. **[220.14(F)]** This VA rating is to be multiplied by **125%**; for the purpose of calculations electric signs are to be considered continuous loads. **[600.5(B)]**

EXAMPLE -   A motel to be constructed will have two (2) 20 ampere, 120-volt branch-circuits provided for the exterior electric signs. Determine the minimum demand load, in VA, on the feeder and service-entrance conductors.

A. 2,400 VA
B. 3,000 VA
C. 4,800 VA
D. 6,000 VA

ANSWER -   (B)   3,000 VA

1,200 VA x 2 (signs) x 125% = 3,000 VA

Receptacle Loads

➤ For non-dwelling occupancies each general-use receptacle outlet is to be calculated at **180 VA** for each single or duplex receptacle on one yoke or strap **[220.14(I)]**; receptacle loads are permitted to be made subject to the demand factors given in **Table 220.44** when calculating the demand loads on feeders and services. **[220.44]** General-use receptacle loads are generally not considered to be a continuous load.

Table 220.44 Demand Factors for Non-dwelling Receptacle Loads

Portion of Receptacle Load to Which Demand Factor Applies (Volt-Ampere)	Demand Factor (Percent)
First 10 kVA or less	100
Remainder over 10 kVA at	50

EXAMPLE –   What is the service demand load, in VA, for one-hundred and fifty (150), 20 ampere, 120-volt general-use duplex receptacles installed in an office building?

A. 27,000 VA
B. 23,125 VA
C. 24,250 VA
D. 18,500 VA

ANSWER -   (D)   18,500 VA

150 receptacles x 180 VA = 27,000 VA (connected load)

First 10 kVA at 100%   = 10,000 VA
remainder (17,000 VA) at 50% =   8,500 VA
                   Total = 18,500 VA

➢ When the exact number of general-use receptacle outlets to be installed in a bank or an office building has not yet been determined, **one (1) VA** per square foot of interior space is to be applied when calculating feeders or services. **[Table 220.12, Note B]** and **[220.14(K)]** When this condition occurs, the receptacle loads are **not** permitted to be made subject to the demand factors given in **Table 220.44. [220.44]**

EXAMPLE -   A 20,000 square foot bank building is to be constructed and the exact number of general-use receptacles to be installed in unknown. Determine the demand load, in VA, on the service-entrance conductors for the unknown receptacles.

A. 20,000 VA
B. 18,000 VA
C. 36,000 VA
D. 60,000 VA

ANSWER -   (A)   20,000 VA

20,000 sq. ft. x 1 VA = 20,000 VA

➢ When calculating the service and/or feeder demand load for multioutlet assemblies installed in commercial, industrial and educational facilities, the calculation is to be based on the use of the supplied cord-connected equipment that is expected to be used at the same time. **[220.14(H)]** (1) Where the cord-connected equipment are **unlikely** to be used simultaneously, each **five (5) feet** or fraction thereof shall be considered as one (1) outlet of not less than **180 VA**. (2) Where the cord-connected equipment are **likely** to be used simultaneously each **one (1) foot** or fraction thereof shall be considered as one outlet of not less than **180 VA**.

➤ The demand factors shown on **Table 220.44** may also be applied to fixed multioutlet assemblies when located in non-dwelling occupancies. Multioutlet assembly receptacles are generally not to be considered a continuous load; if they are **continuous, multiply by 125%.**

EXAMPLE -   What is the service demand load, in VA, for one-hundred (100), 20 ampere, 120-volt, general-use receptacles and one-hundred (100) feet of multioutlet assembly, installed in an office building, where the cord connected appliances are unlikely to be used simultaneously?

A. 21,600 VA
B. 15,800 VA
C. 10,800 VA
D.   8,100 VA

ANSWER -   (B)   15,800 VA

Receptacles – 180 VA x 100   = 18,000 VA
Multioutlet assembly – 100 ft. / 5 = 20 x 180 VA = <u> 3,600 VA</u>
                                        connected load = 21,600 VA

Apply demand factors **[Table 220.44]**

First 10 kVA at 100%   = 10,000 VA
Remainder (11,600 VA) at 50%   = <u> 5,800 VA</u>
                                     demand load   = 15,800 VA

EXAMPLE -   Refer to the previous example and consider the cord-connected appliances are to be used simultaneously and determine the demand load.

A. 15,800 VA
B. 36,000 VA
C. 23,000 VA
D. 18,000 VA

ANSWER -   (C)   23,000 VA

Receptacles – 180 VA x 100   = 18,000 VA
Multioutlet assembly – 100 ft. x 180 VA   = <u>18,000 VA</u>
                                Connected load = 36,000 VA

First 10 kVA at 100%   = 10,000 VA
Remainder (26,000 VA) at 50%   = <u>13,000 VA</u>
                                Demand Load = 23,000 VA

Air Conditioning Loads

➤ When sizing overcurrent protection, branch-circuit, feeder and service conductors for air-conditioning equipment, you will find many air-conditioning condensing units are sized according to **TONS** and not horsepower. The NEC® does not address this issue. A useful and practical method to convert **tons** to **VA** is to consider **one (1) ton** of air-conditioning condensing load equals **2,400 VA**. To find the load, in amperes, simply apply the current formula I = P ÷ E. Multiply 2,400 VA times the tonage of the A/C unit and divide by the voltage. For the purpose of calculating loads in this text this is the method that will be used.

EXAMPLE -   A 240-volt, single-phase, 3½ ton A/C condensing unit will draw_____ of current.

A. 30 amperes
B. 35 amperes
C. 40 amperes
D. 45 amperes

ANSWER -   (B)   35 amperes

$$I = \frac{3.5 \times 2,400 \text{ VA}}{240 \text{ volts}} = \frac{8,400}{240} = 35 \text{ amperes}$$

➤ Branch-circuit conductors supplying a single air-conditioning condensing unit are required to have a current-carrying capacity (ampacity) of not less than **125 percent** of the rated-current of the air-conditioning unit supplied. **[440.32]**

EXAMPLE -   Branch-circuit conductors supplying an air-conditioning condensing unit having a rated-current of 35 amperes, are required to have an ampacity of at LEAST _____.

A. 28 amperes
B. 35 amperes
C. 44 amperes
D. 53 amperes

ANSWER -   (C)   44 amperes

35 amperes x 125% = 43.75 amperes

➤ A value of not less than **100%** of the rated-current of the air-conditioning equipment is to be applied to feeder and service equipment and conductors.

➤ Fuses and circuit breakers provided for the protection of air-conditioning equipment shall be capable of carrying the starting current of the motor. **[440.22(A)]** The overcurrent protection device is mandated to be sized between **175 percent** and no more than **225 percent** of the rated-current of the air-conditioning equipment.

EXAMPLE -   A circuit breaker provided to protect an air-conditioning condensing unit with a rated current of 35 amperes is required to have a MAXIMUM ampere rating of no more than _____.

A. 60 amperes
B. 80 amperes
C. 75 amperes
D. 70 amperes

ANSWER -   (D)   70 amperes

35 amperes x 225% = 78.75 amperes

*NOTE: Under this condition, you must go down to the next standard size circuit breaker, because you may not exceed **225%** of the rated-current of the A/C unit.

Electric Space-Heating Loads

➤ All fixed space heating equipment, including blower motors, shall be considered as **continuous load(s)**, when sizing branch-circuit conductors and overcurrent protection for the heating units. **[424.3(B)]** The branch-circuit conductors supplying electric space-heating equipment are required to have an ampacity of not less than **125 percent** of the current rating of the heating unit(s) to be served.**[210.19(A)(1)]** This rule does not apply when sizing feeders and/or services. The feeder and/or service demand load is calculated at **100 percent** of the total heating load. **[220.51]**

EXAMPLE -   The branch-circuit conductors supplying a 240-volt, single-phase, 15 kW rated fixed electric space heater provided with a 10 ampere blower motor are required to have an ampacity of at LEAST _____.

A. 63 amperes
B. 78 amperes
C. 91 amperes
D. 109 amperes

ANSWER -   (C)   91 amperes

First find the current rating of the heater.

$$I = P \div E \quad I = \frac{15 \text{ kW x 1,000}}{240 \text{ volts}} = 62.5 \text{ amperes}$$

62.5 amperes (heater)
+10.0 amperes (blower)
72.5 amperes x 125% = 91 amperes

EXAMPLE - The overcurrent protection device for the above referenced heating unit is required to have a standard rating of not less than _____.

A. 75 amperes
B. 80 amperes
C. 90 amperes
D. 100 amperes

ANSWER - (D)   100 amperes

The next standard size overcurrent device has a rating of 100 amperes. **[240.6(A)]**

EXAMPLE - Determine the service demand load, in VA, for an office building that has three (3), 208-volt, three-phase, 10 kW fixed electric space heaters, provided with a 1,945 VA blower motor in each heating unit.

A. 35,835 VA
B. 44,794 VA
C. 53,585 VA
D. 55,583 VA

ANSWER - (A)   35,835 VA

10,000 VA + 1,945 VA = 11,945 x 3 units = 35,835 VA

➢ When determining the demand load on the service-entrance conductors for the fixed electric space heating or air-conditioning load, the smaller of the two loads is permitted to be omitted; because both loads are unlikely to be used at the same time. **[220.60]** Apply only the largest load(s) that will be used at one time for calculating the total load on feeder or service conductors.

EXAMPLE -   A retail store is to have a ten (10) ton A/C unit and a thirty-five (35) kW electric heating unit installed. Both units are 240-volts, single-phase. Determine the demand load, in amperes on the service-entrance conductors for the A/C and heating equipment.

A. 100 amperes
B. 125 amperes
C. 146 amperes
D. 183 amperes

ANSWER -   (C)   146 amperes

First compare the two loads.

A/C Unit
10 tons x 2,400 VA = 24,000 VA
$I = \dfrac{24,000 \text{ VA}}{240 \text{ volts}} = 100$ amperes

Heating Unit
$I = \dfrac{35 \text{ kW} \times 1,000}{240 \text{ volts}} = \dfrac{35,000}{240} = 146$ amperes

*NOTE: The heating unit is the larger load therefore, the A/C unit is permitted to be omitted.

➢ Today, many buildings are provided with roof-mounted heating and cooling systems that are in one complete unit in order to save space. The cooling capacity usually range from 5 tons up to 200 tons. Examples of good applications for roof-mounted heating and cooling systems are schools, office buildings, retail stores, super markets and manufacturing facilities.

Kitchen Equipment

➢ For electric kitchen equipment in commercial occupancies the branch circuits and overcurrent protection are sized according to the nameplate rating on the appliance. When sizing feeder and service conductors the demand factors shown on **Table 220.56** may be applied. However, the feeder or service demand load is **not** permitted to be **less** than the sum of the **two (2) largest** kitchen equipment loads. **[220.56]**

EXAMPLE -   A catering service is to have the following cooking related equipment in the kitchen:

- water heater   – 5.5 kW
- booster heater   – 7.0 kW
- dishwasher   – 2.0 kW
- sterilizer   - 2.5 kW
- oven   - 6.0 kW
- grill   - 5.0 kW
- mixer   - 3.0 kW
- freezer   - 3.5 kW
- refrigerator   - 2.5 kW

What is the demand load, in kW, on the service-entrance conductors for the appliances?

A. 37.00 kW
B. 25.90 kW
C. 13.00 kW
D. 24.05 kW

ANSWER -   (D)   24.05 kW

water heater	- 5.5 kW
booster heater	- 7.0 kW
dishwasher	- 2.0 kW
sterilizer	- 2.5 kW
oven	- 6.0 kW
grill	- 5.0 kW
mixer	- 3.0 kW
freezer	- 3.5 kW
refrigerator	- 2.5 kW
(connected load)	37 kW
(demand)	x 65 % **[Table 220.56]**
Demand Load	= 24.05 kW

Laundry Equipment

➢ The branch-circuit conductors and overcurrent protection for laundry equipment in commercial occupancies are to be sized in accordance to the appliance **nameplate rating**. The NEC® does not permit a demand factor to be applied to service, feeder or branch-circuit conductors for commercial laundry equipment therefore, the laundry equipment demand load is to be calculated at **100%.**

EXAMPLE -   The laundry room of a multi-family dwelling will have the following laundry equipment installed:

- two – clothes dryers   - 7,000 VA each
- three – washing machines - 1,920 VA each
- three – washing machines - 1,500 VA each

What is the demand load, in VA, on the service and feeder conductors for the listed appliances?

A. 24,260 VA
B. 18,500 VA
C. 16,982 VA
D. 14,000 VA

ANSWER -   (A)   24,260 VA

clothes dryers	– 2 x 7,000 VA =	14,000 VA
washing machine	– 3 x 1,920 VA =	5,760 VA
washing machine	– 3 x 1,500 VA =	4,500 VA
	TOTAL =	24,260 VA

Mobile Home and Manufactured Home Parks

> The distribution system to mobile home lots is required to be 120/240 volts, single-phase. **[550.30]** Because appliances, luminaries, and other equipment are installed in a mobile home when manufactured and are rated 120/240-volts single-phase; three-phase systems and systems of a different voltage would not be compatible to the loads to be supplied.

> Each mobile home lot is required to be calculated on the basis of the larger of (1) a minimum of not less than **16,000 VA** for each mobile home lot or (2) the calculated load of the largest typical mobile home the lot will accommodate. **[550.31]** However, for each mobile home to be served the service equipment is to be rated at least 100 amperes, **[550.32(C)]** and the mobile home lot feeder conductors shall have a current carrying capacity (ampacity) of not less than 100 amperes. **[550.33(B)]**

> When sizing service-entrance conductors for a mobile home park the demand factors, based on the number of mobile homes in the park, displayed in **Table 550.31** are permitted to be applied.

EXAMPLE -   What is the MINIMUM demand load, in amperes, on the service conductors of a mobile home park consisting of fifteen (15) lots?

A. 250 amperes
B. 260 amperes
C. 400 amperes
D. 1,000 amperes

ANSWER -   (B)   260 amperes

15 lots x 16,000 VA (MINIMUM) = 240,000 VA
                demand   = x   .26 **[Tbl. 550.31]**

demand load   =   62,400 VA

$$I = P \div E$$
$$I = \frac{62,400 \text{ VA}}{240 \text{ volts}} = 260 \text{ amperes}$$

EXAMPLE -   A twenty-five (25) lot mobile home park is to be constructed. Each lot in the park is capable of accommodating a mobile home with a rating of 24,000 VA. Determine the demand load, in amperes, on the park service conductors.

A. 1,000 amperes
B. 650 amperes
C. 400 amperes
D. 600 amperes

ANSWER -   (D)   600 amperes

25 lots x 24,000 VA   = 600,000 VA
                         x   .24   **[Tbl.550.31]**
Demand load   = 144,000 VA

$$I = P \div E$$
$$I = \frac{144,000 \text{ VA}}{240 \text{ volts}} = 600 \text{ amperes}$$

Recreational Vehicle Parks

➢ For recreational vehicle parks the NEC® requires electrical equipment connected line-to-line shall have a voltage rating of 208-230 volts. **[551.40(A)]** Therefore, recreational vehicle parks are permitted to be provided with 120-volt, 120/240-volt, single-phase or 208Y/120-volt, three-phase electrical systems. Typically, most older recreational vehicle parks have 120/240-volt, single-phase distribution systems.

➢ When sizing service-entrance or feeder conductors for a recreational vehicle park, the demand factors, reflected in **Table 551.73(A)**, based on the number of sites in the park, are permitted to be applied.

➢ **Each RV site** supplied with electrical power is required to be provided with at least **one (1) 20 ampere**, 125-volt receptacle outlet. **[551.71]** For the basis of calculation, 20 ampere, 125-volt sites are considered as **2,400 VA per site**. **[551.73(A)]**

➢ At least **20 percent** of all RV sites in the park supplied with electrical power are required to be provided with a **50 ampere**, 125/250-volt receptacle outlet. **[551.71]** The 50 ampere sites are considered as **9,600 VA** per site, for the basis of calculation. **[551.73(A)]** Where the RV site has more than one (1) receptacle outlet, the calculated load shall only be calculated for the highest rated receptacle.

EXAMPLE -   When a forty (40) site RV park supplies all campsites with electrical power, the NEC® requires at LEAST _____ of the sites to be provided with a 50 ampere, 125/250-volt receptacle.

A. eight
B. two
C. twelve
D. forty

ANSWER-   (A)   eight

40 sites x 20% = 8 sites

> At least **70 percent** of all RV sites in the park supplied with electrical power are required to be provided with a **30-ampere**, 125-volt receptacle. **[551.71]** For the basis of calculation 30-ampere, 125-volt, RV sites are considered as **3,600 VA** per site. **[551.73(A)]**

EXAMPLE -   Refer to the previous example. How many sites in the RV park are required to be provided with a 30-ampere, 125-volt receptacle outlet?

A. eight
B. twelve
C. twenty-eight
D. forty

ANSWER -   (C)   twenty-eight

40 sites x 70% = 28 sites

> Dedicated **tent sites** in a RV park that are provided with only 20 ampere, 125-volt receptacles are considered as **600 VA** per site, for the basis of calculation. Because these sites are not intended to accommodate recreational vehicles, the calculated load is permitted to be smaller. **[551.73(A)]**

> When determining the total load for a recreational vehicle park, you must take into consideration the loads required for the recreational buildings, swimming pools, stores, service buildings, etc. These amenities are to be considered commercial loads and are to be sized separately and then added to the value calculated for the RV sites, where they are all supplied by one service. **[551.73(D)]**

> Typically, recreational vehicle parks are provided with one service and the RV sites are supplied from a common feeder through one or more sub-panel(s). The demand factors shown on **Table 551.73(A)** are to be applied when sizing RV site feeders and service-entrance conductors.

EXAMPLE -   What is the feeder/service demand load, in amperes, for the RV sites of a recreational vehicle park that has twenty (20) sites provided with 50 ampere 125/250-volt receptacles, fifteen (15) sites provided with both 30 ampere and 20 ampere receptacles and five (5) RV sites provided with 20 ampere, 125-volt receptacles? The electrical system

is   120/240-volts, single-phase.

A. 392 amperes
B. 441 amperes
C. 213 amperes
D. 1,075 amperes

ANSWER -   (B)   441 amperes

50 ampere sites   – 9,600 VA x 20 sites = 192,000 VA
30/20 ampere sites   – 3,600 VA x 15 sites =   54,000 VA
20 ampere sites   – 2,400 VA x 5 sites =   12,000 VA
                                              258,000 VA
              Table 551.73(A) (demand) x   .41
                            Demand Load   105,780 VA

$$I = P \div E$$
$$I = \frac{105,780 \text{ VA}}{240 \text{ volts}} = 441 \text{ amperes}$$

Electric Welders

➤ The NEC® provides rules governing two general types of electric welding machines.
   1. Arc welders
      Non-motor generator – a transformer supplies current for an AC arc welder.
      Motor generator – A generator or rectifier supplies current for DC arc welder.
   2. Resistance welders, which are commonly referred to as "spot" welders which derive their power from an AC power source.

➤ The ampacity of the supply conductors to individual arc welders is determined by selecting the appropriate factor shown in **Table 630.11(A)** based on the type of welding machine and the duty cycle of the welder. **[630.11(A)]** An arc welder with a 60% duty cycle means the welding machine will be used approximately for 6 minutes out of every 10 minutes. The selected factor is then multiplied by the primary current rating displayed on the welder nameplate to determine the minimum current-carrying capacity (ampacity) of the circuit conductors. The actual size of the conductors are selected from **Table 310.15(B)(16).**

EXAMPLE -   The minimum ampacity of the branch-circuit conductors supplying a transformer arc welder with a 60 percent duty cycle and a primary current of 50 amperes indicated on the nameplate is _____.

A. 40 amperes
B. 44 amperes
C. 39 amperes

D. 50 amperes

ANSWER -   (C)   39 amperes

50 amperes x .78 (multiplier) = 39 amperes

➤ When a feeder supplies more than one arc welding machine the conductor ampacity rating is based on the sum of the current ratings of the individual arc welders determined by applying **Table 630.11(A)** and multiplying by **100 percent** of the **two** largest welders, plus **85 percent** of the **third** largest welder, plus **70 percent** of the **fourth** largest welder, plus **60 percent** of **all remaining** welders in the group. **[630.11(B)]**

EXAMPLE -   A feeder at a school welding shop is to supply the following listed transformer arc welders all with a 50 percent duty cycle.

- two (2) 60 ampere primary current
- two (2) 50 ampere primary current
- two (2) 40 ampere primary current

The feeder is required to have an ampacity of at LEAST _____.

A. 213 amperes
B. 196 amperes
C. 182 amperes
D. 176 amperes

ANSWER -   (D)   176 amperes

60 amperes x .71 = 43 x 100% = 43 amperes
60 amperes x .71 = 43 x 100% = 43 amperes
50 amperes x .71 = 36 x 85% = 31 amperes
50 amperes x .71 = 36 x 70% = 25 amperes
40 amperes x .71 = 28 x 60% = 17 amperes
40 amperes x .71 = 28 x 60% = 17 amperes
                              176 amperes

➤ The ampacity of the supply conductors for a resistance type welder, when the primary current and duty cycle are known, shall not be less than the product of the actual primary current when welding and the multiplication factors shown in **Table 630.31(A)(2).**

EXAMPLE -   A resistance type (spot) welder with a duty cycle of 25 percent and with an actual primary current of 30 amperes is to be served. The conductors supplying the welder are required to have an ampacity of at LEAST _____.

A. 15 amperes
B. 20 amperes
C. 25 amperes
D. 30 amperes

ANSWER -   (A)   15 amperes

30 amperes x .50 = 15 amperes

> When conductors supply two or more resistance type welding machines, the conductors ampacity rating is based on the sum of the primary current of the individual welders determined by applying **Table 630.31(A)(2)** and multiplying by 100% of the largest welder, plus 60 percent of the values obtained for all remaining welders in the group. **[630.31(B)]**

EXAMPLE -   Three (3) spot welders, each having a primary current of 30 amperes and a duty cycle of 10 percent are to be supplied by a common branch circuit. The branch-circuit conductors are required to have an ampacity of at LEAST_____.

A. 15 amperes
B. 22 amperes
C. 66 amperes
D. 99 amperes

ANSWER -   (B)   22 amperes

30 amperes x .32 = 10 amperes x 100% = 10 amperes
30 amperes x .32 = 10 amperes x 60% = 6 amperes
30 amperes x .32 = 10 amperes x 60% = 6 amperes
                                        22 amperes

Commercial Service and Feeder Sizing

> For the purpose of sizing the service for a commercial building, the following steps may be used to determine the demand load.

Step 1   Determine the lighting load. Include:
(1) the **larger** of the area load of the VA per square foot of the facility **[Table 220.12]** or the connected loads of the lighting fixtures **[220.18(B)]** and apply **Table 220.42 if applicable**,

(2) sign lighting, **[220.14(F)]**
(3) show windows, **[220.43(A)]**
(4) track lighting **[220.43(B)]**

Step 2   Calculate the receptacle load. Include:
(1) 180 VA per receptacle outlet **[220.14(I)]**
(2) fixed multi-outlet assemblies **[220.14(H)]** apply demand factors per **Table 220.44**

Step 3   Compare the air-conditioning loads or the space heating loads. Use the **larger** of the two loads at **100%**.

Step 4   Determine the kitchen equipment load. Apply **Table 220.56** for 3 or more units of kitchen equipment.

Step 5   Calculate the laundry equipment at **100%**

Step 6   Add any other miscellaneous loads not covered in the above steps. Examples: walk-in coolers, water heaters, frozen food display cases, welders, exhaust fans, motors, etc.

Step 7   Add the value determined from the above listed steps together to find the volt ampere rating of the service. Next, apply the current formula $(I = P \div E)$ and size the service-entrance conductors using 75°C conductors selected from **Table 310.15(B)(16)**.

EXAMPLE -   A hair salon is 4,000 square feet; the service is 208Y/120-volts, three-phase. Determine the service demand load and the service conductor size for the hair salon which has the following equipment.

- 20 feet of show window lighting
- 150 feet of track lighting
- 120 feet of fixed multi-outlet assembly (appliances will be used simultaneously)
- 50 – 120-volt, 20 ampere duplex receptacles
- one – 12 ton A/C unit, 3-phase (gas heating)
- one – 5 kW cooktop, 208-volt, single-phase
- one – 4 kW oven, 208-volt, single-phase
- one – 1,200 VA, microwave oven
- one – 1,200 VA, refrigerator/freezer
- two – 1,800 VA, washing machines
- one – 5 kW, clothes dryer, 208-volt, single-phase
- one – electric sign circuit

SOLUTION -

LIGHTING

General lighting	– 4,000 sq. ft. x 3 VA x 125%	= 15,000 VA
Show Window	- 20 ft. x 200 VA x 125%	= 5,000 VA
Track Lighting	- 150 ft./2 x 150 VA x 125%	= 14,063 VA
Sign Circuits	- 1 x 1,200 VA x 125%	= 1,500 VA

RECEPTACLES

Multi-outlet Assembly	– 120 ft. x 180 VA	= 21,600 VA
Receptacles	- 50 x 180 VA	= 9,000 VA

                                          30,600 VA

        Table 220.44
                1st 10 kVA @ 100%   = 10,000 VA
                20,600 VA @50%   = 10,300 VA
                                                20,300 VA   = 20, 300 VA

        COMPARE A/C VERSUS HEATING
        A/C – 12 ton x 2,400 VA per ton   = 28,800 VA   = 28,800 VA
        HTG. – N/A   = N/A

        KITCHEN EQUIPMENT
        Cooktop   - 5 kW   = 5,000 VA
        Oven   - 4 kW   = 4,000 VA
        Microwave   - 1,200 VA   = 1,200 VA
        Refrigerator - 1,200 VA   = 1,200 VA
                                                 11,400 VA
                        Table 220.56   x   .8
                                                 9,120 VA   = 9,120 VA

        LAUNDRY EQUIPMENT
        Washing Machine – 2 x 1,800 VA   = 3,600 VA
        Clothes Dryer   - 1 x 5,000 VA   = 5,000 VA
                                                  8,600 VA   = 8,600 VA

                                DEMAND LOAD = 102,383 VA

        I = $\dfrac{102,383 \text{ VA}}{208 \times 1.732}$ = $\dfrac{102,383 \text{ VA}}{368.25}$ = 284 amperes

        Size 300 kcmil copper 75ºC rated service-entrance conductors or size
        500 kcmil aluminum 75ºC rated service-entrance conductors should
        be selected from **Table 310.15(B)(16).**

        *NOTE – See page 182 of this text for an example of this calculation
         method using the following completed form.

+--+
| **COMMERCIAL CALCULATION** |
| **1. LIGHTING:** *Table 220.12 or 220.18(B)* |
| General Lighting: _____ sq. ft. x _____ VA x 125% =   _____ VA |
| 220.18(B):   _____ fixtures x _____ VA x 125% =   _____ VA |
| Show Window: _____ ft. x 200 VA x 125% =   _____ VA |
| Track Lighting: _____ ft. / 2 x 150 VA x 125% =   _____ VA |
| Sign Ckts.   _____ x 1,200 VA x 125% =   _____ VA |
| Misc. Lighting: _____ VA |
| Total Lighting =   (_____) VA   [_____] VA |
+--+

2. RECEPTACLES: 220.14(I) and/or 220.14(H)

Receptacles: 180 VA x _____ receptacles = _____ VA

Multi-outlet Assembly: 180 VA x _____ ft. = _____ VA

Total = (_____) VA

Table 220.44

First 10,000 VA x 100% = _____ VA

Remainder: _____ VA x 50% = _____ VA

Demand = (_____) VA [_____] VA

3. HEATING or A/C at 100% (largest):

Heating unit = _____ VA x _____ units = _____ VA

A/C unit = _____ VA x _____ units = _____ VA

Heat pump = _____ VA x _____ units = _____ VA

Largest Load = _____ VA x _____ units = _____ VA (_____) VA [_____] VA

4. KITCHEN EQUIPMENT: 220.56

Range _____ VA x _____ units = _____ VA

Cooktop _____ VA x _____ units = _____ VA

Oven _____ VA x _____ units = _____ VA

Dishwasher _____ VA x _____ units = _____ VA

Water Heater _____ VA x _____ units = _____ VA

_____ _____ VA x _____ units = _____ VA

_____ _____ VA x _____ units = _____ VA

Total = (_____) VA

Table 220.56 x _____%

Demand = (_____) VA [_____] VA

5. LAUNDRY EQUIPMENT:

Washing Machine _____ VA x _____ units _____ VA

Clothes Dryer _____ VA x _____ units _____ VA

Water Heater _____ VA x _____ units _____ VA

_____ _____ VA x _____ units _____ VA

Total = (_____) VA [_____] VA

6. MISCELLANEOUS LOADS:

_____ VA

_____ VA

Total = (_____) VA [_____] VA

7. TOTAL

[_____] VA

Line I = _____ VA = _____ amperes
volts

Conductors are to be sized per Table 310.15(B)(16)

COMMERCIAL CALCULATION

1. LIGHTING: *Table 220.12 or 220.18(B)*

General Lighting: *4,000* sq. ft. x *3* VA x 125% = *15,000* VA

220.18(B): _____ fixtures x _____ VA x 125% = _____ VA

Show Window: *20* ft. x 200 VA x 125% = *5,000* VA

Track Lighting: *150* ft. / 2 x 150 VA x 125% = *14,063* VA

Sign Ckts. *1* x 1,200 VA x 125% = *1,500* VA

Total Lighting = (*35,563*) VA [*35,563*] VA

2. RECEPTACLES: 220.14(I) and/or 220.14(H)

Receptacles: 180 VA x **50** receptacles = **9,000** VA

Multi-outlet Assembly: 180 VA x **120** ft. = **21,600** VA

Total = (**30,600**) VA

Table 220.44

First 10,000 VA x 100% = **10,000** VA

Remainder: **20,600** VA x 50% = **10,300** VA

Demand = (**20,300**) VA   [**20,300**] VA

3. HEATING or A/C at 100% (largest):

Heating unit = **20,000** VA x **1** units = **20,000** VA

A/C unit = **28,800** VA x **1** units = **28,800** VA

Heat pump = _____ VA x _____ units = _____ VA

Largest Load = **28,800** VA x **1** units = **28,800** VA   (**28,800**) VA   [**28,800**] VA

4. KITCHEN EQUIPMENT: 220.56

Range   _____ VA x _____ units = _____ VA

Cooktop   **5,000** VA x **1** units = **5,000** VA

Oven   **4,000** VA x **1** units = **4,000** VA

Dishwasher   _____ VA x _____ units = _____ VA

_____   _____ VA x _____ units = _____ VA

Microwave   **1,200** VA x **1** units = **1,200** VA

Refrigerator   **1,200** VA x **1** units = **1,200** VA

Total = (**11,400**) VA

Table 220.56 x **80** %

Demand = (**9,120**) VA   [**9,120**] VA

5. LAUNDRY EQUIPMENT:

Washing Machine   **1,800** VA x **2** units   **3,600** VA

Clothes Dryer   **5,000** VA x **1** units   **5,000** VA

Water Heater   _____ VA x _____ units   _____ VA

_____   _____ VA x _____ units   _____ VA

Total = (**8,600**) VA   [**8,600**] VA

6. MISCELLANEOUS LOADS:

_____ VA

_____ VA

Total = (_____) VA   [_____] VA

7. TOTAL

102,383 VA

$$\text{Line} \quad I = \frac{\textbf{102,383} \text{ VA}}{208 \times 1.732} = \textbf{284} \text{ amperes}$$

Conductors are to be sized per Table 310.15(B)(16).

UNIT 10
SELF-ASSESSMENT QUIZ

1. A retail occupancy is to have seventy-five (75) 120-volt, 15-ampere rated duplex receptacle outlets installed. Determine the MINIMUM demand load, in VA, on the service-entrance conductors for these receptacles.

    A. 13,000 VA
    B. 13,500 VA
    C. 12,225 VA
    D. 11,750 VA

2. What is the general lighting demand load, in VA, on the service for a 2,750 square foot office?

    A. 8,250 VA
    B. 9,625 VA
    C. 10,313 VA
    D. 12,031 VA

3. Determine the MINIMUM number of 120-volt, 20-ampere lighting branch circuits required for one-hundred and fifty (150) linear feet of show window lighting in a retail store.

    A. 13
    B. 14
    C. 15
    D. 16

4. A 75,000 sq. ft. office building with 277-volt lighting is required to have at least _____ 20-ampere, single-phase general lighting branch-circuits.

    A. 48
    B. 60
    C. 109
    D. 137

5. A department store is to have 36 linear feet of cord-and-plug connected show window lighting. How many receptacle outlets must be provided directly above the show window for the lighting?

    A. two
    B. three
    C. four
    D. five

6.   A grocery store will have sixty (60) feet of track lighting installed above the meat display case for accent lighting. What demand load, in VA, must be applied to the service for this track lighting?

        A. 11,250 VA
        B. 9,600 VA
        C. 5,625 VA
        D. 4,500 VA

7.   A 208-volt, three-phase, 10 ton A/C condensing unit will draw approximately _____ amperes of current.

        A. 67 amperes
        B. 100 amperes
        C. 115 amperes
        D. 134 amperes

8.   An automobile dealership is to have four (4) 20-ampere, 120-volt branch-circuits provided for the exterior electric signs. What is the MINIMUM demand load, in VA, that must be applied to the service for these signs?

        A. 4,000 VA
        B. 4,800 VA
        C. 6,000 VA
        D. 9,600 VA

9.   A 6,000 square foot bank building to be constructed is to have one (1) electric sign circuit and the exact number of receptacle outlets to be provided is not yet determined. Determine the MINIMUM number of 20-ampere, 120-volt branch-circuits that must be provided for the general lighting, receptacles and the sign.

        A. 14
        B. 15
        C. 16
        D. 12

10.   A 20,000 sq. ft. office building is to be provided with a 208Y/120-volt, 3-phase electrical system. The building will have two-hundred (200), 120-volt, general-use receptacles and seventy-five (75) feet of multioutlet assembly where the cord connected appliances are unlikely to be used simultaneously. Determine the MINIMUM demand load, in amperes, on the ungrounded service conductors for the general lighting and receptacle load.

        A. 262 amperes
        B. 466 amperes
        C. 310 amperes
        D. 538 amperes

11. Branch-circuit conductors supplying a 7½ ton, 208-volt, single-phase, A/C condensing unit are required to have an ampacity of at LEAST _____.

A. 86 amperes
B. 117 amperes
C. 94 amperes
D. 108 amperes

12. When a circuit breaker is provided to protect the previous referenced A/C condensing unit, the circuit breaker is required to have an absolute MAXIMUM ampere rating of no more than _____.

A. 125 amperes
B. 150 amperes
C. 175 amperes
D. 200 amperes

13. A commercial occupancy is to have a fifteen (15) ton A/C unit and a thirty (30) kW electric heating unit installed; both units are 208-volts, 3-phase. What is the demand load, in amperes, to be applied on the service for the A/C and heating equipment?

A. 100 amperes
B. 125 amperes
C. 150 amperes
D. 83 amperes

14. A Mexican food restaurant is to have the following cooking related equipment in the kitchen:

- water heater   - 9.0 kW
- fryer   - 7.5 kW
- grill   - 15 kW
- mixer   - 2.0 kW
- food warmer   - 4.0 kW
- freezer   - 3.5 kW
- refrigerator   - 2.5 kW
- dishwasher   - 2.0 kW
- booster heater - 4.5 kW

What is the demand load, in kW, on the service for the above listed appliances?

A. 50.00 kW
B. 42.75 kW
C. 37.50 kW
D. 32.50 kW

15. Each lot in a fifteen (15) unit manufactured home park is capable of accommodating a manufactured home with a rating of 36,000 VA. The demand load, in amperes, on the park service conductors is _____.

    A. 540 amperes
    B. 585 amperes
    C. 390 amperes
    D. 687 amperes

16. When a one-hundred and twenty-five (125) site RV park supplies all the campsites with electrical power, at LEAST _____ of the sites are required to be provided with a 50-ampere, 125/250-volt receptacle and at LEAST _____ of the sites are required to be provided with a 30-ampere, 125-volt receptacle.

    A. 25, 88
    B. 100, 25
    C. 25, 125
    D. 88, 25

17. An RV park has twenty (20) sites with electrical power reserved as dedicated tent sites. Before demand factors are taken into consideration, what is the MINIMUM total calculated load, in VA, of the tent sites?

    A. 48,000 VA
    B. 36,000 VA
    C. 24,000 VA
    D. 12,000 VA

18. A recreational vehicle park has a total of one hundred and fifty (150) RV sites, all provided with electrical power. Fifty (50) of the sites are provided with 50- and 30-ampere, 125/250-volt receptacles and one-hundred of the sites are provided with 30- and 20-ampere rated 125-volt receptacles. What is the feeder/service demand load, in amperes, for the RV sites where the electrical system is 208Y/120-volts, three-phase?

    A.   956 amperes
    B. 1,670 amperes
    C. 1,435 amperes
    D. 3,500 amperes

19. What MINIMUM size 75°C rated copper branch-circuit conductors are required to supply a 9.0 kW, 208-volt, single-phase storage-type commercial electric water heater?

    A. 10 AWG
    B. 8 AWG
    C. 6 AWG
    D. 4 AWG

20. Refer to the previous question. What MAXIMUM standard size circuit breaker is permitted to be used for overcurrent protection for the water heater?

A. 50 ampere
B. 60 ampere
C. 65 ampere
D. 70 ampere

NOTES

Final Exam

The following questions are based on the 2014 edition of the National Electrical Code® and the related information you have learned in this text. Select the best answer from the choices given and review your answers with the answer key included in this book. If you do not get at least **70 percent** of the questions correct, keep studying and try again. GOOD LUCK!

Final Exam

1. Which of the following listed is/are considered a unit of power?

   A. watt
   B. volt
   C. electromotive force
   D. all of these

2. When determining the current in a single-phase electrical system, which of the following formulas should be used?

   A. P = I x E
   B. I = P x E
   C. I = P ÷ E
   D. I = E ÷ P

3. One kW is equal to _____.

   A. 10,000 watts
   B. 1,000 watts
   C. 100 watts
   D. 10 kilo-watts

4. A 240-volt, single-phase, 7.2 kW electric clothes dryer will draw _____ of current.

   A. 25 amperes
   B. 30 amperes
   C. 35 amperes
   D. 40 amperes

5. When determining the VA of a three-phase electrical system, which of the following formulas should be used?

   A. P = I x E
   B. P = I ÷ E x 1.732
   C. P = E x 1.732 ÷ I
   D. P = I x E x 1.732

6. What is the MAXIMUM demand load, in VA, that may be connected to a 200 ampere, 120/240-volt, single-phase residential service?

   A. 12,000 VA
   B. 24,000 VA
   C. 36,000 VA
   D. 48,000 VA

7. The power factor of a 10 kW load drawing 50 amperes of current when connected to a 240-volt, single-phase source is _____.

    A. 69 percent
    B. 74 percent
    C. 83 percent
    D. 91 percent

8. A single-phase, 120/240-volt residential service with a demand load of 12 kVA will have a MAXIMUM load of _____ on the ungrounded service-entrance conductors.

    A. 100 amperes
    B. 50 amperes
    C. 200 amperes
    D. 75 amperes

9. Determine the current, in amperes, on a balanced three-phase electrical system with a load of 30 kVA per phase and a line voltage of 208Y/120-volts. Total power is 90 kVA.

    A. 250 amperes
    B. 433 amperes
    C. 687 amperes
    D. 749 amperes

10. When connected to a 208-volt, single-phase circuit, a 400 watt industrial type HID luminaire (lighting fixture) with a power factor of 92 percent will draw _____ of current.

    A. 2.0 amperes
    B. 1.0 amperes
    C. 1.5 amperes
    D. 3.0 amperes

11. A one-family dwelling unit with 60 feet by 40 feet of livable space is required to have at least _____ 15-ampere, 120-volt general lighting branch circuits.

    A. two
    B. three
    C. four
    D. five

12. What is the MAXIMUM standard size circuit breaker permitted for overcurrent protection for a 4.5 kW, 240-volt, single-phase water heater?

A. 15 amperes
B. 20 amperes
C. 25 amperes
D. 30 amperes

13. In general, when a branch-circuit supplies a continuous load of 80 amperes, the branch-circuit conductors are required to have an ampacity of at LEAST _____.

A. 64 amperes
B. 80 amperes
C. 100 amperes
D. 125 amperes

14. An apartment house with cooking facilities provided for the tenants, having 20,000 square feet of living area, is required to have at LEAST _____ 20-ampere, 120-volt general lighting and general-use receptacle branch-circuits.

A. 9
B. 34
C. 17
D. 25

15. When protecting a 240-volt, single-phase continuous load, a 2-pole 30-ampere rated circuit breaker is permitted to protect a load having a value of NO more than _____.

A. 5,760 VA
B. 7,200 VA
C. 7,560 VA
D. 9,000 VA

16. A 25,000 square foot retail store to be constructed is to have 15,000 VA of accent lighting in addition to the general lighting. Determine the MINIMUM number of 120 volt, 20-ampere branch-circuits required for the accent and general lighting loads.

A. 42
B. 47
C. 38
D. 59

17. An office building to be constructed will have two-hundred and fifty (250), 20 ampere, 120-volt duplex receptacles installed. Determine the MINIMUM number of 120 volt, 20-ampere branch-circuits required to supply the receptacles.

A. 24

B. 25
C. 18
D. 19

18. Where a circuit breaker is to provide overcurrent protection for a busway having a rating of 1,400 amperes, the circuit breaker is permitted to have a MAXIMUM standard rating of _____.

A. 1,000 amperes
B. 1,200 amperes
C. 1,400 amperes
D. 1,600 amperes

19. A machine shop is to have the following 120-volt receptacle loads:

- 35 – general purpose duplex receptacles
- 10 – single receptacles supplying 100 VA continuous loads.

The demand load, in VA, on the ungrounded service-entrance conductors for the receptacle outlets is _____.

A. 7,550 VA
B. 7,425 VA
C. 8,550 VA
D. 10,125 VA

20. Given: You are to install sixty (60) feet of fixed multioutlet assembly in an appliance store where the cord connected appliances are likely to be used simultaneously and continuously during the business day. Determine the MINIMUM number of 120-volt, 20 ampere branch-circuits required to supply the multioutlet assembly.

A. three
B. four
C. five
D. six

21. An existing office building with a 120/240 volt single-phase service is to have fifty (50) 120-volt receptacles installed. Determine the demand load, in amperes, the additional receptacles will add to each of the ungrounded service-entrance conductors.

A. 37.5 amperes
B. 75 amperes
C. 87.5 amperes
D. 50 amperes

22. What is the MINIMUM number of 30-ampere, 240-volt, single-phase branch-circuits required to supply sixteen (16) residential baseboard heaters each rated 1,500 watts, 240 volts, single-phase?

    A. four
    B. five
    C. six
    D. seven

23. What is the demand load, in kW, on the branch-circuit conductors supplying a 9.5 kW, 240-volt, single-phase residential electric range?

    A. 8 kW
    B. 9.5 kW
    C. 7.6 kW
    D. 12 kW

24. Determine the branch-circuit and feeder demand load, in amperes, for a 14 kW, 240 volt, single-phase residential electric range?

    A. 34 amperes
    B. 50 amperes
    C. 37 amperes
    D. 58 amperes

25. When sizing a branch-circuit supplying a 10 kW, 208-volt, single-phase storage-type water heater, the branch-circuit conductors are required to have the ability to carry at LEAST _____ of current.

    A. 42 amperes
    B. 52 amperes
    C. 60 amperes
    D. 75 amperes

26. A nine (9) unit multi-family dwelling will have a 4 kW storage-type electric water installed in each unit. When applying the standard (general) method of calculation for dwellings, determine the demand load, in kW, on the service conductors for the water heaters.

    A. 45 kW
    B. 36 kW
    C. 32 kW
    D. 27 kW

27. When applying the general method of calculation for dwelling units, each residential electric clothes dryer is to be calculated at a MINIMUM of _____ or the nameplate rating, whichever is larger, when sizing the service conductors.

    A. 4,500 watts (VA)
    B. 5,000 watts (VA)
    C. 6,000 watts (VA)

D. 7,200 watts (VA)

28. A 208Y/120-volt, 3-phase feeder is to supply the following cooking related equipment in the kitchen of a restaurant:

- water heater   - 8.0 kW
- booster heater - 7.5 kW
- dishwasher   - 2.0 kW
- refrigerator   - 2.5 kW
- freezer   - 3.0 kW

What is the demand load, in amperes, on the feeder conductors?

A. 45 amperes
B. 58 amperes
C. 64 amperes
D. 77 amperes

29. A one-family dwelling unit is to have the following fastened in place appliances installed:

- dishwasher   - 1,200 VA
- water heater   - 5,000 VA
- garbage disposer   -   864 VA
- garage door opener - 1,656 VA
- attic fan   - 1,176 VA
- trash compactor   - 1,176 VA

Apply the general (standard) method of calculation for dwellings and determine the service demand load, in VA, for the listed appliances.

A. 7,750 VA
B. 8,304 VA
C. 8,858 VA
D. 11,072 VA

30. Determine the allowable ampacity of a size 4 AWG copper conductor with type THWN insulation installed in a conduit ten (10) feet in length with three (3) other current-carrying conductors of the same size and insulation.

A. 52 amperes
B. 60 amperes
C. 68 amperes
D. 85 amperes

31. A 2-gang metal device box to be installed will contain the following:

- 1 single-pole switch
- 1 duplex receptacle
- 1 bonding jumper

- 4 cable clamps
- 3 spliced equipment grounding conductors

To allow for the grounding and bonding conductors, cable clamps, and devices, the MAXIMUM number of conductors permitted in the box must be reduced by _____ conductors.

A. six
B. seven
C. eight
D. nine

32. Determine the required volume, in cubic inches, for a junction box that contains the following combinations of conductors. Assume all conductors carry current.

- 6 - size 12 AWG with THHN insulation
- 6 - size 10 AWG with THWN insulation
- 4 - size 8 AWG with XHHW insulation

A. 40.50 cubic inches
B. 31.00 cubic inches
C. 50.20 cubic inches
D. 46.50 cubic inches

33. A commercial building with a single-phase, 120/240-volt, 3-wire electrical system has a total load of 40 kVA after all demand factors are taken into consideration. The MINIMUM size 75°C copper conductors required for the ungrounded service-entrance conductors is _____.

A. 4/0 AWG
B. 250 kcmil
C. 3/0 AWG
D. 2/0 AWG

34. When three (3) size 1/0 AWG copper current-carrying conductors are contained within a raceway where the ambient temperature is 120°F, the ampacity (current carrying-capacity) of the conductors is _____.

A. 150 amperes
B. 146 amperes
C. 130 amperes
D. 113 amperes

35. A 60-ampere, 240-volt, single-phase load is located 175 feet from the panelboard and is supplied with size 6 AWG THWN/THHN copper branch-circuit conductors. What is the approximate voltage drop on the branch-circuit conductors? (K=12.9)

A. 7 volts
B. 10 volts
C. 12 volts
D. 15 volts

36. As per the NEC®, what is the recommended MAXIMUM voltage drop for a 120-volt single-phase, lighting branch-circuit?

A. 2.0 volts
B. 2.4 volts
C. 3.6 volts
D. 6.0 volts

37. For the purpose of determining allowable fill in raceways, what is the total area, in square inches, of three (3) size 2/0 AWG THWN and three (3) size 1/0 AWG THWN copper conductors?

A. 1.1355 square inches
B. 1.3602 square inches
C. 2.6320 square inches
D. 1.2234 square inches

38. Refer to the previous question. If the conductors are to be installed in an electrical metallic tubing (EMT) 25 feet long; as per the NEC®, what MINIMUM standard trade size EMT is required?

A. 1½ inch
B. 2 inches
C. 2½ inches
D. 3 inches

39. The area, in square inches, of a bare copper conductor can be found in Chapter 9, Table _____ of the NEC®.

A. 8
B. 5 A
C. 4
D. 2

40. A 12 inch long electrical metallic tubing (EMT) is to contain the following listed insulated conductors:

- four - size 12 AWG THHN
- three - size 6 AWG THW
- three - size 4 AWG THW
- three - size 2 AWG XHHW

Determine the MINIMUM trade size EMT the NEC® requires for this installation.

A. 1¼ inches
B. 1½ inches
C. 2 inches
D. 2½ inches

41. The MINIMUM standard size device box required to enclose six (6) size 12 AWG THHN conductors, and one (1) three-way switch is _____.

A. 4 x 2 1/8 x 1½ in.
B. 3 x 2 x 3½ in.
C. 4 x 2 1/8 x 2 1/8 in.
D. None of these

42.What is the MAXIMUM number of size 4/0 AWG copper conductors with XHHW insulation the NEC® permits to be installed in an 18 inch long trade size 2½ inch intermediate metal conduit (IMC)?

A. seven
B. eight
C. nine
D. ten

43. A one-family dwelling has an air-conditioning load of 8,400 VA. (3½ ton, 240-volt, single-phase unit.) The house also has a central space heating unit rated at 15 kVA. When applying the optional calculation method for dwellings, a connected load of _____ is to be added to the service load calculation for the A/C and/or heating loads.

A. 15,000 VA
B. 9,750 VA
C. 14,430 VA
D. 8,400 VA

44. What is the ampacity of a size 10 AWG 75°C rated copper conductor enclosed in a conduit, greater than 24 inches on length, with seven (7) other conductors of the same size and insulation? Given: all conductors are current-carrying and the ambient temperature is 100°F.

A. 30 amperes
B. 28 amperes

C. 26 amperes

D. 22 amperes

45. Determine the MINIMUM size copper branch-circuit conductors required to supply a 120-volt, 16 ampere load, located 100 feet from the panelboard, where limiting the voltage drop to 3 percent. (K=12.9)

    A. 6 AWG

    B. 8 AWG

    C. 10 AWG

    D. 12 AWG

46. Determine the allowable ampacity of a size 12/2 with ground NM copper cable, when the cable is bundled together for six (6) feet with three (3) other 120-volt branch-circuits using the same cable.

    A. 17.5 amperes

    B. 14 amperes

    C. 21 amperes

    D. 25 amperes

47. A one-family dwelling with a 120/240-volt, single-phase service has a calculated demand load of 36,000 VA. Determine the MINIMUM size ungrounded service-entrance conductors the NEC® permits when using aluminum conductors with THWN/THHN insulation.

    A. 1 AWG

    B. 1/0 AWG

    C. 2/0 AWG

    D. 3/0 AWG

48. A commercial building has a calculated non-continuous demand load of 12,200 VA and a continuous demand load of 16,200 VA. Determine the MINIMUM standard size fuses to be used for overcurrent protection on the disconnecting means. The building is provided with a 120/240-volt, single-phase electrical system.

    A. 110

    B. 135

    C. 200

    D. 150

49. How many size 12 AWG conductors may be installed in 3½ inch deep, 4-gang masonry box that contains two (2) three-way switches and (2) single-pole switches?

    A. 28
    B. 26
    C. 36
    D. 32

50. An electrical conduit is installed in an equipment room of a commercial building having an ambient temperature of 97°F. The conduit contains one (1) size 4/0 AWG THWN copper grounded conductor and three (3) size 4/0 AWG THWN copper ungrounded conductors. What is the ampacity of the ungrounded conductors where all the conductors are considered as current-carrying?

    A. 202 amperes
    B. 162 amperes
    C. 184 amperes
    D. 230 amperes

51. Determine the MAXIMUM number of size 2/0 AWG XHHW compact aluminum conductors the NEC® permits to be installed in a 4 in. x 4 in. metal raceway.

    A. 17
    B. 18
    C. 20
    D. 30

52. A wireway is to contain the following listed copper conductors.

    • three – size 500 kcmil THWN
    • three – size 250 kcmil THWN
    • three – size 4/0 AWG THWN

Which one of the following listed wireways is the MINIMUM size required to house the conductors?

    A. 4 in. x 1 in.
    B. 6 in. x 6 in.
    C. 8 in. x 8 in.
    D. 12 in. x 12 in.

53. Which of the following formulas, if any, may be used to determine the MINIMUM number of branch-circuits required to serve continuous loads such as commercial lighting?

      I. Number of Circuits $= \dfrac{\text{Load VA x 125\%}}{\text{Circuit VA}}$

      II. Number of Circuits $= \dfrac{\text{Load VA}}{\text{Circuit VA x 80\%}}$

      A. I only
      B. II only
      C. neither I nor II
      D. either I or II

54. As mandated by the NEC®, the MINIMUM ampacity of the conductors supplying a 5 hp, 208-volt, single-phase, continuous-duty, induction type ac electric motor, with a nameplate ampere rating of 28.5 amperes is _____.

      A. 30.8 amperes
      B. 20.8 amperes
      C. 38.5 amperes
      D. 35.6 amperes

55. Refer to the motor in the previous question. What MINIMUM size 75°C rated copper branch-circuit conductors are required to supply the motor? Assume all terminations are rated for 75°C.

      A. 6 AWG
      B. 8 AWG
      C. 10 AWG
      D. 12 AWG

56. When the ambient temperature is not a consideration, a size 8 AWG XHHW insulated aluminum conductor has an ampacity of _____, when installed in free air.

      A. 55 amperes
      B. 70 amperes
      C. 45 amperes
      D. 50 amperes

57. The absolute MAXIMUM standard rating of an inverse time circuit breaker for branch-circuit, short-circuit, and a ground-fault protection allowed for a 40 hp, 230-volt, 3-phase, continuous-duty, Design C, ac motor is _____.

      A. 150 amperes
      B. 200 amperes
      C. 250 amperes

D. 300 amperes

58. Refer to the motor in the previous question. Determine the absolute MAXIMUM size time-delay (dual-element) fuse that may be used for overcurrent protection for the motor.

A. 150 amperes
B. 200 amperes
C. 225 amperes
D. 250 amperes

59. Where an apartment complex has a calculated connected lighting load of 205.4 kVA, what is the DEMAND load in, kVA, on the service for the lighting load? Given: Each unit in the apartment complex has cooking facilities provided. Apply the general (standard) method of calculation for dwellings.

A. 58.9 kVA
B. 60.2 kVA
C. 16.5 kVA
D. 65.3 kVA

60. When a 15-ampere rated ac general-use snap switch is to serve as a disconnecting means for a motor of a 2 hp or less and rated at 240-volts, the NEC® requires the MAXIMUM full-load current rating of the motor to be no more than _____.

A. 7.5 amperes
B. 10 amperes
C. 12 amperes
D. 15 amperes

61. Feeder conductors are to supply the following ac motors, used in a continuous duty application, from a panelboard:

- motor #1 – FLC rating 10 amperes
- motor #2 – FLC rating 20 amperes
- motor #3 – FLC rating 30 amperes

The feeder conductors must have an ampacity of at LEAST _____.

A. 60.0 amperes
B. 67.5 amperes
C. 75.0 amperes
D. 90.0 amperes

62. When there are no more than three (3) current-carrying size 2 AWG XHHW aluminum conductors in a raceway at an ambient temperature of 86°F, when terminated on a circuit breaker rated at 60°C the conductors have an allowable ampacity of _____.

A. 100 amperes

B. 95 amperes
C. 90 amperes
D. 75 amperes

63. When a size 8/3 AWG with ground copper NM cable is installed in the attic of a dwelling unit where the attic temperature reaches 130°F during the summer months, the cable has an allowable ampacity of _____.

A. 40.0 amperes
B. 41.8 amperes
C. 33.5 amperes
D. 16.4 amperes

64. Where a building or structure is supplied from a 4-wire, 3-phase, electrical system where the major portion of the load consists of _____ loads, the neutral conductor shall be considered a current-carrying conductor.

A. nonlinear
B. inductive
C. 3-phase
D. single-phase

65. When serving a 36,000 VA, 240-volt, single-phase load in an area where the ambient temperature reaches 119°F, determine the MINIMUM size 75°C rated copper conductors required to supply the load.

A. 1/0 AWG
B. 2/0 AWG
C. 3/0 AWG
D. 4/0 AWG

66. Refer to the previous question and assume the same conditions exist, with one exception; the load is continuous. Now, determine the MINIMUM size conductors required.

A. 2/0 AWG
B. 3/0 AWG
C. 4/0 AWG
D. 250 kcmil

67. An existing school with a 480Y/277-volt, 3-phase service is to add seventy-five (75) 120-volt, 20-ampere general-use duplex receptacle outlets. What demand load,

in amperes, will the additional receptacles add to each of the ungrounded service-entrance conductors?

    A. 14 amperes
    B. 24 amperes
    C. 49 amperes
    D. 113 amperes

Questions 68 through 74 are based on the following information given for a retail store building with dimensions of 100 feet by 75 feet.

- Service is 208/120-volts, 3-phase, 4-wire
- Actual connected general lighting load of 14,000 VA
- The store has 50 feet of show window lighting.
- The building is provided with 115 general use-receptacle outlets
- Fifty (50) feet of multioutlet assembly where the cord-connected appliances are likely to be used simultaneously will be installed.
- Forty (40) feet of track lighting will be installed for accent lighting.
- The store will have two (2) 20-ampere, 120-volt exterior electric sign circuits.
- Consider all overcurrent protection devices not to be listed for continuous use.

68. When calculating the service for the building, what MINIMUM VA must be included for the general lighting load?

    A. 14,000 VA
    B. 18,000 VA
    C. 22,500 VA
    D. 28,125 VA

69. Determine the MINIMUM number of 20-ampere, 120-volt, branch-circuits required for the general lighting load of the store.

    A. eight
    B. ten
    C. eleven
    D. twelve

70. When sizing the service what MINIMUM value, in VA, must be included for the show window lighting?

    A. 10,000 VA
    B. 12,500 VA
    C. 11,250 VA
    D. 9,375 VA

71. Determine the MINIMUM number of 20-ampere, 120-volt, branch-circuits required for the general-use receptacle outlets.

    A. seven
    B. eight
    C. nine
    D. ten

72. Determine the demand load, in VA, on the service for the general-use receptacles and the multioutlet assembly.

    A. 29,700 VA
    B. 20,700 VA
    C. 14,850 VA
    D. 19,850 VA

73. What is the MINIMUM service demand load, in VA, for the two (2) exterior sign circuits?

    A. 4,800 VA
    B. 5,875 VA
    C. 2,400 VA
    D. 3,000 VA

74. Determine the service demand load, in VA, for the track lighting.
    A. 3,000 VA
    B. 3,750 VA
    C. 6,000 VA
    D. 7,500 VA

75. Given: A 3-phase, 480-volt, 30 hp, induction type ac motor has a FLA of 38 amperes and a service factor of 1.15 indicated on the nameplate. The MINIMUM setting in amperes of the overload device used to protect this motor as required by the NEC® is _____.

    A. 53.2 amperes
    B. 43.7 amperes
    C. 47.5 amperes
    D. 50.0 amperes
76. Refer to the previous question. Assume the minimum rating of the overload device you have selected will not allow the motor to start without tripping. Determine the MAXIMUM setting, in amperes, of the overload device the NEC® permits to be used to protect the motor.

A. 53.2 amperes
B. 49.4 amperes
C. 52.0 amperes
D. 56.0 amperes

77. Determine the allowable ampacity of size 1/0 AWG THHW copper conductors when used as service-entrance conductors, installed in a conduit mast, in a commercial occupancy, when given the following conditions:

- wet location
- four (4) current-carrying conductors in the conduit
- conduit length, six (6) feet
- ambient temperature, 110°F

A. 98 amperes
B. 112 amperes
C. 123 amperes
D. 150 amperes

78. Determine the MINIMUM size THWN/THHN copper feeder conductors required by the NEC® to supply the following 480-volt, continuous duty, 3-phase, induction type ac motors. Assume all terminations are rated for 75°C.
- two (2) – 50 HP
- one (1) – 40 HP

A. 2/0 AWG
B. 3/0 AWG
C. 4/0 AWG
D. 250 kcmil

79. Determine the MINIMUM required length of a junction box that has a trade size 3½ inch conduit containing four (4) size 250 kcmil conductors, pulled through the box for a 90° angle pull. Exceptions are not to be applied.

A. 21 inches
B. 24 inches
C. 28 inches
D. 34 inches

80. What MINIMUM size THWN/THHN copper conductors are required to supply a continuous-duty, 25 hp, 208-volt, 3-phase ac motor? Given: The ambient temperature is 50°C and all terminations are rated for 75°C.

A. 6 AWG
B. 3 AWG
C. 2 AWG
D. 1 AWG

81. A ten (10) unit apartment building has the following total connected loads:

- general lighting & receptacles   - 25,200 VA
- small appliances & laundry circuits   - 45,000 VA
- Fixed appliances   - 150,500 VA
- A/C- Heating equipment   - 48,800 VA

Apply the optional method of calculation for multi-family dwellings and determine the DEMAND load, in VA, on the ungrounded service-entrance conductors.

    A. 121,275 VA
    B. 118,580 VA
    C. 115,885 VA
    D. 269,500 VA

82. What is the feeder/service demand load, in amperes, for a recreational vehicle park that has the following sites provided with electrical facilities? The electrical system is 208Y/120-volts, 3-phase, 4-wire.

- 30 RV sites with 50-ampere, & 30-ampere, receptacles
- 30 RV sites with 30-& 20-ampere, receptacles
- 10 RV sites with 20-ampere, receptacles
- 5 tent sites with 20-ampere, receptacles

    A. 723 amperes
    B. 642 amperes
    C. 481 amperes
    D. 519 amperes

83. A twenty-five (25) lot mobile home park is to be designed for mobile homes that have a load of 15,000 VA per lot. The service demand load, in VA, for the park is

_____.

    A. 84,000 VA
    B. 96,000 VA
    C. 100,000 VA
    D. 108,000 VA

84. Determine the MAXIMUM initial standard rating of time-delay (dual-element) fuses permitted for branch-circuit, short-circuit and ground-fault protection for a 10 hp, 208 volt, three-phase, induction type, continuous-duty ac motor.

    A. 70 amperes
    B. 50 amperes
    C. 55 amperes

D. 60 amperes

85. Refer to the previous question. Where exceptions are not to be applied, what is the MAXIMUM permitted operational setting for an adjustable inverse-time circuit breaker when used for overcurrent protection of the motor?

    A. 77 amperes
    B. 54 amperes
    C. 93 amperes
    D. 62 amperes

86. What MAXIMUM standard size time-delay (dual-element) fuses are required for the feeder overcurrent protection of a feeder supplying three (3), 20 hp, 480-volt, three-phase, continuous-duty, ac motors? Consider each of the motors are protected with 50-ampere rated time-delay (dual-element) fuses.

    A. 100 amperes
    B. 110 amperes
    C. 125 amperes
    D. 150 amperes

87. Approximately, what is the MAXIMUM distance size 10 AWG copper, 120-volt, branch-circuit conductors may ran to a 16-ampere load when the voltage drop is to be limited to 3 percent? (K=12.9)

    A. 100 feet
    B. 60 feet
    C. 180 feet
    D. 90 feet

88. A metal junction box has a volume of 30 cubic inches and contains a total of seven (7) size 12 AWG wires. Additional size 10 AWG conductors are needed to be added in the box. No devices or fittings are contained in the box. What is the MAXIMUM number of size 10 AWG conductors permitted to be added in this junction box?

    A. three
    B. four
    C. five
    D. six

89. An existing trade size 1½ inch rigid metal conduit (RMC) nipple contains four (4) size 6 AWG THWN/THHN copper conductors. In compliance with the NEC®, how many additional size 10 AWG THWN/THHN copper conductors are permitted to be installed in the pipe?

     A. 12
     B. 26
     C. 32
     D. 49

90. Where a rooftop mounted air conditioning unit is supplied with three (3) size 8 AWG THWN copper current-carrying conductors, enclosed in an electrical metallic tubing (EMT) within three (3) inches of the rooftop, and exposed to direct sunlight and an ambient temperature of 100°F, the allowable ampacity of the conductors is _____ .

     A. 50 amperes
     B. 44 amperes
     C. 29 amperes
     D. 25 amperes

NOTES

PRACTICAL CALCULATIONS FOR ELECTRICIANS
UNIT 1
SELF ASSESSMENT QUIZ
ANSWER KEY

ANSWER

REFERENCE

1. C

Trade Knowledge

$$1 \text{ kVA} \times 1,000 = 1,000 \text{ VA}$$

2. B

Trade Knowledge

$$\frac{5,000}{1,000} = 5 \text{ kW}$$

3. C

Current Formula

$$I = \frac{1,200 \text{ watts}}{120 \text{ volts}} = 10 \text{ amperes}$$

4. A

Power Formula

$$P = 6 \text{ amperes} \times 120 \text{ volts} = 720 \text{ watts}$$

5. D

Ohm's Law

$$R = \frac{240 \text{ volts}}{20 \text{ amps}} = 12 \text{ ohms resistance}$$

6. B

Current Formula

$$I = \frac{2 \text{ kW} \times 1,000}{240 \text{ volts}} = \frac{2,000}{240} = 8.33 \text{ amperes}$$

7. D

Power Formula

$$P = 8 \text{ amperes} \times 115 \text{ volts} \times .8 \text{ (pf)} = 736 \text{ VA}$$

8. C

Power Formula

$$P = 240 \text{ volts} \times 150 \text{ amperes} = 36,000 \text{ VA}$$

9. A

Current Formula

$$I = \frac{15\ kW\ x\ 1{,}000}{208\ volts} = \frac{15{,}000}{208} = 72\ amperes$$

10. B   Power Factor Formula

$$PF = \frac{6{,}500\ watts}{240\ volts\ x\ 33\ amps} = \frac{6{,}500\ watts}{7{,}920\ VA} = .82 = 82\%$$

11. A   Ohm's Law

$$I = \frac{240\ volts}{22\ ohms} = 10.90\ amperes$$

12. C   Power Factor Formula

$$PF = \frac{5\ kW\ x\ 1{,}000}{208\ volts\ x\ 30\ amps} = \frac{5{,}000\ watts}{6{,}240\ VA} = .80 = 80\%$$

13. D   Power Formula, 3-phase

$$VA = 208\ volts\ x\ 1.732\ x\ 200\ amps = 72{,}051\ VA$$

14. C   Ohm's Law

$$\frac{volts}{current\ x\ resistance} \qquad \frac{E}{I\ x\ R}$$

15. D   Current Formula

$$I = \frac{600\ VA}{15\ volts} = 40\ amperes$$

   *NOTE – The VA rating of the transformer is the same on both the primary and
         on the secondary.

16. C   Current Formula, 3-phase

$$I = \frac{75{,}000\ VA}{208\ volts\ x\ 1.732} = \frac{75{,}000}{360.25} = 208.30\ amperes$$

17. A   Power Factor Formula

$$PF = \frac{300\ watts}{120\ volts \times 3\ amps} = \frac{300}{360} = .83\ (83\%)$$

18. B   General Knowledge

5 HP x 746 watts   = 3,730 watts

19. C   Current Formula

$$I = \frac{400\ watts}{277\ volts \times .86} = \frac{400}{238.22} = 1.679\ amperes$$

1.679 amperes x 8 (luminaires) = 13.43 amperes

20. D   Power Formula, 3-phase

$$P = \frac{400A \times 480V \times 1.732}{1,000} = \frac{332,544\ VA}{1,000} = 332.5\ kVA$$

PRACTICAL CALCULATIONS FOR ELECTRICIANS
UNIT 2
SELF-ASSESSMENT QUIZ
ANSWER KEY

ANSWER	**REFERENCE**	**NEC PG. #**
1. D	Article 100	pg. 29
2. C	210.19(A)(1)(a)	pg. 57
3. C	General Knowledge	

100 ft. x 150 ft. x 6 stories = 90,000 sq. ft.

4. B	240.6(A)	pg. 96
5. A	240.4(D)(7)	pg. 95
6. C	Table 220.12	pg. 68

70 ft. x 30 ft. = 2,100 sq. ft. x 3 VA = 6,300 VA

$$\text{number of circuits} = \frac{6,300 \text{ VA}}{120 \text{ volts x 15 amps}} = 3.5 = 4 \text{ circuits}$$

7. A	220.14(J)	pg. 69
8. D	220.14(I)	pg. 69
9. C	210.20(A)	pg. 59

240 volts x 20 amperes x 80% = 3,840 VA

10. B	220.12	pg. 67
	Table 220.12	pg. 68

2,600 sq. ft. + 1,300 sq. ft. = 3,900 sq. ft. total

$$\frac{3,900 \text{ sq. ft. x 3 VA}}{120 \text{ volts x 15 amps}} = \frac{11,700 \text{ VA}}{1,800 \text{ VA}} \begin{array}{l} \text{(load)} \\ \text{(circuit)} \end{array} = 6.5 = 7 \text{ circuits}$$

11. D	422.11(E)(3)	pg. 303

Current Formula
240.6(A)   pg. 96

I = $\dfrac{3,600 \text{ VA}}{240 \text{ volts}}$ = 15 amps x 150% = 22.5 amperes

*NOTE- The **next** size circuit breaker has a rating of 25 amperes.

12.   C   Table 220.12   pg. 68

$\dfrac{16,000 \text{ sq. ft. x 3 VA}}{120 \text{ volts x 20 amps}} = \dfrac{48,000 \text{ VA (load)}}{2,400 \text{ VA (circuit)}}$ = 20 circuits

*NOTE- Apartments **with** cooking facilities are considered dwelling units.

13.   D   Table 220.12   pg. 68
                                 210.19(A)(1)(a)   pg. 57

$\dfrac{6,000 \text{ x 3.5 VA x } \textbf{125\%}}{120 \text{ volts x 20 amps}} = \dfrac{26,250 \text{ VA (load)}}{2,400 \text{ VA (circuit)}}$ = 10.9 = 11 circuits

14.   A   220.18(B)   pg. 69
                                 210.20(A)   pg. 59

$\dfrac{120 \text{ volts x 20 amps x } \textbf{80\%}}{120 \text{ volts x 1.6 amps}} = \dfrac{1,920 \text{ VA (circuit)}}{192 \text{ VA (fixture)}}$ = 10 luminaires

15.   A   220.14(I)   pg. 69

$\dfrac{120 \text{ volts x 15 amps}}{180 \text{ VA}} = \dfrac{1,800 \text{ VA (circuit)}}{180 \text{ VA (recpt.)}}$ = 10 receptacles

16.   B   220.14(H)(2)   pg. 69

$\dfrac{200 \text{ ft. x 180 VA}}{120 \text{ volts x 20 amps}} = \dfrac{36,000 \text{ VA (load)}}{2,400 \text{ VA (circuit)}}$ = 15 circuits

17.   C   422.13   pg. 304
                                 422.10(A)   pg. 303

18.   D   220.18(B)   pg. 69

$$\frac{100 \text{ x } 277 \text{ V x .75 A}}{277 \text{ V x } 20 \text{ A x } \textbf{80\%}} = \frac{20{,}775 \text{ VA (load)}}{4{,}432 \text{ VA (circuit)}} = 4.6 = 5 \text{ circuits}$$

19. B   210.19(A)(1)(a)   pg. 57

160 amps x **125%** = 200 amperes

20. D   Current Formula
                                      424.3(B)   pg. 308
                                      210.20(A)   pg. 59
                                      240.4(B)(1),(2)&(3)   pg. 94 & 95
                                      240.6(A)   pg. 96

$$I = \frac{18 \text{ x } 1{,}000}{240 \text{ volts}} = \frac{18{,}000}{240} = 75 \text{ amps x } 125\% = 93.73 \text{ amperes}$$

*NOTE- The **next** size circuit breaker has a rating of 100 amperes.

ANSWER	REFERENCE	NEC PG.#
1. A	Table 220.55, Column B	pg. 72

8.5 kW x 80% = 6.8 kW demand

| 2. D | Table 220.54 | pg. 71 |
| 3. A | Table 220.55 & Note 3 | pg. 72 |

Use Column B – 5 appliances = 45% demand
6 kW + 8 kW + 3.5 kW + 6 kW + 3.5 kW = 27 kW connected load
27 kW x 45% = 12.15 kW demand load

4. B	220.53	pg. 70
5. C	220.54	pg. 71
6. B	210.19(A)(3)	pg. 57
7. A	220.53	pg. 70

4,800 VA – water heater
1,200 VA – dishwasher
1,150 VA – garbage disposal
   800 VA – trash compactor
1,200 VA – attic fan
9,150 VA connected load x 75% demand = 6,863 VA demand load

| 8. C | Note 4 to Table 220.55
Current Formula | pg. 72 |

$$I = \frac{6 \text{ kW} \times 1,000}{240 \text{ volts}} = \frac{6,000}{240} = 25 \text{ amperes}$$

9. D   220.54   pg. 70 & 71
                                         Power Formula

    VA = 240 volts x 30 amperes = 7,200 VA

10. A   Table 220.55, Column C   pg. 72
                                         220.61(B)(1)   pg. 71

    Column C demand (1 range) = 8 kW x 70% = 5.6 kW

11. B   Table 220.55, Column C   pg. 72
                                         Note 1 to Table 220.55

    18 kW – 12 kW = 6 kW x 5% = 30% increase in Column C
    Column C demand (1 range) = 8 kW x 130% = 10.4 kW demand

12. C   220.56   pg. 71
                                         Current Formula

    $I = \dfrac{5\ kW \times 1,000}{240\ volts} = \dfrac{5,000}{240} = 20.8$ amperes

13. D   Table 220.55, Column C   pg. 72

14. B   Table 220.55, Note 4   pg. 72
                                         Current Formula

    6 kW + 4.5 kW + 4.5 kW = 15 kW connected load
    Treat as one range
    15 kW – 12 kW = 3 kW x 5% = 15% increase in Column C
    Column C demand (1 range) = 8 kW x 115% = 9.2 kW demand load

    $I = \dfrac{9.2\ kW \times 1,000}{240\ volts} = \dfrac{9,200}{240} = 38.3$ amperes

15. A   Article 100   pg. 29

16. C   220.53   pg. 70

    6 water heaters x 5 kW = 30 kW connected load
    30 kW x 75% (demand factor) = 22.5 kW demand load

17. D   220.61(B)(1)   pg. 71

18. B   Table 220.55, Notes 1 & 4   pg. 72

216   Copyright © 2016 - WWW.BROWNTECHNICAL.ORG

13.5 kW (rounded up) = 14 kW
14 kW – 12 kW = 2 kW x 5% = 10% increase in Column C
Column C demand (1 range) = 8 kW x 110% = 8.8 kW demand

$$I = \frac{8.8 \text{ kW} \times 1,000}{240 \text{ volts}} = \frac{8,800}{240} = 36.6 \text{ amperes}$$

19. B   220.56   pg. 71
                                Table 220.56   pg. 71

6.0 kW – water heater
2.0 kW – dishwasher
7.5 kW – booster heater
6.0 kW – oven
1.5 kW – waste disposal
2.5 kW – mixer
25.5 kW connected load x 65% demand = 16.5 kW demand load

20. A   Table 220.55, Column C   pg. 72
                                220.61(B)(1)   pg. 71

21 kW demand (6 ranges) in Column C
21 kW x 70% (neutral demand) = 15 kW demand load

PRACTICAL CALCULATIONS FOR ELECTRICIANS
UNIT 4
SELF-ASSESSMENT QUIZ
ANSWER KEY

ANSWER		REFERENCE	NEC PG. #
1.	A	Table 310.15(B)(3)(a)	pg. 160
2.	D	Table 310.104(A)	pg. 177
3.	A	Table 310.15(B)(2)(a)	pg. 158
4.	B	310.15(B)(7)(1)	pg. 160
		Table 310.15(B)(16)	pg. 161

150 amperes x 83% = 124.5 amperes

Size 1 AWG XHHW copper conductors with an ampacity of 130 amperes should be selected from the 75°C column of Table 310.15(B)(16).

5.	A	Table 310.15(B)(17)	pg. 162
6.	C	Table 310.15(B)(16)	pg. 161
7.	A	Table 310.15(B)(16)	pg. 161
		Table 310.15(B)(2)(a)	pg. 158

Size 1/0 AWG THW ampacity (before derating) = 150 amperes
150 amperes x .75 (temperature correction) = 112.5 amperes

8.	D	Table 310.15(B)(16)	pg. 161
		Table 310.15(B)(3)(a)	pg. 160

Size 4 AWG THWN ampacity (before derating) = 85 amperes
85 amperes x .8 (adjustment factor) = 68 amperes

9.	C	Table 310.15(B)(16)	pg. 161
		Table 310.15(B)(2)(a)	pg. 158

Required ampacity = $\dfrac{200 \text{ amperes}}{.82 \text{ (temp. correction)}}$ = 243.9 amperes

Table 310.15(B)(16) requires size 350 kcmil aluminum conductors rated for 75 deg. C with an ampacity of 250 amperes.

10.	B	Table 310.15(B)(16)	pg. 161

| 11. | D | Table 310.15(B)(16) | pg. 161 |
| | | Table 310.15(B)(2)(a) | pg. 158 |

3/0 AWG THHN ampacity (before derating) = 225 amperes
225 amperes x .82 (temp. correction) = 184.5 amperes

12.	A	Table 310.104(A)	pg. 176
		Table 310.15(B)(16)	pg. 161
		310.15(A)(2)	pg. 157

13.	C	Current Formula	
		310.15(B)(7)(1)	pg. 160
		Table 310.15(B)(16)	pg. 161

$$I = \frac{P}{E} \quad I = \frac{45,000 \text{ VA}}{240 \text{ volts}} = 187.5 \text{ amperes} \times 83\% = 155.625 \text{ amperes}$$

Table 310.15(B)(16) requires a size 4/0 AWG aluminum USE cable.

| 14. | D | Table 310.15(B)(3)(c) | pg. 160 |

15.	C	110.14(C)	pg. 38
		Table 310.15(B)(16)	pg. 161
		240.4(B)(2)	pg. 95

| 16. | B | 310.15(B)(3)(2) | pg. 158 |
| | | Table 310.15(B)(16) | pg. 161 |

| 17. | A | 310.15(B)(5)(a)&(b) | pg. 158 |

| 18. | D | Table 310.104(A) | pg. 177 |

19.	B	310.15(B)(5)(c)	pg. 158
		215.2(A)(1)(a)	pg. 64
		Table 310.15(B)(3)(a)	pg. 160
		Table 310.15(B)(16)	pg. 161

$$\text{Required ampacity} = \frac{104 \text{ amperes} \times 125\%}{.8 \text{ (adj. factor)}} = \frac{130}{.8} = 162.5 \text{ amperes}$$

20.	C	210.19(A)(1)(a)	pg. 57
		Table 310.15(B)(2)(a)	pg. 158
		Table 310.15(B)(3)(a)	pg. 160
		Table 310.15(B)(16)	pg. 161

$$\text{Required ampacity} = \frac{15 \text{ amps} \times 125\%}{.7 \text{ (adj. factor)} \times .88 \text{ (temp. cor.)}} = \frac{18.75}{.616} = 30.4 \text{ amperes}$$

PRACTICAL CALCULATIONS FOR ELECTRICIANS
UNIT 5
SELF-ASSESSMENT QUIZ
ANSWER KEY

ANSWER	REFERENCE	NEC PG. #
1. B	Table 314.16(A)	pg. 186
2. A	314.16(B)(3)	pg. 185
3. C	Table 314.16(B)	pg. 186
4. C	314.16(B)(4)	pg. 185
5. B	314.16(B)(4) Table 314.16(B)	pg. 185 pg. 186

$$\frac{18 \text{ cu. in. (box)}}{2.25 \text{ cu. in. (\#12 wire)}} = 8 \text{ wires (allowable fill)}$$

8 wires (allowable fill) – 2 (device) = 6 wires may be added

#12/2 with ground NM cable = 3 wires per cable

$$\frac{6 \text{ wires (allowed)}}{3 \text{ wires (per cable)}} = 2 \text{ cables are permitted}$$

6. B	ANNEX C, Table C.4	pg. 804
7. C	314.16(B)(1),(2),(4)&(5) Table 314.16(B)	pg. 185 pg. 186

size 14/2	= 2.00 cu. in. x 4 =	8.00
size 12/2	= 2.25 cu. in. x 4 =	9.00
equip. grnd.	= 2.25 cu. in. x 1 =	2.25
clamps	= 2.25 cu. in. x 1 =	2.25
receptacle	= 2.25 cu. in. x 2 =	4.50
switch	= 2.00 cu. in. x 2 =	4.00
	TOTAL =	30.00 cubic inches

*NOTE – One or more clamps are counted as equal to the largest wire in the box per 314.16(B)(2). One or more equipment grounding conductors are counted as equal to the largest equipment grounding conductor in the box per 314.16(B)(5). Devices are counted as equal to two (2) conductors, based on the largest wire connected to the device per 314.16(B)(4).

8. A	Table 314.16(A)	pg. 186

9. D   314.16(B)(1)   pg. 185
                               Table 314.16(B)   pg. 186

    2.25 cu. in. x 4 wires = 9.00 cubic inches

10. C   314 28(A)(1)   pg. 190

11. A   Chapter 9, Table 1   pg. 756

12. B   Chapter 9, Note 4   pg. 756

13. A   Chapter 9, Table 5   pg. 763

    4/0 THWN - .3237 sq. in. x 4 wires = 1.2948 sq. in.
    3/0 THWN - .2679 sq. in. x 3 wires = 0.8037 sq. in.
                        TOTAL = 2.0985 sq. in.

14. C   Chapter 9, Table 4   pg. 757
                               Chapter 9, Table 5   pg. 762

    Allowable fill of 4 in. EMT @ 60% = 8.852 square inches
    Area of 300 kcmil RHW w/o covering = .5281 square inches

    number of wires = 8.852 (allowable fill) = 16.76 = 16 wires
                      .5281 (one wire)

15. D   314.28(A)(2)   pg. 190

    2.5 in. (conduit) x 6 = 15 inches

16. B   314.28(A)(2)   pg. 190

    Top to bottom – 3 in. (largest conduit) x 6 = 18 in. + 3 in. = 21 inches
    Side to side – 3 in. (largest conduit) x 6 = 18 in. + 2½ in. = 20½ inches

17. B   Chapter 9, Table 5   pg. 764
                               Chapter 9, Table 8   pg. 766
                               Chapter 9, Table 4   pg. 760

    size 1 AWG XHHW = .1534 sq. in. x 4 wires = .6136 sq. in.
    size 6 AWG bare =   .0270 sq. in.
                                                .6406 sq. in.

    *NOTE – A trade size 1½ in. Schedule 40 PVC with an allowable fill of .794 sq.
            in. should be selected.

18. A   376.22(A)   pg. 237

19. D   376.22(A)   pg. 237
                          Chapter 9, Table 5A   pg. 765

4 in. x 4 in. = 16 sq. in. x 20% = 3.2 sq. in. permitted fill

number of wires = $\dfrac{\text{3.2 sq. in. (permitted fill)}}{\text{.3421 sq. in. (one wire)}}$ = 9.3 = 9 wires

20. C   Chapter 9, Table 5   pg. 763
                          376.22(A)   pg. 237

500 kcmil THWN = .7073 sq. in. x 8 wires = 5.6584 sq. in.
2 AWG THWN   = .1158 sq. in. x 24 wires = 2.7792 sq. in.
                                  TOTAL = 8.4376 sq. in.

required area = $\dfrac{\text{8.4376 sq. in. (wire)}}{\text{20\% (permitted fill)}}$ = 42.188 sq. in.

*NOTE – An 8 in. x 8 in. wireway with an area of 64 square inches is required.

PRACTICAL CALCULATIONS FOR ELECTRICIANS
UNIT 6
SELF-ASSESSMENT QUIZ
ANSWER KEY

ANSWER	REFERENCE	NEC PG. #
1. C	Trade Knowledge	
2. A	210.19(A)(1) IN#4	pg. 57

120 volts x 0.03 = 3.6 volts

3. D	Chapter 9, Table 8	pg. 766
4. D	Trade Knowledge	
5. B	Chapter 9, Table 8	pg. 766
6. D	Trade Knowledge	
7. B	Single-phase Voltage Drop Formula Chapter 9, Table 8	pg. 766

$$VD = \frac{2 \times K \times I \times D}{CM} = \frac{2 \times 12.9 \times 32 \times 80}{16{,}510} = \frac{66{,}048}{16{,}510} = 4 \text{ volts}$$

8. C   Ohms Law

$$\text{Resistance} = \frac{4 \text{ ohms}}{1{,}000} = 0.004 \text{ ohms per ft.}$$

0.004 ohms x 300 ft. = 1.2 ohms total resistance
VD = I x R   VD = 5 amperes x 1.2 ohms = 6 volts dropped

9. A   Current Formula

First, determine the current.

I = $\frac{10,800 \text{ VA}}{240 \text{ volts}}$ = 45 amperes

VD = $\frac{2 \times K \times I \times D}{CM}$

VD = $\frac{2 \times 12.9 \times 45 \times 200}{26,240}$ = $\frac{232,200}{26,240}$ = 8.84 volts

10. B   Chapter 9, Table 8   pg. 766
                          1 Φ Voltage Drop Formula

VD = $\frac{2 \times K \times I \times D}{CM}$

VD = $\frac{2 \times 21.2 \times 100 \times 140}{83,690}$ = $\frac{551,200}{83,690}$ = 7.09 volts

11. A   Chapter 9, Table 8   pg. 766
                          3 Φ Voltage Drop Formula

VD = $\frac{1.732 \times K \times I \times D}{CM}$

VD = $\frac{1.732 \times 12.9 \times 275 \times 125}{300,000}$ = $\frac{768,034}{300,000}$ = 2.5 volts

12. D   Chapter 9, Table 8   pg. 766
                          1 Φ Wire Size Formula

First find allowable voltage drop:

VD = 240 x .03 = 7.2 volts

CM = $\frac{2 \times K \times I \times D}{VD}$

CM = $\frac{2 \times 12.9 \times 114 \times 160}{7.2}$ = $\frac{470,592}{7.2}$ = 65,360 CM

*NOTE – Size 2 AWG copper conductors with a CMA of 66,360 CM are required.

13. C   210.19(A)(1)(a)   pg. 57

3 Φ Wire Size Formula
Chapter 9, Table 8   pg. 766

Allowable voltage drop (VD) – 208 volts x 3% = 6.24 volts
Load (I) – 40 amperes x 125% (continuous load) = 50 amperes

$$CM = \frac{1.732 \times K \times I \times D}{VD}$$

$$CM = \frac{1.732 \times 12.9 \times 50 \times 300}{6.24} = \frac{335{,}142}{6.24} = 53{,}709 \text{ CM}$$

NOTE – Size 2 AWG copper conductors with a CMA of 66,360 CM are
required.

14.   B   Current Formula
                           215.2(A)(1)(a)   pg. 64
                           3 Φ Wire Size Formula
                           Chapter 9, Table 8   pg. 766

First find current:

$$I = \frac{kVA \times 1{,}000}{E \times 1.732} = \frac{36 \times 1{,}000}{208 \times 1.732} = \frac{36{,}000}{360.25} = 100 \text{ amperes}$$

100 amperes x 125% (continuous load) = 125 amperes

$$CM = \frac{1.732 \times K \times I \times D}{VD}$$

$$CM = \frac{1.732 \times 21.2 \times 125 \times 200}{6} = \frac{917{,}960}{6} = 152{,}993 \text{ CM}$$

NOTE – Size 3/0 AWG aluminum conductors with a CMA of 167,800 CM are
required.

15.   A   1 Φ Distance Formula
                           Chapter 9, Table 8   pg. 766

First find permitted VD:

240 volts x .03 = 7.2 volts

$$D = \frac{CM \times VD}{2 \times K \times I}$$

$$D = \frac{16{,}510 \times 7.2}{2 \times 12.9 \times 32} = \frac{118{,}872}{826} = 144 \text{ feet}$$

PRACTICAL CALCULATIONS FOR ELECTRICIANS
UNIT 7
SELF-ASSESSMENT QUIZ
ANSWER KEY

ANSWER	REFERENCE	NEC PG. #
1. D	430.6(A)(1)	pg. 324
2. D	430.6(A)(2)	pg. 324
3. C	430.22	pg. 329
4. A	430.6(A)(1)	pg. 324
5. A	Table 430.52 430.52(C)(1), Exception 1	pg. 335 pg. 335
6. B	430.32(A)(1)	pg. 332
7. C	Table 430.248	pg. 350
8. C	430.6(A)(1) Table 430.250 430.22	pg. 324 pg. 351 pg. 329

10 hp FLC = 30.8 amperes x 125% = 38.5 amperes

9. B	430.32(A)(1)	pg. 332

motor FLA = 54 amperes x 115% = 62.1 amperes

10. C	430.32(C)	pg. 333

motor FLA = 54 amperes x 130% = 67.5 amperes

11. A	430.6 & 430.6(A)(1)	pg. 324

Table 430.250	pg. 351
430.22	pg. 329
Table 400.5(A)(1), Column A	pg. 269

40 hp FLC = 52 amperes x 125% = 65 amperes

Table 400.5(A)(1) indicates a size 2 AWG SO cord having an ampacity of 80 amperes is required.

12. D

430.6(A)(1)	pg. 324
Table 430.248	pg. 350
430.22	pg. 329
Table 310.15(B)(16)	pg. 161

7½ hp FLC = 40 amperes x 125% = 50 amperes

Table 310.15(B)(16) indicates size 8 AWG 75°C copper conductors should be selected.

13. D

430.32(A)(2)	pg. 332
Table 430.248	pg. 350

2 hp FLC = 24 amperes x 140% = 33.6 amperes

14. B

430.24(1)&(2)	pg. 330
Table 430.250	pg. 351
Table 310.15(B)(16)	pg. 161

10 hp FLC = 14 amperes x 100% = 14.00
15 hp FLC = 21 amperes x 100% = 21.00
20 hp FLC = 27 amperes x 125% = 33.75
                        TOTAL = 68.75 amperes

Table 310.15(B)(16) indicates size 4 AWG 75°C conductors with an ampacity of 85 amperes should be selected.

15. C

430.6(A)(1)	pg. 324
Table 430.248	pg. 350
Table 430.52	pg. 335

7½ hp FLC = 40 amperes x 175% = 70 amperes

16. B   430.52(C)(1), Exception 2(b)   pg. 335

7½ hp FLC = 40 amperes x 225% = 90 amperes

17.　D　　　　　　　　　　　Table 430.52　　　　　　　　pg. 335

7½ hp FLC = 40 amperes x 250% = 100 amperes

18.　A　　　　　　　　　　　430.6(A)(1)　　　　　　　　pg. 324
　　　　　　　　　　　　　　Table 430.250　　　　　　　pg. 351
　　　　　　　　　　　　　　430.110(A)　　　　　　　　pg. 344

25 hp FLC = 34 amperes x 115% = 39.1 amperes

19.　C　　　　　　　　　　　430.62(A)　　　　　　　　　pg. 338
　　　　　　　　　　　　　　Table 430.250　　　　　　　pg. 351

Largest OCP in group　= 70 amperes
30 hp FLC　　　　　　= 40 amperes
20 hp FLC　　　　　　= 27 amperes
20 hp FLC　　　　　　= 27 amperes
　　　　　　　TOTAL = 164 amperes

*NOTE – You are required to go down to 150 ampere rated fuses.

20.　B　　　　　　　　　　　Table 430.250　　　　　　　pg. 351
　　　　　　　　　　　　　　430.22　　　　　　　　　　pg. 329
　　　　　　　　　　　　　　Table 310.15(B)(2)(a)　　　pg. 158
　　　　　　　　　　　　　　Table 310.15(B)(16)　　　　pg. 161

15 hp FLC = 46.2 amperes

46.2 amperes x 125% = 57.75 amperes

$$\frac{57.75 \text{ amps}}{.75 \text{ (temp. cor.)}} = 77 \text{ amperes}$$

Size 4 AWG copper conductors rated for 75°C with an ampacity of 85 amperes should be selected.

PRACTICAL CALCULATIONS FOR ELECTRICIANS
UNIT 8
SELF-ASSESSMENT QUIZ
ANSWER KEY

___

ANSWER	REFERENCE	NEC PG. #
1. B	230.42(B)	pg. 87
	230.79(C)	pg. 91
2. A	220.12	pg. 67
3. C	Table 220.12	pg. 68
4. B	310.15(B)(7)(1)	pg. 160
	Table 310.15(B)(16)	pg. 161

150 amperes x 83% = 124.5 amperes
Size 1 AWG THHW copper conductors rated 75ºC with an ampacity of 130 amperes should be selected from Table 310.15(B)(16).

5. D	220.52(A)	pg. 70
	210.11(C)(1)	pg. 55

1,500 VA x 2 circuits = 3,000 VA

6. A	220.53	pg. 70
7. C	220.54	pg. 70 & 71
8. B	220.61(B)(1)	pg. 71
9. A	220.53	pg. 70
	Table 430.248	pg. 350

water heater	- 4.5 kW x 1,000	= 4,500 VA
dishwasher	- 1,250 VA	= 1,250 VA
garbage disposal	- 3/4 HP – 13.8 amps x 120 volts	= 1,656 VA
trash compactor	- 1/2 HP – 9.8 amps x 120 volts	= 1,176 VA
attic fan	- 1/3 HP – 7.2 amps x 120 volts	= 864 VA
	Connected Load	= 9,446 VA
	(Demand)	x 75%
	Demand Load	= 7,085 VA

| 10. | D | Table 220.55 | pg. 72 |
| | | 220.61(B)(1) | pg. 71 |

8kW (Tbl. 220.55) x 70% = 5,600 VA

| 11. | C | Power Formula | |
| | | 220.54 | pg. 70 |

P = I x E = 30 amperes x 240 volts = 7,200 VA

| 12. | D | Table 220.12 | pg. 68 |

35 feet x 75 feet = 2,625 square feet
2,625 square feet x 3 VA = 7,875 VA

| 13. | A | Table 220.42 | pg. 70 |

14.	D	220.12	pg. 67
		Table 220.12	pg. 68
		220.52(A)&(B)	pg. 70
		Table 220.42	pg. 70

2,500 sq. ft. + 1,250 sq. ft. = 3,750 sq. ft.

3,750 sq. ft. x 3 VA	= 11,250 VA
3 small appl. circuits x 1,500 VA	= 4,500 VA
1 laundry circuit x 1,500 VA	= 1,500 VA
TOTAL CONNECTED LOAD	= 17,250 VA

First, 3,000 VA at 100%	= 3,000 VA
remainder (17,250 – 3,000) 14,250 VA at 35%	= 4,988 VA
	7,988 VA

| 15. | A | 220.82(C)(1) | pg. 73 |

| 16. | D | 220.82(C)(5) | pg. 73 |

| 17. | C | 220.82(B)(3)b. | pg. 73 |

10 kw x 1,000 = 10,000 VA

| 18. | B | 220.82(A) | pg. 73 |

220.61(B)(1)   pg. 71

10,000 VA x 70% = 7,000 VA

19. D   220.82(B)   pg. 73

20. B   220.82(B)   pg. 73

- General lighting and receptacles   = 17,500 VA
- Small appliance and laundry circuits   =   7,500 VA
- Fastened in place appliances and motors   = 40,500 VA
- TOTAL GENERAL LOAD   = 65,500 VA

1st 10,000 VA @ 100%   = 10,000 VA
Remainder (total – 10,000) = 55,500 VA @ 40%   = 22,200 VA
DEMAND LOAD   = 32,200 VA

PRACTICAL CALCULATIONS FOR ELECTRICIANS
UNIT 9
SELF-ASSESSMENT QUIZ
ANSWER KEY

ANSWER	REFERENCE	NEC® PG. #
1. B	310.15(B)(7)(1) Table 310.15(B)(16)	pg. 160 pg. 161
2. D	210.11(C)(1) 220.52(A)	pg. 55 pg. 70
3. A	220.53	pg. 70
4. B	220.54	pg. 70
5. D	220.61(B)(1)	pg. 71
6. C	220.61(B)(2)	pg. 71
7. A	220.82(A)	pg. 73
8. D	220.84(A)(1)&(3)	pg. 74
9. D	220.60	pg. 71
10. B	General Knowledge	

900 sq. ft. x 4 units = 3,600 sq. ft.
1,100 sq. ft. x 6 units = 6,600 sq. ft.
        Total   = 10,200 sq. ft.

| 11. B | Table 220.12
210.11(C)(1)
220.52(A) | pg. 68
pg. 55
pg. 70 |

General Lighting – 840 sq. ft. x 20 units x 3 VA = 50,400 VA
Small appl. circuits – 15,000 VA x 2 x 20 units = 60,000 VA
Laundry Circuit   =   -0-
            Total Connected Load   = 110,400 VA

Apply demand factors – Table 220.42
First 3,000 VA @ 100%   =   3,000 VA
Remainder (110,400 – 3,000) 107,400 @ 35% = 37,590 VA
            Demand Load   = 40,590 VA

| 12. C | 220.53 | pg. 70 |

Disposal –   846 VA x 16 units = 13,824 VA
Dishwasher –   1,250 VA x 16 units = 20,000 VA
Water Heater – 3,600 VA x 16 units = 57,600 VA
                                                              91,424 VA
                    (Demand Factor)   x 75%
                                                              68,568 VA

13. C   220.54   pg. 70
                                 Table 220.54   pg. 71

        5,000 VA (MINIMUM) x 10 units = 50,000 VA
                        (demand)   x   50%
                                                      25,000 VA

14. A   Table 220.55   pg. 72

        Col. B – 8,000 VA x 6 units = 48,000 VA x 43% = 20,640 VA
        Col. C – 9,000 VA – demand for 6 ranges   = 21,000 VA
                                                                                41,640 VA

        *NOTE: Column C of Table 220.55 indicates a demand of 27 kW for twelve
        ranges. The smaller value is permitted to be used instead of the higher value.

15. A   Table 220.42   pg. 70

        Connected Load = 200.2 kW x 1,000 = 200,200 VA

        First 3,00 VA @ 100%   =   3,000 VA
        Next 117,000 VA @ 35%   = 40,950 VA
        Remainder (200.2 kW -120 kW) = 80,200 VA @ 25% = 20,050 VA
                                                        Demand   = 64,000 VA

16. A   220.84(A)(1)&(2)   pg. 74
                                   210.11(C)(1)&(2)   pg. 55
                                   Table 220.84   pg. 74

        General lighting   1,250 sq. ft. x 3 VA x 14 units = 52,500 VA
        Small appl. circuits 1,500 VA x 2 x 14 units   = 42,000 VA
        Laundry Circuits   1,500 VA x 1 x 14 units   = 21,000 VA
                                                                        115,500 VA
                                             (demand)   x 40%
                                    demand load =   46,200 VA

17. A   220.84(C)(3)c.   pg. 74

Table 220.84   pg. 74

4,000 VA x 14 units = 56,000 VA
     (demand)   x 40%
                   22,400 VA

18. D   220.84(C)(3)b.   pg. 74
                              220.84(A)(3)   pg. 74
                              220.61(B)(1)   pg. 71

8,000 VA x 14 units = 112,000 VA (Connected load)
                   x 40%   [Table 220.84]
                   44,800
                   x 70%   [220.61(B)(1)]
               31,360 VA (demand)

19. B   220.84(C)(5)   pg. 75
                              Table 430.248   pg. 350

First, compare the two loads.

A/C = 17 amperes x 240 volts = 4,080 VA
Heat = 5,000 VA

Circulating motor – 4.9 amperes x 240 volts = 1,176 VA

Under this condition the heating load is the larger load, omit the smaller A/C load.

Heating = 5,000 + 1,176 VA (cir. motor) = 6,176 VA
                                     x 16 units
                               98,816 VA
                                x 39%
          (demand load)   38,538 VA

20. B   Current Formula
                          Table 310.15(B)(16)   pg. 161

$$I = P \div E \qquad I = \frac{90 \text{ kW x } 1{,}000}{240 \text{ volts}} = \frac{90{,}000}{240} = 375 \text{ amperes}$$

*NOTE: Table 310.15(B)(16) indicates 75°C rated size 500 kcmil conductors with an ampacity of 380 amperes should be selected.

PRACTICAL CALCULATIONS FOR ELECTRICIANS
UNIT 10
SELF-ASSESSMENT QUIZ
ANSWER KEY

ANSWER	REFERENCE	NEC PG. #
1. D	220.14(I)	pg. 69
	Table 220.44	pg. 70

75 receptacles x 180 VA = 13,500 VA (connected load)

$$1^{st} \ 10{,}000 \ VA \ at \ 100\% \ = \quad 10{,}000 \ VA$$
$$\text{Remainder (3,500 VA) at 50\%} \ = \quad \underline{1{,}750 \ VA}$$
$$11{,}750 \ VA \ \text{(demand load)}$$

| 2. D | Table 220.12 | pg. 68 |
| | 230.42(A)(1) | pg. 87 |

2,750 sq. ft. x 3.5 VA x 125% = 12,031 VA

| 3. D | 220.43(A) | pg. 69 |
| | 210.19(A)(1)(a) | pg. 57 |

200 VA x 150 ft. x 125% = 37,500 VA (load)

$$\text{circuits} \ = \ \frac{37{,}500 \ VA}{120 \ volts \ x \ 20 \ amps} \ = \ \frac{37{,}500 \ VA}{2{,}400} \ = \ 15.6 = 16 \ circuits$$

| 4. B | Table 220.12 | pg. 68 |
| | 210.19(A)(1)(a) | pg. 57 |

75,000 sq. ft. x 3.5 VA x 125% = 328,125 VA (load)

$$\text{circuits} \ = \ \frac{328{,}125 \ VA}{277 \ volts \ x \ 20 \ amps} \ = \ \frac{328{,}125}{5{,}540} \ = \ 59.2 = 60$$

| 5. B | 210.62 | pg. 63 |

$$\frac{36 \text{ ft. (length of show window)}}{12 \text{ ft. (length per receptacle)}} = 3 \text{ receptacles}$$

6. C   220.43(B)   pg. 70

$$\frac{150 \text{ VA} \ \text{x} \ 60 \text{ ft x} \ 125\%}{2} = \frac{11,250}{2} = 5,625 \text{ VA}$$

7. A   Trade Knowledge

*NOTE: 1 ton of A/C load = 2,400 VA
$$I = P \div E$$
$$I = \frac{10 \text{ tons} \ \text{x} \ 2,400 \text{ VA}}{208 \text{ volts x} \ 1.732} = \frac{24,000}{360.25} = 66.6 \text{ amperes}$$

8. C   220.14(F)   pg. 68
                               600.5(B)   pg. 543

1,200 VA x 4 circuits x 125% = 6,000 VA

9. B   Table 220.12   pg. 68
                               210.19(A)(1)(a)   pg. 57
                               220.14(K)(2)   pg. 69
                               600.5(A)   pg. 543

(lighting) 6,000 sq. ft. x 3.5 VA x 125% =   26,250 VA
(receptacles) 6,000 sq. ft. x 1 VA   =   6,000 VA
                                                    32,250 VA

$$\frac{32,250 \text{ VA}}{120 \text{ volts x} \ 20 \text{ amps}} = \frac{32,250}{2,400} = 13.4 = 14 \text{ ltg. & recpt. circuits}$$
$$+ \ 1 \text{ sign circuit}$$
$$\text{TOTAL} \ \ 15 \text{ circuits}$$

10. C   Table 220.12   pg. 68
                               230.42(A)(1)   pg. 87

	220.14(H)&(I)	pg. 68 & 69
	Table 220.44	pg. 70
	Current Formula	

<u>Lighting</u> 20,000 sq. ft. x 3.5 VA x 125%   =[87,500 VA]

<u>Receptacles</u> 180 VA x 200 =   36,000 VA
<u>Multioutlet Assembly</u> 75 ft ÷ 5 = 15 x 180 VA =   2,700 VA
                                        38,700 VA

Apply demand factors (Table 220.44)
First 10 kVA at 100% =   10,000 VA
28,700 VA (remainder) at 50% =   14,350 VA
                                      24,350 VA =[24,350 VA]

                        TOTAL =111,850 VA

I = P ÷ E x 1.732
I =   111,850 VA   =   111,850 = 310.4 amperes
       208 volts x 1.732   360.25

11. D   Current Formula
                         440.32   pg. 356

*NOTE: 1 ton of A/C = 2,400 VA

I = P ÷ E
I = 7.5 tons x 2,400 VA =   18,000 = 86 amperes
         208 volts   208

86 amperes x 1.25 = 107.5 amperes

12. C   440.22(A)   pg. 355 &
356
                         240.6(A)   pg. 96 & 97

86 amperes x 225% = 193.5 amperes

*NOTE: Under this condition, you must go down to the next standard
      size circuit breaker which has a rating of 175 amperes.

13. A   220.60   pg. 71
                                Current Formula

              A/C Unit
              15 tons x 2,400 VA = 36,000 VA

              $I = \dfrac{36,000\ VA}{208\ volts\ x\ 1.732} = \dfrac{36,000}{360.25} = 100\ amperes$

              Heating Unit
              $I = \dfrac{30\ kW\ x\ 1,000}{208\ x\ 1.732} = \dfrac{30,000}{360.25} = 83\ amperes$

              *NOTE: The A/C unit is the larger load therefore the heating unit is
                     permitted to be omitted.

14. D   Table 220.56   pg. 71

              Water heater   - 9.0 kW
              fryer   - 7.5 kW
              grill   - 15 kW
              mixer   - 2.0 kW
              food warmer   - 4.0 kW
              freezer   - 3.5 kW
              refrigerator   - 2.5 kW
              dishwasher   - 2.0 kW
              booster heater   - 4.5 kW
                                   50 kW (connected load)
                                 x   65% [Table 220.56]
                                 32.5 kW (demand load)

15. B   550.30   pg. 512
                                  Table 550.31   pg. 512
                                  Current Formula

              15 lots x 36,000 VA =   540,000 VA
                                          x .26 [Table 550.31]
                                        140,400 VA (demand)

              $I = P \div E$
              $I = \dfrac{140,400\ VA}{240\ volts} = 585\ amperes$

16. A   551.71   pg. 524

        50 ampere – 125 sites x 20% = 25 receptacle outlets
        30 ampere – 125 sites x 70% = 88 receptacle outlets

17. D   551.73(A)   pg. 524

    20 sites x 600 VA = 12,000 VA

18. A   551.73(A)   pg. 524
                                  Table 551.73(A)   pg. 525
                                  Current Formula

    50/30 ampere sites – 9,600 VA x 50 sites =   480,000 VA
    30/20 ampere sites – 3,600 VA x 100 sites =   360,000 VA
                                                  840,000 VA
                                              x   .41 [Table
551.73(A)]

                                  344,400 VA (demand load)

    I = P ÷ E
    I = ___344,400 VA___   = _344,400_ = 956 amperes
           208 volts x 1.732   360.25

19. C   Current Formula
                                  422.13   pg. 304
                                  422.10(A)   pg. 303
                                  Table 310.15(B)(16)   pg. 161

    I = P ÷ E
    I = _9 kW x 1,000 x 125%_ = _11,250_ = 54 amperes
               208 volts   208

    *NOTE: Table 310.15(B)(16) indicates size 6 AWG conductors should
be   selected.

20. D   Current Formula
                                422.11(E)(3)   pg. 303
                                240.6(A)   pg. 96 & 97

$$I = P \div E$$
$$I = \frac{9\ kW \times 1{,}000 \times 150\%}{208\ volts} = \frac{13{,}500}{208} = 65\ amperes$$

*NOTE: A circuit breaker with a 70 ampere rating is permitted because you are allowed to go up to the next standard size circuit breaker.

PRACTICAL CALCULATIONS FOR ELECTRICIANS
FINAL EXAM
ANSWER KEY

ANSWER	REFERENCE	NEC® PG #
1. A	General Knowledge	
2. C	Current Formula	
3. B	General Knowledge	
4. B	Single-Phase Current Formula	

$$I = P \div E$$
$$I = \frac{7.2 \text{ kW} \times 1{,}000}{240 \text{ volts}} = \frac{7{,}200}{240} = 30 \text{ amperes}$$

5. D	General Knowledge	
6. D	Single-Phase Power Formula	

$$P = I \times E$$
$$P = 200 \text{ amperes} \times 240 \text{ volts} = 48{,}000 \text{ VA}$$

7. C	Power Factor Formula	

$$PF = \frac{10 \text{ kW} \times 1{,}000}{240 \text{ volts} \times 50 \text{ amps}} = \frac{10{,}000}{12{,}000} = .83 \text{ or } 83\%$$

8. B	Single-Phase Current Formula	

$$I = P \div E$$
$$I = \frac{12 \text{ kVA} \times 1{,}000}{240 \text{ volts}} = \frac{12{,}000}{240} = 50 \text{ amperes}$$

9. A	Three-Phase Current Formula	

$$I = P \div E \times 1.732$$
$$I = \frac{90 \text{ kVA} \times 1{,}000}{208 \text{ volts} \times 1.732} = \frac{90{,}000}{360.25} = 249.8 \text{ amperes}$$

10. A	Single-Phase Current Formula	

$$I = \frac{\text{watts}}{\text{volts} \times PF} = \frac{400}{208 \times .92} = \frac{400}{191} = 2 \text{ amperes}$$

11. C   220.12   pg. 67 & 68

Table 220.12   pg. 68

60 ft. x 40 ft. = 2,400 sq. ft. x 3 VA = 7,200 VA

$$\text{Circuits} = \frac{7,200 \text{ VA}}{120 \text{ volts x 15 amps}} = \frac{7,200 \text{ VA}}{1,800 \text{ VA}} = 4 \text{ circuits}$$

12. D   Single-Phase Current Formula

422.11(E)(3)   pg. 303

240.6(A)   pg. 96

$$I = P \div E$$
$$I = \frac{4.5 \text{ kW x 1,000}}{240 \text{ volts}} = \frac{4,500}{240} = 18.75 \text{ amperes}$$
$$18.75 \text{ amperes x } 150\% = 28 \text{ amperes}$$

* The next higher standard circuit breaker has a rating of 30 amperes.

13. C   210.19(A)(1)(a)   pg. 57

80 amperes x 125% = 100 amperes

14. D   220.12   pg. 67 & 68

Table 220.12   pg. 68

20,000 sq. ft. x 3 VA = 60,000 VA
$$\text{Circuits} = \frac{60,000 \text{ VA}}{120 \text{ volts x 20 amps.}} = \frac{60,000 \text{ VA}}{24,000 \text{ VA}} = 25 \text{ circuits}$$

15. A   Power Formula

210.20(A)   pg. 58

$$P = I \text{ x } E \text{ x } 80\%$$
$$P = 30 \text{ amperes x } 240 \text{ volts x } 80\% = 5,760 \text{ VA}$$

16. B   Table 220.12   pg. 68
210.19(A)(1)(a)   pg. 57

$$\text{General ltg. circuits} = \frac{25,000 \text{ x 3 VA}}{120 \text{ x 20 x } 80\%} = \frac{75,000}{1,920} = 39 \text{ circuits}$$

$$\text{Accent ltg. circuits} = \frac{15,000 \text{ VA}}{120 \text{ x 20 x } 80\%} = \frac{15,000}{1,920} = 7.8 = 8 \text{ circuits}$$

39 circuits + 8 circuits = 47 Total Lighting Circuits

17. D   220.14(I)   pg. 69

        Circuits = $\dfrac{180\ VA \times 250}{120\ volts \times 20\ amps}$ = $\dfrac{45,000}{2,400}$ = 18.75 = 19 circuits

18. B   240.4(C)   pg. 95
                               240.6(A)   pg. 96

19. C   220.14(I)   pg. 69
                               230.42(A)(1)   pg. 87

        Duplex receptacles – 35 x 180 VA =   6,300

VA
        Single receptacles – 10 x 180 VA (minimum) x 125% = 2,250 VA
                                                           8,550 VA

20. D   220.14(H)(2)   pg. 69
                               210.19(A)(1)(a)   pg. 57

        Circuits = $\dfrac{60\ ft. \times 180\ VA \times 125\%}{120\ volts \times 20\ amps}$ = $\dfrac{13,500}{2,400}$ = 5.6 = 6 circuits

21. A   220.14(I)   pg. 69
                               Single-Phase Current Formula

        180 VA x 50 (receptacles) = 9,000 VA
        I = P ÷ E
        I = $\dfrac{9,000}{240\ volts}$ = 37.5 amperes

22. B   424.3(B)   pg.
308
                               210.19(A)(1)(A)   pg. 57

        Circuits = $\dfrac{1,500\ VA \times 16 \times 125\%}{240\ volts \times 30\ amps}$ = $\dfrac{30,000}{7,200}$ = 4.1 = 5 circuits

23. A   Note 4 to Table 220.55   pg. 72
                               Table 220.55, Column C   pg. 72

24. C   Notes 1 & 4 to Table 220.55   pg. 72
                               Table 220.55, Column C   pg. 72
                               Current Formula

14 kW – 12 kW = 2 kW x 5% = 10% increase in Column C
Column C demand (1 range) = 8 kW x 110% = 8.8 kW

$I = P \div E$
$I = \dfrac{8.8 \text{ kW} \times 1{,}000}{240 \text{ volts}} = \dfrac{8{,}800}{240} = 36.6 \text{ amperes}$

25. C   422.13   pg. 304

                          422.10(A)   pg. 303

                   Single-Phase Current Formula

$I = P \div E$
$I = \dfrac{10 \text{ kW} \times 1{,}000}{208 \text{ volts}} = \dfrac{10{,}000}{208} = 48 \text{ amperes}$

48 amperes x 125% = 60 amperes

26. D   220.53   pg. 70

9 units x 4 kW x 75% (demand) = 27 kW

27. B   220.54   pg. 70

28. A   Table 220.56   pg. 71
                          Current Formula

8 kW + 7.5 kW + 2 kW + 2.5 kW + 3 kW = 23 kW Total
23 kW x 70% (demand) = 16.1 kW demand load

$I = P \div E$
$I = \dfrac{16.1 \text{ kW} \times 1{,}000}{208 \text{ volts} \times 1.732} = \dfrac{16{,}100}{360.25} = 44.6 \text{ amperes}$

29. B   220.53   pg. 70

dishwasher	- 1,200 VA
water heater	- 5,000 VA
garbage disposer	- 864 VA
garage door opener	- 1,656 VA
attic fan	- 1,176 VA
trash compactor	- 1,176 VA
	11,072 VA
	x 75% Demand
	8,304 VA

30. C   Table 310.15(B)(16)   pg. 161

Table 310.15(B)(3)(a)
pg. 160

size 4 AWG THWN ampacity (before derating) — 85 amperes
85 x .8 (adjustment factor) = 68 amperes

31. A   314.16(B)(2)(4)&(5)   pg. 185

single-pole switch   = 2 conductors
duplex receptacle   = 2 conductors
bonding jumper   = 0 conductors
cable clamps   = 1 conductor
grounding conductors   = <u>1 conductor</u>
Total = 6 conductors

32. A   Table 314.16(B)   pg. 186

*NOTE: Disregard conductor insulation when doing box fill calculations.

Size 12 AWG - 2.25 x 6 = 13.5 cubic inches
Size 10 AWG - 2.50 x 6 = 15.0 cubic inches
Size 8 AWG - 3.00 x 4 = <u>12.0 cubic inches</u>
Total = 40.5 cubic inches

33. D   Single-Phase Current Formula

Table 310.15(B)(16)   pg. 161

$$I = \frac{kVA \times 1{,}000}{volts}$$

$$I = \frac{40\ kVA \times 1{,}000}{240\ volts} = \frac{40{,}000}{240\ volts} = 167\ amperes$$

*NOTE: Size 2/0 AWG 75°C conductors with an ampacity of 175 amperes should be selected.

34. D   Table 310.15(B)(16)   pg. 161

Table 310.15(B)(2)(a)
pg. 158

1/0 THW ampacity (before derating) = 150 amperes
150 amps x .75 (temp. correction) = 112.5 amperes

35. B   Chapter 9, Table 8   pg. 766

Single-Phase Voltage Drop Formula

$$VD = \frac{2 \times K \times I \times D}{CM}$$

$$VD = \frac{2 \times 12.9 \times 60 \text{ amps} \times 175 \text{ ft.}}{26,240 \text{ cm}} = \frac{270,900}{26,240} = 10.3 \text{ volts}$$

36. C   210.19(A)(1), IN #4   pg. 57

120 volts x 3% = 3.6 volts

37. D   Chapter 9, Table 5   pg. 763

1/0 THWN = .1855 sq. in x 3 = .5565 square inches
2/0 THWN = .2223 sq. in. x 3 = .6669 square inches
                    Total =   1.2234 square inches

38. B   Chapter 9, Table 4   pg. 757

39. A   Chapter 9, Table 8   pg. 766

40. B   Chapter 9, Table 5   pg. 762-764

                                   Chapter 9, Table 4   pg. 757

#12 THHN   - .0133 x 4 = .0532 square inches
6 THW   - .0726 x 3 = .2178 square inches
4 THW   - .0973 x 3 = .2919 square inches
2 XHHW   - .1146 x 3 = .3438 square inches
              Total   = .9067 square inches

*NOTE: This installation requires a trade size 1½ in. EMT with an allowable fill of 1.221 sq. in. at 60% permitted fill.

41. B   314.16   pg. 185

                                   314.16(B)(1),(2) &(4)   pg. 185

                                   Table 314.16(B)   pg. 186

                                   Table 314.16(A)   pg. 186

```
Size 12 AWG THHN              =  2.25 x 6  =  13.50 cu. in.
switch  =  2 size 12 AWG wires  =  2.25 x 2  =   4.50 cu. in.
                                      Total    18.00 cu. in.
```

42. C   Chapter 9, Note 4   pg. 756

                         Chapter 9, Table 4   pg. 758

                         Chapter 9, Table 5   pg. 764

2½ in. IMC @ 60% fill = 3.081 sq. in. (allowable fill)

$$\frac{3.081 \text{ sq. in. (allowable fill)}}{.3197 \text{ sq. in. (wire)}} = 9.6 \text{ or } 9 \text{ wires}$$

43. B   220.82(C)(4)   pg. 73
                         220.60   pg. 71

15,000 VA (heating load) x 65% = 9,750 VA
*NOTE: The heating load is greater than the 100% demand load of the
            A/C unit, so the smaller of the two is permitted to be omitted.

44. D   Table 310.15(B)(16)   pg. 161

                         Table 310.15(B)(2)(a)   pg. 158

                         Table 310.15(B)(3)(a)   pg. 160

#10 - 75°C rated ampacity (before derating) = 35 amperes
35 amperes x .88 (temp. cor.) x .7 (adjustment factor) = 21.5 amperes

45. B   Chapter 9, Table 8   pg. 766
                         Wire Size Formula

$$CM = \frac{2 \times K \times I \times D}{VD}$$

$$CM = \frac{2 \times 12.9 \times 16 \text{ amps} \times 100 \text{ ft.}}{3.6 \text{ volts (3\% of 120 volts)}} = \frac{41,288}{3.6} = 11,467 \text{ CM}$$

*NOTE: Size 8 AWG with a CMA of 16,510 should be selected.

46. C   334.80   pg. 205

                         Table 310.15(B)(16)   pg. 161

                         310.15(B)(3)(a)   pg. 157

247

Table 310.15(B)(3)(a)
pg. 160

30 amps. x 70% (adj. factor) = 21 amperes

*NOTE: Under this condition, all grounded and ungrounded conductors
are considered to be current-carrying.

47. C   Single-Phase Current Formula
                                    310.15(B)(7)(1)   pg.
160
                                              Table 310.15(B)(16)   pg.
161

I = P ÷ E

I = $\underline{36,000 \text{ VA}}$ = 150 amperes x 83% = 124.5 amperes
            240 volts

*NOTE- Size 2/0 AWG aluminum 75°C conductors with an ampacity
of
                        135 amperes should be selected from Table
310.15(B)(16).

48. D   230.42(A)(1)   pg. 87
                                    240.4(B)(1),(2),&(3)   pg. 94 &
95
                                    240.6(A)   pg. 96 & 97
                                    Single-Phase Current Formula

Continuous load = 16,200 VA x 125% = 20,250 VA
Non-Continuous load   = $\underline{12,200 \text{ VA}}$
                                Total   = 32,450 VA
I = P ÷ E
I = $\underline{32,450 \text{ VA}}$ = 135 amperes
            240 volts

*NOTE: Under this condition you are permitted to go up to the next
standard size fuses.

49. A   Table 314.16(A)   pg.
186
                                    314.16(B)(1)(4)   pg.
185

allowable #12 per gang = 9 conductors
switch   = $\underline{\text{-2 conductors}}$
                                7 conductors per gang may be added
                              $\underline{\text{x 4 gang}}$
                                28 total conductors may be added

50. B   Table 310.15(B)(16)   pg. 161

               Table 310.15(B)(2)(a)
pg. 158
               Table 310.15(B)(3)(a)
pg. 160

4/0 THWN ampacity (before derating) = 230 amperes
230 amps. x .88 (temp. correction) x .8 (adj. factor) = 161.9 amperes

51. A   376.22(A)   pg. 237
237
               Chapter 9, Table 5A   pg. 765
765

4" x 4" = 16 sq. in. x 20% = 3.2 sq. in. (allowable fill)

$$\frac{3.2 \text{ sq. in. (allowable fill)}}{.1855 \text{ sq. in. (wire)}} = 17.2 \text{ or } 17 \text{ wires}$$

52. B   Chapter 9, Table 5   pg. 763
763
               376.22(A)   pg. 237
237

500 kcmil THWN = .7073 x 3 = 2.1219 sq. in.
250 kcmil THWN = .3970 x 3 = 1.1910 sq. in.
4/0 AWG THWN = .3237 x 3 = .9711 sq. in.
                 Total   = 4.2840 sq. in.

$$\frac{4.2840 \text{ sq. in. (area of wires)}}{20\% \text{ (permitted fill)}} = 21.42 \text{ sq. in. required}$$

A 6 in. x 6 in. wireway with an area of 36 square inches is required.

53. D   Trade Knowledge

54. C   430.6(A)(1)   pg. 324
324
               Table 430.248
pg. 350
               430.22   pg. 329
329

5 hp FLC = 30.8 amperes x 125% = 38.5 amperes

55. B	Table 310.15(B)(16)	pg. 161
56. A	Table 310.15(B)(17)	pg. 162
57. D	430.6(A)(1)	pg. 324
	Table 430.250	
pg. 351	430.52(C)(1), Ex. 2(C)	
pg. 335		
	240.6(A)	pg. 96 & 97

40 hp, 3 ph., 230 volt, FLC = 104 amperes
104 amperes x 300% = 312 amperes

*NOTE: Under this condition, you must go down to the next standard size circuit breaker.

58. C	430.52(C)(1),Ex.2(b)	
pg. 335		
	240.6(A)	pg. 96 & 97

104 amperes x 225% = 234 amperes
*NOTE: Exceeding 225% of the FLC of the motor is not permitted when using time-delay fuses therefore, fuses with a rating of no more than 225 amperes should be selected.

| 59. D | Table 220.42 | pg. 70 |

205.4 kVA x 1,000 = 205,400 VA

First 3,000 VA @ 100%   = 3,000 VA
3,001 to 120,000 VA @ 35% = 117,000 VA @ 35%   = 40,950 VA
Remainder 205,400 VA – 120,000 VA = 85,400 @ 25% = 21,350 VA
                                    Demand   = 65,300 VA

$\frac{65,300 \text{ VA}}{1,000}$ = 65.3 kVA

| 60. C | 430.109(C)(2) | |
| pg. 344 | | |

15 amperes x 80% = 12 amperes

61. B   430.24(1) & (2)   pg. 330

Motor #1 - 10 amperes x 100% = 10.0 amperes
Motor #2 - 20 amperes x 100% = 20.0 amperes
Motor #3 - 30 amperes x 125% = 37.5 amperes
                    Total   = 67.5 amperes

62. D   110.14(C)   pg. 38
                                Table 310.15(B)(16)   pg. 161

63. B   334.80   pg. 205

                                Table 310.15(B)(16)   pg. 161

                                Table 310.15(B)(2)(a)   pg. 158

size 8 AWG before derating (90°C column) = 55 amperes
55 amperes x .76 (temp. correction) = 41.8 amperes

64. A   310.15(B)(5)(c)   pg. 158

65. C   Single-Phase Current Formula
                                Table 310.15(B)(16)   pg. 161

                                Table 310.15(B)(2)(a)   pg. 158

$$I = \frac{36{,}000 \text{ VA}}{240 \text{ volts}} = 150 \text{ ampere load}$$

$$\text{required ampacity} = \frac{150 \text{ amperes}}{.75 \text{ (temp. correction)}} = 200 \text{ amperes}$$

66. D   Table 310.15(B)(16)   pg. 161

                                Table 310.15(B)(2)(a)   pg. 158

$$\text{Required Ampacity} = \frac{150 \text{ amperes} \times 125\%}{.75 \text{ (temp. correction)}} = \frac{187.5}{.75} = 250 \text{ amperes}$$

67. A   220.14(I)   pg. 69
                      Table 220.44   pg. 70
                      Current Formula

75 receptacles x 180 VA = 13,500 VA

First 10,000 VA @ 100%   = 10,000 VA
3,500 VA (remainder) @ 50%   =   1,750 VA
             Demand   = 11,750 VA

$$I = \frac{11,750 \text{ VA}}{480 \times 1.732} = \frac{11,750}{831.36} = 14 \text{ amperes}$$

68. D   220.12   pg. 67 & 68
                      Table 220.12   pg. 68
                      230.42(A)(1)   pg. 87

100 ft. x 75 ft. = 7,500 sq. ft. x 3 VA = 22,250 VA
22,250 VA x 125% = 28,125 VA

69. A   210.19(A)(1)(a)   pg. 57
                      210.11(A)   pg. 55

$$\text{\# of circuits} = \frac{14,000 \text{ VA} \times 125\%}{120 \text{ volts} \times 20 \text{ amps}} = \frac{17,500 \text{ VA}}{2,400 \text{ VA}} = 7.2 = 8 \text{ circuits}$$

*NOTE: Branch circuits need only to supply the actual connected load.

70. B   220.43(A)   pg. 69
                      230.42(A)(1)   pg. 87

50 ft. x 200 VA = 10,000 VA x 125% = 12,500 VA

71. C   220.14(I)   pg. 69

180 VA x 115 receptacles = 20,700 VA (load)

$$\text{\# of circuits} = \frac{20,700 \text{ VA}}{120 \text{ volts} \times 20 \text{ amps}} = \frac{20,700 \text{ VA}}{2,400 \text{ VA}} = 8.6 = 9 \text{ circuits}$$

72. D   220.14(H)(2)   pg. 69
                      220.14(I)   pg. 69
                      Table 220.44   pg. 70

multioutlet assembly – 180 VA x 50 ft. =   9,000 VA
Receptacles - 180 VA x 115   = 20,700 VA
                                    29,700 VA

Table 220.44
First 10,000 VA @ 100%   = 10,000 VA
19,700 VA (remainder) @ 50%   = <u>9,850 VA</u>
                    Demand   = 19,850 VA

73. D   220.14(F)   pg. 68
543   600.5(B)   pg.

1,200 VA x 2 signs x 125% = 3,000 VA

74. B   220.43(B)   pg. 70
                         230.42(A)(1)   pg. 87

40 ft. ÷ 2 x 150 VA x 125% = 3,750 VA

75. C   430.6(A)(2)   pg.
324
                         430.32(A)(1)   pg.
332

38 amperes x 1.25 = 47.5 amperes

76. A   430.32(C)   pg.
333

38 amperes x 140% = 53.2 amperes

77. A   Table 310.104(A)   pg.
176
                         Table 310.15(B)(16)   pg.
161
pg. 158   Table 310.15(B)(2)(a)

                         Table 310.15(B)(3)(a)
pg. 160

1/0 THHW @ 75°C ampacity (before derating) = 150 amperes
150 amperes x .82 (temp. corrrection) x .8 (adj. factor) = 98.4
amperes

78. B   430.6(A)(1)   pg.
324
                         Table 430.250
pg. 351

430.24(1) & (2) pg. 330

Table 310.15(B)(16) pg. 161

FLC of 50 hp = 65 x 125% = 81.25 amperes
FLC of 50 hp = 65 x 100% = 65.00 amperes
FLC of 40 hp = 52 x 100% = 52.00 amperes
                Total   = 198.25 amperes

*NOTE: Size 3/0 AWG 75ºC conductors with an ampacity of 200 amperes
should be selected.

79. A 314.28(A)(2) pg. 190

3.5 in. x 6 = 21 inches

80. D 430.6(A)(1) pg. 324

Table 430.250 pg. 351

430.22 pg. 329

Table 310.15(B)(16) pg. 161

Motor FLC = 74.8 amperes x 125% = 93.5 amperes

$$\frac{93.5 \text{ amperes}}{.75 \text{ (temp. correction)}} = 124.6 \text{ amperes}$$

*NOTE: Size 1 AWG 75ºC conductors with an ampacity of 130 amperes
should be selected.

81. C 220.84(A) pg. 74
Table 220.84 pg. 74

    25,200 VA
    45,000 VA
   150,500 VA
    48,800 VA
   269,500 VA (connected load)
   x   43%   [Tbl. 220.84]
   115,885 VA

82. C   551.73(A)   pg. 524

                                Table 551.73(A)   pg. 525

                                3-Phase Current Formula

50/30 ampere RV sites - 9,600 VA x 30 = 288,000 VA
30/20 ampere RV sites - 3,600 VA x 30 = 108,000 VA
20 ampere RV sites -   2,400 VA x 10 =   24,000 VA
20 ampere tent sites -   600 VA x 5 =   3,000 VA
                                                        432,000 VA
              Tbl. 551.73 (demand)   x   .41
              Demand Load   173,430 VA

I = $\frac{173,430 \text{ VA}}{208 \times 1.732}$ = $\frac{173,430}{360.25}$ = 481 amperes

83. B   550.31(1)   pg. 512

                                Table 550.31   pg. 512

16,000 VA (minimum) x 25 lots = 400,000 VA
        Tbl. 550.31 (demand) =   x .24
              Demand Load   96,000 VA

84. D   430.6(A)(1)   pg. 324

                                Table 430.250   pg. 351

                                Table 430.52   pg. 335

                                430.52(C)(1), Ex. 1   pg. 335

                                240.6(A)   pg. 96

        10 hp FLC = 30.8 amperes x 175% = 53.9 amperes

*NOTE: The next standard size fuses have an ampere rating of 60 amperes.

85. A   Table 430.52   pg. 335

        10 hp FLC = 30.8 amperes x 250% = 77 amperes

86. A   Table 430.250   pg. 351

                         430.62(A)   pg. 338

                         240.6(A)   pg. 96 & 97

20 hp, 480 volts, 3-phase, FLC = 27 amperes

50 A (largest OCP in group) + 27 A + 27 A = 104 amperes

*NOTE: When sizing overcurrent protection for motor feeder conductors   you are NOT permitted to go up to the next standard size fuses
                         or circuit breaker.

87. D   Chapter 9, Table 8   pg. 766

VD = 120 volts x 3% = 3.6 volts

$$D = \frac{CM \times VD}{2 \times K \times I}$$

$$D = \frac{10,380 \times 3.6}{2 \times 12.9 \times 16} = \frac{37,368}{413} = 90 \text{ feet}$$

88. C   Table 314.16(B)   pg. 186

Size 12 AWG = 2.25 cu. in. x 7 wires = 15.75 cu. in.

30 cu. in. (total) – 15.75 cu. in. = 14.25 cu. in. (remaining space)

$$\frac{14.25 \text{ cu. in}}{2.5 \text{ cu. in. (#10)}} = 5.7 = 5 \text{ size 10 AWG wires may be added}$$

89. D   Note 4, to Chapter 9 Tables   pg. 756

                         Chapter 9, Table 4   pg. 759

                         Chapter 9, Table 5   pg. 763

1½ in. rigid metal conduit @ 60% fill   = 1.2430 sq. in.
6 AWG THWN/THHN = .0507 x 4 wires   = -.2028 sq. in.
                         Remaining Space= 1.0402 sq. in.

$$\frac{1.042 \text{ sq. in. (remaining space)}}{.0211 \text{ sq. in. (#10 THWN/THHN)}} = 49 \text{ #10 AWG wires may be added}$$

Outside temp.   = 100 ° F
Adder (3 in. above roof) = <u>40 ° F</u>
Total Temp.   = 140 ° F (for derating purposes)

Size 8 AWG ampacity (before derating) = 50 amperes
50 amperes x .58 (temperature correction) = 29 amperes

NOTES

Glossary

Adjustable-trip circuit breakers: Circuit breakers whose trip setting can be changed by adjusting the ampere rating, trip time characteristics, or both, within a
   particular range.

Aluminum wire: An electrical conductor composed of aluminum metal.

Ambient temperature: The surrounding temperature present in a specific area.

American Wire Gauge (AWG): Standard used to identify the size of a wire.

Ampacity: The maximum current, in amperes that a conductor can carry continuously, under the conditions of use without exceeding the temperature rating.

Ampere: The unit of current measurement. The amount of current that will flow through a one ohm resistor when one volt is applied.

Appliance: Utilization equipment, installed to perform one or more functions, such as clothes washing, air conditioning, cooking, etc.

Appliance branch circuit: A branch circuit that supplies energy to one or more outlets to which appliances are to be connected.

Arc-Fault Circuit Interrupter (AFCI): A device intended to provide protection from the effects of arc faults by recognizing characteristics unique to arcing and by functioning to de-energize the circuit when an arc fault is detected.

Automatic: Performing a function without the necessity of human intervention.

Balanced load: The load of an electrical system, in which two or more branches are balanced and symmetrical with respect to voltage and intensity of current.

Ballast: An electrical circuit component used with discharge lighting luminaires to provide the voltage necessary to strike the mercury arc within the lamp, and then to limit the amount of current that flows through the lamp. (Examples of discharge lighting luminaires are fluorescent and HID lighting fixtures.)

Bare conductor: A conductor with no insulation or covering of any type.

Bonded (Bonding): Connected to establish electrical continuity and conductivity.

Bonding conductor: The conductor that connects the non-current carrying parts of electrical equipment, cable raceways or other enclosures to the approved system ground conductor.

Bonding jumper: A conductor used to assure the required electrical connection between metal parts of an electrical system.

Bonding jumper, System: The connection between the grounded circuit conductor and the supply-side bonding jumper, or the equipment grounding conductor, or both, at a separately derived system.

Box: A metallic or nonmetallic electrical enclosure used to house utilization equipment and devices, the support of luminaires and pulling or terminating conductors.

Branch circuit: That portion of a wiring system beyond the final overcurrent protection device protecting the circuit and the outlet(s).

Branch circuit, Multiwire: A branch circuit that consists of two or more ungrounded conductors that have a voltage between them, and a grounded conductor that has equal voltage between it and each ungrounded conductor of the circuit and that is connected to the neutral or grounded conductor of the system.

Branch-circuit rating: The ampere rating or setting of the overcurrent device protecting the conductors.

Building: A stand-alone structure or a structure which is separated from adjoining structures by fire walls.

Buried cable: A cable laid directly in the ground without being enclosed or protected in an electrical conduit.

Bus: A conductor, or group of conductors, that serve as a common connection for two or more circuits.

Busway: A sheet metal enclosure that contains factory assembled aluminum or copper busbars which are supported on insulators.

Cable: One or more insulated or non-insulated wires used to conduct electrical current.

Cable assembly: A flexible assembly containing multiconductors with a protective outer sheath.

Cablebus: An assembly of insulated conductors and terminations in an enclosed, ventilated protective metal housing.

Cable tray system: An assembly of sections and associated fittings which form a rigid structural system used to support cables and raceways.

Carrying capacity: The MAXIMUM current strength, in amperes, that a conductor can safely carry continuously. (See ampacity)

Celsius: A unit of measurement, in degrees, for temperature at which the freezing point is 0° and the boiling point is 100°. It is commonly represented by the letter "C".

Circuit: A complete path over which an electric current can flow.

Circuit breaker: A device which opens and closes circuits by nonautomatic means and opens circuits automatically when a predetermined overcurrent exists.

Circuit voltage: The greatest effective difference of potential between any two conductors in a given circuit.

Circular mil (CM): A measurement of the cross-sectional area of a conductor. The area of one circular mil equals .001 inches in diameter.

Circular mil foot: A unit of conductor size, equal to a portion of the conductor having a cross-sectional area of one circular mil and length of one foot.

Clamp: A device intended to secure raceways, tubing or cables.

Commercial equipment: Equipment intended to be used on commercial, industrial or institutional premises, such as schools, hotels, office buildings, manufacturing facilities, libraries and other public buildings.

Computer: An electronic machine which, by means of stored instructions and information, performs rapid, often complex calculations or compiles, correlates and selects data.

Conductor: A wire that is used to transmit the flow of electrons in an electrical circuit. Copper wire is the most common conductor used today in the electrical industry.

Conduit: A metallic or nonmetallic pipe or tubing used to enclosed conductors.

Connected load: The sum of the rating(s) of the load consuming equipment, connected to an electrical system or any part thereof.

Contactor: An electrically operated switch, usually by a coil or solenoid. The switch contains one or more sets of contacts which controls one or more circuits.

Continuous duty: Operation at a substantially constant load for an indefinitely long time.

Continuous load: A load in which the MAXIMUM current may continue for three hours or more.

Controller: A device, or group of devices, which serves to govern in some predetermined manner the electric power delivered to the apparatus to which it is connected.

Control panel: A panel containing switches and other protective, controlling and measuring devices for electrical equipment, motors, and/or machinery.

Copper: A brownish-red, malleable, ductile, metallic element that is an excellent conductor of electricity and heat. The most common element used for conductors in the electrical industry.

Copper Wire: An electrical conductor composed of copper metal.

Cord: A small cable, very flexible, and substantially insulated to withstand wear. There is no sharp dividing line in respect to size between a cord and a cable, and likewise no sharp dividing line in respect to the character of insulation between a cord and a stranded wire.

Cord-and-plug connected appliance: An appliance to be connected to the power source by means of a supply cord.

Cord-connected unit: A unit intended for connection to the power source by means of a supply cord to prevent vibration or enable the unit to be moved.

Cross-section: A cutting or piece of something cut off at right angles to an axis. The cross-sectional area is 100% of the cross-section.

Current: The flow of electricity in a circuit, measured in amperes. Represented by the letter "I" or "A".

Current transformer (CT): An instrument transformer with a primary winding in series with a current-carrying conductor and secondary winding connected to a meter or device which is actuated by conductor current and current changes.

Demand factor: The ratio of the MAXIMUM demand of a system, or part of a system, to the total connected load of a system or the part of the system under consideration. All the loads of a system are usually never used all at the same time due to the many uses of the power.

Device box: A box which houses an electrical device(s), such as receptacles and switches.

Device: Electrical components, such as receptacles, switches and dimmers, that are designed to carry and/or control electric energy as its principle function, but not use electricity.

Disconnecting means: A device, or group of devices, by which the circuit conductors are disconnected from their source of supply.

Double pole: Switch or device connected to both lines of a circuit or controlling both lines of a circuit.

Dry location: A location not normally subject to dampness or wetness. A location classified as dry may be temporarily subject to dampness or wetness, as in the case of a building under construction.

Duty cycle: The time interval occupied by a device on intermittent duty in starting, running, stopping and idling.

Dwelling: A structure that contains eating, living and sleeping space and permanent provisions for cooking and sanitation.

Dwelling unit: A dwelling with one or more rooms used by one or more people for housekeeping.

Effectively grounded: Grounded with sufficient low impedance and current-carrying capacity to prevent hazardous voltage build-ups.

Efficiency: The ratio of output power to input power, expressed as a percentage.

Electrical discharge luminaire: A luminaire (lighting fixture) that utilizes a ballast for the operation of the lamp.

Electrical metallic tubing (EMT): A lightweight tubular steel raceway used to enclosed conductors.

Electric circuit: The complete path of an electric current.

Electric power production and distribution network: Power production, distribution, and utilization equipment and facilities, such as electric utility systems that deliver electric power to the connected loads, that are external to and not controlled by an interactive system.

Electric sign: A fixed, stationary, or portable self-contained, electrically illuminated, utilization equipment with words or symbols designed to convey information or attract attention.

Electrode: A conducting substance through which electric current enters or leaves.

Enclosed: Surrounded by a case, housing, fence or walls which will prevent persons from accidentally contacting energized parts.

Enclosure: The case or housing of equipment or other apparatus which provides protection from live or energized parts.

Equipment: A general term including devices, luminaires, appliances, materials, machinery, apparatus, etc. used in conjunction with electrical installations.

Equipment bonding jumper: A conductor that connects two or more parts of the equipment grounding conductor.

Equipment grounding conductor: An electrical conductor that provides a low-impedance path between electrical equipment and enclosures and the system grounded conductor and grounding electrode conductor.

Explosionproof equipment: Equipment enclosed in a case that is capable of withstanding an explosion of a specified gas or vapor that may occur within it and is capable of preventing the ignition of a specified gas or vapor surrounding the enclosure by sparks, flashes, or explosion of the gas or vapor within, and that is operated at such an external temperature that a surrounding flammable atmosphere will not be ignited thereby.

Fahrenheit: A unit of measurement, in degrees, for temperature at which the freezing point is 32° and the boiling point is 212°. It is commonly represented by the letter "F".

Fault: An electrical defect.

Fault current: Any current that travels an unwanted path, other than the normal operating path of an electrical system.

Feeder: All circuit conductors between the service equipment or the source of a separately derived system and the final branch circuit overcurrent device.

Feeder neutral load: The maximum unbalanced load between any of the ungrounded conductors and the grounded conductor of a feeder.

Fished: A means of installing electrical wiring in existing inaccessible hollow spaces of buildings with a minimum damage to the building finish.

Fixed appliance: An appliance which is fastened or otherwise secured at a specific location.

Fixed equipment: Equipment intended to be permanently connected electrically and not easily moved.

Flexible cord: An assembly of two or more insulated conductors, with or without braids, contained within an overall outer covering and used for the connection of equipment to a power source.

Flexible metal conduit (FMC): A raceway consisting of metal strips which are formed into a circular cross-sectional raceway, which is used to enclose conductors.

Fluorescent light: A method of lighting which makes use of ultraviolet energy to activate a fluorescent material coated inside of the bulb's surface.

Full-load amperes (FLA): The amount of current, in amperes, in an electrical circuit when the load is operating in a full-capacity condition.

Full-load current (FLC): The current required by a motor to produce the full-load torque at the motor's rated speed.

Fuse: A protective device with a fusible element that opens the circuit by melting when subjected to excessive current.

Galvanizing: The process of coating metals with zinc to prevent corrosion.

Ganged switch box: A box containing more than one switch.

General lighting: Lighting designed to provide a substantially uniform level of illumination throughout an area, exclusive of any provision for special local requirements.

General-purpose branch circuit: A branch circuit that supplies a number of outlets for lighting and appliances.

General-use snap switch: A form of general-use switch constructed so that it can be installed in device and/or outlet boxes.

General-use switch: A switch for use in general distribution and branch circuits. The ampere rated switch is capable of interrupting its rated current at its rated voltage.

General-use receptacle: 125-volt, single-phase, 15-or-20 ampere receptacles connected to a branch-circuit supplying two or more receptacles provided for the purpose of supplying cord-and-plug connected loads. Not provided for specific loads such as small appliances or laundry equipment.

Generator: A device that is used to convert mechanical energy to electrical energy.

Grade: The final level or elevation of the earth at a given location.

Ground: A conducting connection between electrical circuits or equipment and the earth.

Grounded (Grounding): Connected to the earth or a conducting body connected to the earth.

Grounded circuit: A circuit in which one conductor or point (usually the neutral) is intentionally grounded, either solidly or through a grounding device.

Grounded conductor: A conductor that has been intentionally grounded.

Ground-fault: An unintentional connection between an ungrounded conductor and any grounded raceway, box, enclosure, fitting, etc.

Ground-fault circuit interrupter: An electrical device which protects personnel by detecting hazardous ground faults and quickly disconnects power from the circuit.

Grounding: The connection of all exposed non-current carrying metal parts to the earth.

Grounding conductor: A conductor used to connect equipment or the grounded circuit of a wiring system to a grounding electrode or electrodes.

Grounding electrode: A conducting object through which a direct connection to earth is established.

Grounding electrode conductor: The conductor used to connect the system grounded conductor and/or the equipment to a grounding electrode or to a point on the grounding electrode system.

Handhole enclosure: An enclosure for use in underground systems, provided with an open or closed bottom, and sized to allow personnel to reach into, but not enter, for the purpose of installing, operating, or maintaining equipment or wiring or both.

Health care facility: A location, either a building or a portion of a building, which contains occupancies such as, hospitals, nursing homes, limited or supervisory care facilities, clinics, medical and dental offices, and ambulatory care facilities.

Hermetic refrigerant motor-compressor: A combination of a compressor and motor enclosed in the same housing, having no external shaft or shaft seals, with the motor operating in the refrigerant.

Hickey (fitting): A fitting used to mount a lighting fixture in an outlet box or on a pipe or stud. It has openings through which fixture wires may be brought out of the fixture stem.

HID lamp: A high-intensity discharge lamp.

High-intensity discharge (HID) luminaire: A luminaire (lighting fixture) that generates light from an arc lamp contained within an outer tube.

Horsepower (hp): A unit of power equal to 746 watts that describes the output of electric motors.

Hybrid system: A system comprised of multiple power sources. These power sources may include photovoltaic, wind, micro-hydro generators, engine-driven generators, and others, but do not include electrical production and distribution network systems. Energy storage systems, such as batteries, do not constitute a power source for the purpose of this definition.

Identified: Recognized as suitable for the use, purpose, etc.

Illumination: The supplying of light or lighting up a given area. The density of light flux projected on a surface, measured in footcandles (FC).

Impedance: The total opposition to the flow of current in an AC circuit.

Incandescent lamp: A lamp in which the light is produced by a filament of conducting material contained in a vacuum and heated to incandescence by an electric current.

Individual branch circuit: A branch circuit that supplies only one unit of utilization equipment.

Induction: The process by which an electrical conductor becomes electrified when near a charged body and becomes magnetized.

Information Technology Equipment (ITE): Equipment and systems rated 600 volts or less, normally found in offices or other business establishments and similar environments classified as ordinary locations, that are used for creation and manipulation of data, voice, video, and similar signals that are not communications equipment as defined in the NEC®.

Instantaneous: A qualifying term used in giving properties and characteristics of apparatus indicating that no delay is purposely introduced in its action. Done in an instant.

Instantaneous-trip circuit breakers: Circuit breakers with no delay between the fault or overload sensing element and the tripping action of the device.

Insulated: Separated from other conducting surfaces by a dielectric substance or air space permanently offering a high resistance to the passage of current and to disruptive discharge through the substance or space.

Insulated conductor: A conductor covered with a material identified as electrical insulation.

Intensity of current: The strength of an electric current. It is the quantity of electricity that flows past any point in a circuit in one second, and is measured by a unit called the ampere. Represented by the letter "I".

Interactive system: A solar photovoltaic system that operates in parallel with and may deliver power to an electrical production and distribution network. For the purpose of this definition, an energy storage subsystem of a solar photovoltaic system, such as a battery, is not another electrical production source.

Intermittent duty: Operation for alternate intervals of (1) load and no load; or (2) load and rest; or (3) load, no load, and rest. A requirement of operation or service consisting of alternate periods of load and rest so apportioned and regulated that the temperature rise at no time exceeds that specified for the particular class of apparatus under consideration.

Intermittent load: A load in which the MAXIMUM current does not continue for three hours.

Interrupt: To stop a process in such a way that it can be resumed.

Interrupting rating: The maximum rating, in amperes, of an overcurrent protective device (OCPD).

Intersystem bonding termination: A device that provides a means for connecting bonding conductors for communications systems to the grounding electrode system.

Inverse-time circuit breakers: Circuit breakers with an intentional delay between the time when the fault or overload is sensed and the time when the circuit breaker operates. The greater the overload the less time the circuit breaker takes to trip. Conversely, the smaller the overload the more time the circuit breaker takes to trip.

Inverter: Equipment that is used to change voltage level or waveform, or both, of electrical energy. Commonly, an inverter [also known as a power conditioning unit (PCU) or power conversion system (PCS)] is a device that changes dc input to an ac output. Inverters may also function as battery chargers that use alternating current from another source and convert it into direct current for charging batteries.

Junction box: A box in which splices, taps or terminations are made.

kcmil: One thousand circular mils. Conductor sizes from 250 kcmil through 2,000 kcmil are expressed in this manner.

Kilo: A prefix often used with a physical unit to designate a quantity one thousand times as great. Designated by the letter "K".

Kilo-volt amperes (kva): One thousand (1,000) volt amperes.

Kilowatt (kw): One thousand (1,000) watts.

Lamp: A light source. Reference is to a light bulb, rather than a lamp.

Lampholders: Devices designed to accommodate a lamp for the purpose of illumination.

Lighting outlet: An outlet intended for the direct connection of a lampholder, a lighting fixture or pendant cord terminating in a lampholder.

Lighting track: An assembly consisting of an energized track and luminaire units which can be positioned along the track.

Liquidtight flexible metal conduit (LFMC): A flexible metal raceway of circular cross-section with an outer liquidtight, non metallic, sunlight-resistant jacket over an inner helically-wound metal strip.

Liquidtight flexible nonmetallic conduit (LFNC): A flexible nonmetallic raceway of circular cross-section with an outer jacket which is resistant to oil, water, sunlight, corrosion, etc. The inner core varies based on intended use.

Load: The amount of electric power used by any electrical unit or appliance at any given moment.

Location, damp: Partially protected locations under canopies, marquees, roofed open porches and like locations and interior locations subject to moderate degrees of moisture, such as some basements, barns and cold storage warehouses.

Location, dry: A location not normally subject to dampness or wetness. A location classified as dry may be temporarily subject to dampness or wetness, as in the case of a building under construction.

Location, wet: Installations underground or in concrete slabs or masonry, in direct contact with the earth and locations subject to saturation with water or other liquids, such as vehicle washing areas and locations exposed to weather and unprotected.

Locked rotor: The condition when a motor is loaded so heavily that the shaft can not turn.

Locked rotor current: The steady-state current taken from the line with the rotor locked and with rated voltage applied to the motor.

Luminaire: A complete lighting fixture consisting of the lamp or lamps, reflector or other parts to distribute the light, lamp guards and lamp power supply.

Main bonding jumper: The connection at the service equipment that bonds together the equipment grounding conductor, the grounded conductor and the grounding electrode conductor.

MAXIMUM: The greatest value in any given group. A value greater than any which precedes or follows it in succession of values.

Metal wireway: A sheet metal raceway with a hinged or removable cover that houses and protects wires and cables laid in place after the wireway has been installed.

Mil: One thousandths of an inch (0.001").

Mobil home: A transportable factory assembled structure or structures constructed on a permanent chassis for use as a dwelling. A mobile home is not constructed on a permanent foundation but is connected to the required utilities. The term "mobile home" does not include manufactured homes.

Module: A complete, environmentally protected unit consisting of solar cells, optics, and other components, exclusive of tracker, designed to generate dc power when exposed to sunlight.

Motor: A device for converting electrical energy into mechanical energy.

Motor branch circuit: The point from the last fuse or circuit breaker in the motor circuit out to the motor.

Motor control center: An assembly of one or more enclosed sections with a common power bus and primarily containing motor control units.

Motor efficiency: The effectiveness of a motor to convert electrical energy in to mechanical energy. The more efficient a motor is the less current it draws. Conversely, the less efficient a motor is the more current it draws.

Motor starter: An electrically operated switch (contactor) that includes overload protection.

Multiconductor cable: It consists of a number of individually insulated wires, either solid or stranded, which may or may not be grouped together within an outer covering. Sometimes an outer sheath of aluminum or steel is placed over the cable.

Multifamily dwelling: A dwelling with three or more dwelling units.

Multioutlet assembly: A metal raceway with factory-installed conductors and attachment plug receptacles. Usually surface mounted.

Multiwire branch circuit: A branch circuit with two or more ungrounded conductors having a potential difference between them, and is connected to the neutral or grounded conductor or the system.

Nameplate: A plaque giving the manufacturer's name, current rating and voltage of a transformer, generator, motor, appliance, etc.

Neutral: Neither positive nor negative; having zero potential; having electrical potential intermediate between the potentials of other associated parts of the circuit, positive with reference to some parts, negative with reference to others.

Nipple: A short piece of conduit or tubing having a length not exceeding 24 inches.

Noncoincidental loads: Loads that are not on at the same time.

Nonlinear load: A load where the wave shape of the steady-state current does not follow the wave shape of the applied voltage. Examples of nonlinear loads are electronic equipment, such as computers and HID and fluorescent lighting.

Nonmetallic-sheathed cable (NM): A factory assembly of two or more insulated conductors having an outer sheath of moisture-resistant, flame-retardant, non-metallic material.

Non-time delay fuses: Fuses that may detect an overcurrent and open the circuit without any delay.

Ohm: The unit of measurement of electrical resistance. One ohm of resistance will allow one ampere of current to flow through a pressure of one volt.

Ohm's Law: A law which describes the mathematical relationship between voltage, current and resistance.

One-family dwelling: A dwelling with one dwelling unit.

Outlet: Any point in the electrical system where current supplies utilization equipment.

Overcurrent: Any current in excess of that for which the conductor or equipment is rated. It may result from overload, short circuit, or ground fault.

Overload: Operation of equipment in excess of normal, full-load rating, or of a conductor in excess of its rated ampacity that, when it persists for a sufficient length of time, would cause damage or dangerous overheating. A fault, such as a short circuit or ground fault, is not an overload.

Overload protection: A device that prevents overloading a circuit or motor such as a fuse or circuit breaker.

Panelboard: A single panel or group of assembled panels with buses and overcurrent devices, which may have switches to control light, heat or power circuits.

Parallel conductors: Two or more conductors that are electrically connected at both ends to form a single conductor.

Pendants: Hanging luminaires (lighting fixtures), that use flexible cords to support the lampholder.

Permanently-connected appliance: A hard-wired appliance that is not cord-and-plug connected.

Permanently installed swimming pool: A pool constructed in ground or partially above ground and designed to hold over 42 inches of water and all indoor pools regardless of depth.

Phase: Used in ac terminology, refers basically to time. Usually the phase position is defined by specifying the number of electrical degrees between the phase and the reference position. The number of electrical degrees that two quantities are out of phase is called the phase angle.

Phase conductor: The conductors other than the neutral conductor.

Phase converter: An electrical device that converts single-phase power to three-phase power.

Phase-to-ground voltage: The maximum voltage between any two phases of an electrical distribution system.

Portable appliance: An appliance which is actually moved or can be easily moved from one place to another in normal use.

Power (watts): A basic unit of electrical energy, measured in watts. Power is usually expressed as the letter "P" or "W".

Power (volt- amperes): The apparent power in an ac circuit or electrical system. Represented by the letters "VA".

Power factor: The ratio of the voltage and current, or volt-amperes that do useful work in an ac circuit or equipment, to the total voltage and current, volt-amperes, flowing in the circuit. Power factor is usually expressed as "pf."

Premises wiring: Basically all interior and exterior wiring installed on the load side of the service point or the source of a separately derived system.

Primary: The part of a motor or transformer having windings that are connected to the power supply line.

Primary current: The current in the primary of a transformer.

Primary winding: The coil of a transformer which is energized from a source of alternating voltage and current. The input side.

Pull box: A box used as a point to pull or feed electrical conductors in the raceway system.

Rated current: The load, in amperes, that a circuit breaker is intended to carry continuously without opening of the circuit.

Raceway: A metal or nonmetallic channel for enclosing and protecting conductors.

Receptacle outlets: Outlets that provide power for cord-and-plug connected equipment.

Recreational vehicle: A vehicular type unit which is self-propelled or is mounted on or pulled by another vehicle and is primarily designed as temporary living quarters for camping, travel or recreational use.

Resistance: That property of a conductor by which it opposes the flow of an electric current, resulting in the generation of heat in the conducting material. Usually measured in ohms. Resistance is usually represented by the letter "R".

Rigid metal conduit (RMC): A conduit used to enclose conductors, made of metal with a galvanized protective coating.

Rigid nonmetallic conduit (RNC): A conduit made of materials other than metal, usually polyvinyl chloride (PVC).

Secondary current: The current induced in the secondary of a transformer or induction coil.

Separately derived system: A premises wiring system whose power is derived from a source of electric energy or equipment other than a service. Examples of separately derived systems are transformers, generators and storage batteries. Such systems have no direct connection from circuit conductors of one system to circuit conductors of another system, other than connections through the earth, metal enclosures, metallic raceways, or equipment grounding conductors.

Series circuit: A circuit supplying energy to a number of loads connected in series. The same current passes through each load in completing its path to the source of supply.

Service: The conductors and equipment for delivering electric energy from the serving utility to the wiring system of the premises served.

Service conductors: The conductors from the service point or other source of power to the service disconnecting means.

Service drop: The overhead service conductors that extend from the last pole of the utility supply system to the service-entrance conductors at the building or structure.

Service-entrance cable (SE): A single or multiconductor assembly with or without an overall covering.

Service-entrance conductors: Conductors that connect the service equipment for the building or structure with the electrical utility supply conductors.

Service equipment: All of the necessary equipment to control the supply of electrical power to a building or a structure.

Service lateral: The underground service conductors that connect the utility's electrical distribution system with the service-entrance conductors.

Service mast: An assembly consisting of a service raceway, guy wires or braces, service head and any fittings necessary for the support of service drop conductors.

Sheath: The final outer protective coating applied to a cable.

Short circuit: The unintentional connection of two ungrounded conductors that have a potential difference between them. The condition that occurs when two ungrounded conductors (hot wires), or an ungrounded and grounded conductor of a circuit, come in contact with each other.

Short circuit protection: Any automatic current-limiting system that enables a power supply to continue operating at a limited current. and without damage, into any output overload including short-circuits.

Show window: Any window used or designed to be used for the display of goods, products, services, or advertising material. Usually visible by the general public from street or floor level.

Single phase: A term applied to a simple alternating current of uniform frequency as distinguished from polyphase currents.

Single phase circuit: An ac circuit consisting of two or three intentionally interrelated conductors.

Solar cell: The basic photovoltaic device that generates electricity when exposed to light.

Solar photovoltaic system: The total components and subsystems that, in combination, convert solar energy into electric energy suitable for connection to a utilization load.

Spa (hot tub): An indoor or outdoor hydromassage pool or tub that is not designed to have the water discharged after each use.

Special permission: The written approval of the authority having jurisdiction.

Splice: A joint used for connecting conductors together.

Stationary appliance: A cord-connected appliance that is intended to be fastened in place or located in a dedicated space.

Switch: A device, with a current and voltage rating, used to open or close an electrical circuit.

Switchboard: A single panel or group of assembled panels with buses, overcurrent devices and instruments.

Temperature rise: The amount of heat that an electrical component produces above the ambient temperature.

Thermal protection: Refers to an electrical device which has inherent protection from overheating. Typically in the form of a bimetal strip which bends when heated to a certain point.

Three-phase circuit: a combination of circuits energized by AC that differ in phase by one third of a cycle, which is 120 degrees.

Three phase power: A combination of three alternating currents (usually denoted as A, B and C) in a circuit with their voltages displaced 120 degrees or one third of a cycle.

Three-phase transformer: A combination in one unit of three single phase transformers with separate electric circuits, but having certain magnetic circuits in common. There are three magnetic circuits through the core and the fluxes in the various circuits are displaced in phase.

Time delay fuse: Fuses designed to provide a time interval upon detection of an overload, before blowing. This type of fuse is used primarily for overcurrent protection for motors.

Transformer: An electrical device that contains no moving parts, which converts or "transforms" electrical power at one voltage or current to another voltage or current.

Transformer vault: An isolated enclosure either above or below ground, with fire-resistant walls, ceiling and floor, for unattended transformers.

True power: The actual power used in an electrical circuit measured in watts or kilowatts. Represented by the letter "P" or the letter "W".

Unfinished basement: The portion of area of a basement which is not intended as a habitable room, but is limited to storage areas, work areas, etc.

Ungrounded: A system, circuit or apparatus without an intentional connection to ground except through potential indicating or measuring devices or other very high impedance devices.

Uninterruptible power supply: A power supply used to provide alternating current power to a load for some period of time in the event of a power failure.

Utilization equipment: Any electrical equipment which uses electrical energy for electronic, mechanical, heating, lighting, or similar purposes.

Ventilated: Provided with a means to permit circulation of air sufficient to remove an excess of heat, fumes or vapors.

Volt: The practical unit of electric pressure. The pressure which will produce a current of one ampere against a resistance of one ohm.

Voltage: The greatest root-mean-square (effective) difference of potential between any two conductors or the circuit concerned.

Voltage drop: The drop of pressure in an electric circuit due to the resistance of the conductor. This loss exists in every circuit. It is directly proportional to the length of the conductor, and is inversely proportional to its cross-sectional area.

Voltage, nominal: A nominal value assigned to a circuit or system for the purpose of conveniently designating its voltage class (e.g., 120/240 volts, 480Y/277 volts, 600 volts). The actual voltage at which a circuit operates can vary from the nominal within a range that permits satisfactory operation of equipment.

Voltage-to-ground: The difference of potential between a given conductor and ground.

Volt-ampere: the volt-ampere is the apparent power in an AC circuit. Represented by the letters "VA".

Wall mounted oven: An oven for cooking purposes designed for mounting in or on a wall or other surface and consisting of one or more heating elements.

Watt: The practical unit of power, being the amount of energy expended per second by an unvarying current of one ampere under a pressure of one volt.

Weatherproof: So constructed or protected that exposure to the weather will not interfere with successful operation.

Wireway: A metallic or nonmetallic trough with a hinged or removable cover designed to house and protect conductors and cables.

Wye connection: A connection that has one end of each coil connected together and the other end of each coil left open for external connections.

TITLES AVAILABLE BASED ON THE 2014 NEC©

Electricians Exam Book   ISBN

Electricians Practice Calculations Exams   ISBN

Practical Calculations for Electricians   ISBN

Texas Electricians Practice Exams & Study Guide   ISBN

TITLES AVAILABLE BASED ON THE 2011 NEC©

Electricians Exam Book   ISBN

Electricians Handbook of NEC® Questions   ISBN

Electricians Practice Calculations Exams   ISBN

Practical Calculations for Electricians   ISBN

TO ORDER ONLINE VISIT:
WWW.BROWNTECHNICAL.ORG
BROWN TECHNICAL PUBLICATIONS INC

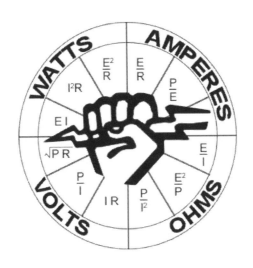

Made in the USA
Lexington, KY
13 May 2017